THE MAYA 4.5 HANDBOOK

THE MAYA 4.5
HANDBOOK

ADAM WATKINS

CHARLES RIVER MEDIA, INC.

Hingham, Massachusetts

Publisher: Jenifer Niles
Production: Publishers' Design and Production Services, Inc.
Cover Design: The Printed Image
Cover Image: Adam Watkins

CHARLES RIVER MEDIA, INC.
20 Downer Avenue, Suite 3
Hingham, Massachusetts 02043
781-740-0400
781-740-8816 (FAX)
info@charlesriver.com
www.charlesriver.com

This book is printed on acid-free paper.

Adam Watkins. *The Maya 4.5 Handbook*.
ISBN: 1-58450-234-7

Library of Congress Cataloging-in-Publication Data

Watkins, Adam.
     The Maya 4.5 handbook / Adam Watkins. — 1st ed.
        p. cm.
     ISBN 1-58450-234-7 (paperback with CD-ROM : alk. paper)
     1. Computer animation. 2. Three-dimensional display systems. 3. Maya
  (Computer file) I. Title.
     TR897.7 .W38 2003
     006.6'96—dc21

                                                    2002154402

Printed in the United States of America
02 7 6 5 4 3 2 First Edition

As always, to my beautiful wife Kirsten. It just keeps getting better and better.

ABOUT THE FIGURES

Most of the figures in this text were meant to be generated in color and are provided on the CD-ROM as they would be viewed on your monitor.

CONTENTS

Acknowledgments xi
Preface xiii

CHAPTER 1 **MAYA WORK FLOW AND INTERFACE** **1**

A General 3D Work Flow 2
    Step 1: Project Conceptualization 2
    Step 2: Modeling 2
    Step 3: Shading (Texturing) 3
    Step 4: Lighting 3
    Step 5: Animation 4
    Step 6: Rendering 4
    Work Flow Wrap-up 4
An Interface Overview 5
    Modules 5
    Menu Bar 7
    Status Line 9
Shelf 26
Toolbox 26
    Quick Setup 27
Workspace 28
Channel/Layer Box/Tool Settings/Attribute Editor 29
Time and Range Slider 31
Command Line and Help Line 31
Conclusion 31

CHAPTER 2 **GETTING STARTED WITH MODELING** **33**

Setting Up Your Project 34
Maneuvering in Maya 35
TUTORIAL 2.1: Exploring the Manipulator 36

	Understanding States of Object Display	39
	Moving On	41
	TUTORIAL 2.2: Primitive Room Forms	42
	Conclusion	61

CHAPTER 3   **NURBS AND COMPONENT-LEVEL EDITING**   **63**

	Curves	65
	TUTORIAL 3.1: Getting Started with Curves	66
	NURBS	74
	TUTORIAL 3.2: NURBS Modeling in "The Room"	78
	Conclusion	96

CHAPTER 4   **NURBS CONTINUED**   **97**

| | TUTORIAL 4.1: NURBS Surfaces Continued | 98 |
| | Conclusion | 118 |

CHAPTER 5   **COMPONENT LEVEL EDITING AND BOOLEANS**   **121**

	Power of the Duplication Tool	122
	TUTORIAL 5.1: Exploring Duplicate Tool	122
	TUTORIAL 5.2: Finishing the Room	127
	Conclusion	147

CHAPTER 6   **SUBDIVISION MODELING**   **149**

	The States of a Subdivision Surface	150
	Standard Mode	151
	Polygon Mode	152
	TUTORIAL 6.1: Creating a Hummingbird	156
	Conclusion	172

CHAPTER 7   **MATERIALS AND TEXTURING**   **173**

	The Texturing Paradigm	174
	Terms	175
	Types of Materials	175
	Anatomy of a Material	177
	Texture Creation and Editing	181
	TUTORIAL 7.1: Texturing the Room	184
	Conclusion	201

CHAPTER 8   CUSTOM TEXTURE MAPS IN MATERIALS   203

TUTORIAL 8.1: Texturing the Room, Continued   204

Conclusion   226

CHAPTER 9   LIGHTING AND RENDERING   227

Light Attributes   230

Light Types   233

    Ambient Light   233

    Directional Light   235

    Point Light   236

    Decay   237

    Spot Light   238

    Area Lights   239

    Volume Light   240

Light Anatomy   241

TUTORIAL 9.1: Nighttime   245

TUTORIAL 9.2: Daytime Lighting   258

Rendering   270

Image File Output   270

Resolution   271

Field Options   272

Anti-aliasing Quality   272

Raytracing Quality   273

Modify Extensions and Renumber Frames   274

Motion Blur   274

Render Options   274

Memory and Performance Options   275

IPR Options   275

Render Layer/Pass Control   276

Conclusion   276

CHAPTER 10   ANIMATION   279

What Is It?   280

Keyframe Animation   281

Setting Up Maya for Animation   282

The Animation Tools   283

    Time Slider and Current Time Marker   284

    Playback Controls   284

    Range Bar   284

    Auto Keyframe Button   285

    Animation Preferences Button   285

Animatable Elements   285
TUTORIAL 10.1: Mechanical Hummingbird   286
Conclusion   304

APPENDIX A   WHICH HARDWARE TO USE?   305
Maya's Qualified Hardware   305
Mac Systems   306
Linux Systems   307
PC Systems   307
Important Components   309
    Processor(s)   309
    A Note on Multiple Processors   310
    Video Cards   310
    RAM   312
    Monitor   312
    Mouse   313
Conclusion   313

APPENDIX B   CUSTOMIZING THE MAYA USER INTERFACE   315
General Overview   315
    Windows   316
    Managing Panels   317
Showing and Hiding Parts of the Interface   322
Adjusting UI Elements through Preferences   324
Editing Interaction   326
Editing Hotkey Configurations   326
Changing Interface Colors   327
Customizing Marking Menus   329
Creating Marking Menus from Scratch   332
Controlling Shelves   336
    Editing Shelf Content   337
    Creating New Shelves   337
Conclusion   338

APPENDIX C   CREATING EFFECTIVE TEXTURE MAPS   339
TUTORIAL C.1: Creating Seamless Textures   341
Conclusion   350

APPENDIX D   ABOUT THE CD-ROM   351
System Requirements   351

ACKNOWLEDGMENTS

Again, many thanks to Jenifer for her never-ending patience and encouragement. You are truly great to work with.

Thanks to the folks at Boxx Technologies. The 3DBoxx that I used to write this book performed flawlessly. I'd recommend it to anyone (*www.boxxtechnologies.com*).

Special thanks to Goose, Fish, Tick, Jenny, and The Creature (a.k.a. Mr. Beans the Psycho Kitty) for keeping me happy and sane through the writing process.

Special appreciation to my folks. Sorry we haven't been to visit too much these last few months—your support and visits make for fun times and good memories.

PREFACE

Maya is powerful and it's everywhere. One needn't look any further than virtually any popular media to see its influence. From films, to television, to one of its newest hardcore targets—games, the power of Maya is everywhere.

Maya is deep. If there is one thing I have learned in the classes that I have taught it's that Maya can do about anything imaginable if you can just find where it is. Unfortunately, many students of Maya, in pursuit of that elusive command or function, end up in dark corners of the program that are spooky when unfamiliar and which allow them to do things to their projects that really should not be done. So, the real question is how to wield this powerful multifunctional weapon without hurting yourself.

This book is designed to point out the vital aspects of Maya. Will we cover every nook and cranny of Maya? No, it would take many, many volumes to do that. What we will do is start from the beginning and move toward creating truly professional-grade projects.

To learn these vital skills, we will study two areas. First, we will look at the theory and background of the Maya paradigm and work flow. Without an understanding of the ideas behind the buttons, you are forever limited to the last manual you read. Once we discuss these ideas, we will move right into step-by-step tutorials.

These tutorials have been developed through class experimentation here at the University of the Incarnate Word. They are designed to provide very detailed information on where to get which commands but also to give further rationale behind why and when to use commands.

Included with the explanations and the tutorials, you will find screen shots and renders of the projects as we work. The grayscale images contained in this book are usually more than enough to guide you in the direction we are going. However, if you need more visual information, all the images included in the book are also contained on the CD-ROM in full color.

ON THE CD

In addition, the results of the tutorials and several in-process versions of the tutorial files are included on the CD-ROM. Sometimes, picking apart an already altered file can teach volumes.

ORGANIZATION

For the most part, this book assumes that you have a good understanding of 3D. Perhaps this knowledge comes from using another software package. Although we will look at a few general ideas behind 3D and how they relate to Maya, we will not spend a whole lot of time on general vocabulary or concepts. (If you need this sort of theoretical base to work from, check out *3D Animation: From Models to Movies* ©2001 Charles River Media, Inc.)

This book is organized so that you can jump ahead to any area you wish. Whether a beginning or intermediate Maya user, there is something here for you (for you advanced users, we will get to you in a future volume). If you are just starting out with the program, start from the beginning of the book. We'll look at how Maya organizes its Workspace, how it "thinks" of digital space, and how to work within that space. Immediately after, we will dive into the many levels of modeling within Maya. After modeling, we will jump into Maya's shading methods, then onto animation, and finally, character animation.

As Maya is a node-based program, this book is a node-based volume. Each node (modeling, shading, and animation) has its own eccentricities and can be used powerfully just by itself. However, to create the most powerful effects, all the nodes have a synergistic effect when used together. A quick look through the book will show that the projects are interdependent; one builds on the next. So, if you do jump to a different place in the book, be mindful that sometimes core information has been presented earlier.

Keep in mind that although this is not a reference book, there are some sections included in the appendices that can be used as reference sections. Largely, the appendices are short articles that cover issues of what software is needed to run Maya effectively, how to change the Maya interface, and information about the machine used to create the Maya projects in this book. In general, if you are looking for a general background discussion of a concept, check the appendices.

RATIONALE

The core idea of this volume is to make sure that after you are done reading it, you can do more than what is presented in the tutorials. After all, you cannot use the tutorials in your demo reel because they will look just like what everyone else produced who followed these tutorials. If after reading a tutorial, you have a completed project but not a good understanding, please reread the tutorial. The goal is to teach a fundamental understanding of the techniques, not an understanding of how to follow tutorial instructions.

Having said this, it is also important to point out that lots of detail is written into each chapter and tutorial. Because this volume covers both Maya for the PC and the Mac, occasionally there will be instances where the instructions may differ a bit. So, watch out for any platform-specific quirks that may arise during tutorial exercises.

CONVENTIONS

Because of Maya's slightly unconventional method of hiding different parts of its tool set, it will be important to point out some conventions we will use in the process of this volume.

- Things that should be typed into input fields will be listed in this font.
- Keystrokes, hotkeys, keyboard shortcuts (for things like Marking menus) will be in bold. For example, the keystroke for duplicating an object is **CTRL-D**.
- Maya hides different collections of tools depending on which module you are in. Do not worry too much about what *module* means now, but if you look at your interface, in the top-left corner is a pop-down menu that allows you to change the module you are in (Animation, Modeling, Dynamics, Rendering, and so on). To make sure that you are always in the right module, when pull-down menus are listed, if they are module-specific, the module will be listed as Modeling|Surfaces>Loft. This means, "Make sure you are in Modeling module, go to the Surfaces pull-down menu, and select Loft."

Using the mouse is a complex operation in Maya.

    a. LMB = left mouse button
    b. MMB = middle mouse button
    c. RMB = right mouse button
    d. LMMB = left and middle mouse button at the same time
    e. Unless otherwise stated, "click" or "double-click" means to click the LMB.

CONCLUSION

Above all, make sure you are having fun. If you are not, stop, rest, and then tackle it again. Writing and reading tutorials can be a tricky business. Something that seems obvious to one writer or reader may not be to another. Please be patient with things that move too slowly and with the other parts that seem to move too quickly.

So, without further ado, let's get started. There is plenty of ground to cover and lots of fun to be had.

MAYA WORK FLOW AND INTERFACE

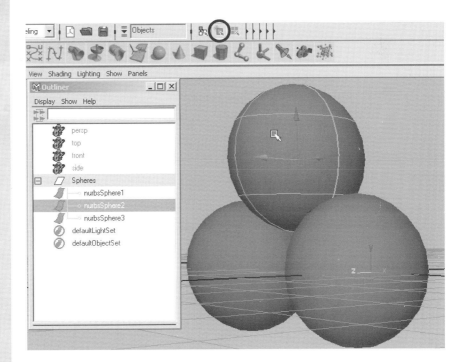

L
ater in this chapter, we are going to get into the reasons behind the organization of Maya's interface. This will help define why the interface has been often admired and often imitated. But to better understand the reasoning behind the organization, it's important to first look briefly at a general 3D work flow and specifically, at Maya's work flow. Through the process, we will have an opportunity to discuss Maya's working paradigm—the rationale behind the software as well as the benefits and drawbacks of this way of thinking.

A GENERAL 3D WORK FLOW

Every 3D artist works a little differently than the next. The goal of this section is not to define a definitive step-by-step progression, because the steps may shift depending on your project or your team. In general, however, most 3D projects can be broken down into the following steps.

Step 1: Project Conceptualization

Okay, so this is actually a huge step and includes an incredible amount of sub-steps including research, sketches, storyboards, perhaps clay models, and a video asset collection. The importance of building, defining, and refining a solid concept is immense. The process is also highly individualized. What needs to happen before a project "goes digital" depends largely on an animator's strengths and weaknesses. Because of this, we will leave this discussion at that. But if you are just getting started in 3D, make sure you build the habit of playing with ideas on paper before pounding polygons. Usually, a couple of hours in traditional pencil and paper land can save you many, many hours in the digital realm.

For further information on general work flow in 3D creation see my book, *3D Animation: From Models to Movies* (©2000. Charles River Media, Inc.).

Step 2: Modeling

Modeling is a specific term that covers a lot of concepts and a large amount of techniques. At its simplest, modeling is the process of constructing the virtual shapes that make up your scene. These objects can be anything from clouds to worms to furniture to caricatures to photo-realistic people.

How these objects are constructed largely depends on a myriad variables including what the object is, how it's going to move, if it's going to move, how it needs to be textured, how detailed it is, and what the final output is, games, TV, movies, etc., to name a few. Basically, the idea here is that before anything else can be done on the project—including lighting, shading, or animation—there must first be models with which to work.

Over the course of this volume, we will be talking about several modeling methods. Of course, these are by no means exhaustive and many artists use techniques and methods that are specific to their style or the pipeline of their workplace. So, take these techniques as a very general look at basic building blocks. Put them together in ways that make sense to you and create new methods.

Step 3: Shading (Texturing)

Texturing is the process of giving the gray models created in earlier steps surface characteristics including color, specular highlights, luminance, diffuse, and others. Tactile characteristics like bumps are also controlled through the texturing process. Most of these texturing processes are a type of *veneer*—a flat kind of painting across the surface of the model; however, there are some texturing techniques such as displacement that actually alter the geometry of the model.

Basically, texturing makes a volleyball look different than a bowling ball that looks different than a tennis ball that is still different than an eyeball. Maya's texturing capabilities are incredibly powerful and deep. Again, will take time to explore a whole lot of interesting techniques for using Maya's texturing tools. Once again, this will not be an exhaustive exploration—just enough to introduce you to many of the levers of this texturing tool; you will even get to pull a few. The mastering of the texture techniques will be up to you.

Step 4: Lighting

Virtual lighting is one of the most fun but most challenging parts of 3D. Not many people take enough time with it and unfortunately, that means not very many people do it well. A well-lit scene can hide problems or highlight strengths. Lighting is largely a subconscious aesthetic so folks do not often understand that they are being affected by it.

Lighting in 3D has some interesting challenges as virtual lights don't behave quite like "real" lights. Because of the different rules of light in a virtual world, a bit of different thinking must go into your virtual lighting design. Throughout this volume, we'll look closely at how Maya's lighting tools work and how we can manipulate them to produce the desired image.

Step 5: Animation

Perhaps the most fun, dynamic, and difficult of the whole process is animation. Everyone thinks they can do it but few people are really very good at it. *Animation* is the process of making the objects modeled earlier move, or even making objects such as lights or virtual cameras move. The key to it all is movement.

The problem is that movement is very hard to cover in a book. It's very hard to teach in general and requires quite a bit of physical face-to-face time. So, we won't be going into the physics of movement much. Neither will we go much beyond a cursory look at movement aesthetics and issues of timing. What we'll cover are the tools that Maya brings to the table to allow you to make your textured, lit models come to life.

Maya's animation tools—and especially the character animation tools—are truly at the top of their class. We'll look at the core of this robust animation tool set over the course of this book. The animations we'll create will be basic but sound. You can use the techniques and skill set from these tutorial animations to create great masterpieces that will amaze your family and impress your friends.

Step 6: Rendering

You're the god of the 3D world you're creating. You define the objects therein, what characteristics they have, and how they move. When you've finished creating and animating your world, you then tell Maya (the camera) how to take a picture or draw the world you've created. You can define all sorts of minute details of how Maya will understand the light, how large it'll draw or render the image, how many images in a second it's going to draw to create movement, and how much detail to put into the final rendering. The core idea though is that Maya, under your direction, is drawing or rendering the world you've created. You define the rules but Maya does little without your telling it to.

The truth is, Maya's rendering isn't as intuitive as many of the 3D applications that you might be coming from. The power is great within the renderer but with this power comes endless options, each of which can tweak your project closer to the illustrative perfection you see in your mind's eye.

Work Flow Wrap-up

Now of course the steps outlined so far are a gross underrepresentation of the cyclical nature of the creation process. Hardly any of the steps outlined are done and then totally left behind for the remainder of the creation process. Usually, you model, texture, rework the model, rework the texture, then light a bit, then rework a texture or two, touch up the model a bit, then readjust the lighting, and so on. But in general, it's nice to think of your project in this linear process.

As we work through the book, we'll follow this general process. We'll start out by looking at the general layout of the tools. Then we'll move right into creating some objects through various modeling techniques. After we have our mini-worlds created, we'll color them through the texturing process. Then we'll illuminate the world through lighting, animate some of the characters in this world, and finally have Maya render the whole thing out for us. It's a complex and fun process but it will take a while. So, let's move right into how Maya organizes the tools it gives us to create our virtual worlds.

AN INTERFACE OVERVIEW

3D interfaces have come a long way over the years. The trend has shifted and evolved as the interface aesthetic has changed. An interesting development is their tendency to mimic Maya's interface. This is especially true of mid-range 3D applications. It's no wonder because the Maya interface has a fairly intuitive organization and an extremely customizable toolbox from which to grab the tools to create your masterpiece.

Part of what makes the initial Maya interface so powerful is that it packs so much into so little space. This efficiency can be incredibly intimidating at first but don't lose hope. In all actuality, the interface is well organized and once you understand the organization, it becomes much easier to grab the tool you need (Figure 1.1).

Modules

Maya is so deep that it "hides" many of its tools so that the user isn't overwhelmed by the incredible options it provides. There are several ways that Maya organizes tools but the broadest method is through *modules*. Modules are general collections of tools and pull-down menus that are organized specifically for one aspect of Maya. To access or change modules, use the first Menu Set pop-up menu on the Status Line (Figure 1.2).

In Maya Complete the Modules are Animation, Modeling, Dynamics, and Rendering. In Maya Unlimited the Modules include Animation, Modeling, Dynamics, Rendering, Live, and Cloth.

As discussed in the Preface, varying collections of tools and pull-down menus are available depending on what module is active. Be sure to take note of which module you're in when working.

FIGURE 1.1   A general overview and breakdown of the Maya default user interface.

FIGURE 1.2   Shift modules through the Menu Set in the Status Line.

Menu Bar

Like most any application in the Mac or Windows worlds, the menu bar includes the main pull-down menus in Maya. Unlike most applications, there are so many pull-down menus that they aren't all displayed at once. The File, Edit, Modify, Create, Display, and Window pull-down menus are always visible, regardless of which module you're in. However, to the right of these six pull-down menus are others that will change depending on your module (Figure 1.3).

FIGURE 1.3   A brief overview of the varying pull-down menus available with different modules.

Converting Pull-down Menus to Floating Menus and Palettes

The Menu Bar, with its pull-down menus, also has some user-friendly options of note. First, notice that pull-down menus need not remain pull-down menus. When a pull-down menu is first activated, a set of double lines is highlighted (Figure 1.4a). When these double lines are selected, the pull-down menu becomes a floating palette of sorts (Figure 1.4b). This is a nice temporary modification to the interface that allows you to have a collection of tools you're going to be using repeatedly in your process.

Appendix B, "Customizing the Maya User Interface," is all about modifying the interface to adjust to your work flow. As you work and become more familiar with Maya, be sure to take a look at that appendix for tips on putting together Maya's user interface just the way you want it.

FIGURE 1.4   (a-b) Change pull-down menus into floating palettes.

Option Boxes

Notice that within many of the pull-down menus, items will have a small square to their right (Figure 1.5). This is referred to as the Option box.

The presence of the Options box signifies that this particular tool has some customizable options that you may or may not want to adjust before using the tool. Simply move your mouse over the box before releasing the LMB to open the options dialog box.

Be aware that when you change the settings in an Options dialog box, Maya remembers those changes. So, if you choose that tool again,

FIGURE 1.5   Select an Option box to specify aspects of the tool.

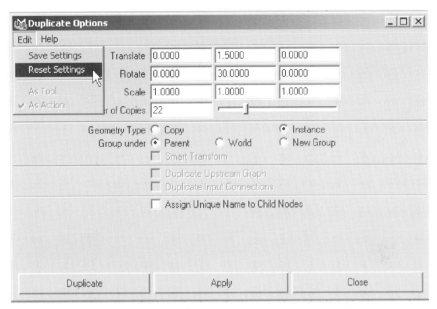

FIGURE 1.6   This Options dialog box allows you to reset the settings for this tool.

all of the altered options remain in effect. In general, if you are using a machine that's in a lab, that other people have worked with, or that you haven't worked with for a while, be sure to open the options for tools the first time to use them to reset your options (Figure 1.6).

We will talk much more about manipulating dialog boxes in the tutorials of later chapters.

Status Line

Moving straight down the interface, the next collection of tools below the pull-down menus is the Status Line (Figure 1.7). The Status Line is an interesting collection of tools. We will not talk in great detail here about each of these tools individually; rather, we will cover broad collections of tools. Because of this, notice the circled elements that are called *collapsers*. When you click the LMB, they allow you to hide or show the tools to their right. We will talk about tools in the context of collections between collapsers.

As we talk about collections of tools within the Status Line, we will start with a completely "collapsed" Status Line. We will uncollapse the collections as we go.

FIGURE 1.7   The collapsers in the Status Line are circled.

Module Menu Set

The first part of the Status Line consists of the previously discussed module menu sets. Remember, you get an entirely new collection of pull-down menus when these are changed (Figure 1.8).

New, Open, and Save

The New, Open, and Save tools are fairly standard options for many applications (Figure 1.9). They are just visual representations of File>New Scene . . . , File>Open Scene . . . , and File>Save Scene . . . Remember that **Ctrl-N** (New), **Ctrl-O** (Open), and **Ctrl-S** (Save) are still faster ways to create, open, or save scenes.

FIGURE 1.8   The Menu Set module allows you to bring up new collections of tools depending on the point in your creation process.

FIGURE 1.9   The New, Open, and Save tools are available within the Status Line.

Selection Masks

As your projects become more complex, the number of objects, lights, or animation tools will begin to increase dramatically. As time goes on, it can become nearly impossible to select the object you want as you work. This Selection Mask (Figure 1.10) allows you to define what objects are selectable.

When the time comes for animation, being able to select the right object in your Workspace becomes especially important. It is important to

FIGURE 1.10   The Selection Mask allows you to define what items may be selected within your Workspace.

have an eye for this tool and remember that it is there. Often, problems that students have when working with a complex scene can be solved by simply taking time to hone in on the types of objects they wish to select.

The setting listed in the Selection Mask is linked to the next two collections of tools:

- Hierarchy, Object, and Component Modes
- Select by Object or Component Types

Hierarchy, Object, Component Mode

The Hierarchy, Object, and Component modes (Figure 1.11) affect what part or parts of the scene you are able to select and alter. All three of these modes refer to a level of organization within your scene.

The ability to alter and control which Mode you are in is an incredibly important part of working effectively in Maya. We will explore this aspect much more in depth in the course of the tutorials, but it is important to understand a bit about the theory behind them.

When you create a primitive form or a surface in Maya, you have created an *object*. This object consists of sub-parts called *components*. A polygon object is made of vertex, face, and edge components. Non-uniform Rational B-Splines (NURBS) objects contain components such as control vertices, isoparms, and hulls. When objects are grouped they become part of *hierarchies*.

Consider Figure 1.12, which shows three spheres (objects) grouped into a group (a hierarchy) called *Spheres*, which is displayed in the Outliner to the left.

If the Hierarchy button is pressed, notice that the Selection Mask changes to Hierarchy, meaning of course that if we LMB-click anywhere in the scene, we're limited to selecting hierarchies. Indeed, if any of the spheres in the scene are clicked, Maya does not select the sphere, but the hierarchy that that sphere resides in (Figure 1.13).

Similarly, if the Object mode is selected, the Selection Mask accordingly changes to Objects and we can select individual objects within the scene by LMB-clicking on them (Figure 1.14).

Finally, if Components mode is chosen, we can select components that are parts of objects. In the case shown in Figure 1.15, we're selecting Control Vertices that are part of the first object, NURBS Sphere.

FIGURE 1.11   Hierarchy, Object, and Component mode items.

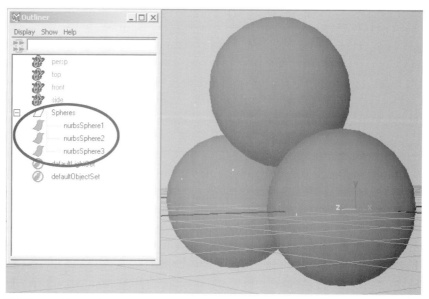

FIGURE 1.12 Three spheres (NURBS) are collected into the group, *Spheres*.

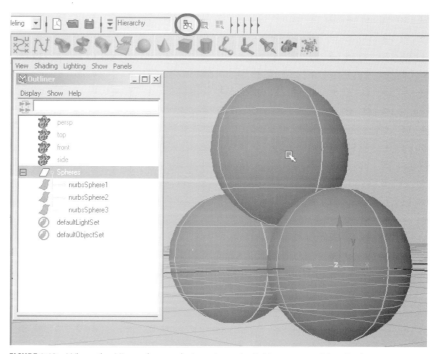

FIGURE 1.13 When the Hierarchy mode is activated, clicking on an object in the scene selects the hierarchy that that object is in.

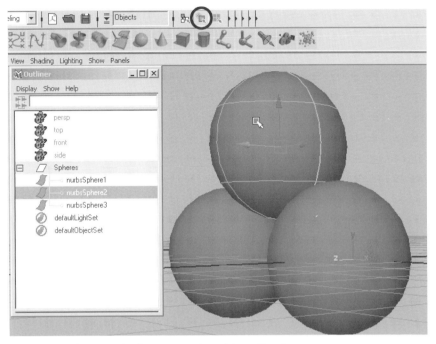

FIGURE 1.14   Object mode allows us to select objects directly.

FIGURE 1.15   Components mode allows you to select a part or building component tool of an object.

Now this may seem rather simple and redundant because you could do much the same thing by simply altering the Selection Mask. It would be redundant if not for the next collection of tools.

Select by Hierarchy:Type, Select by Object:Type, and Select by Component:Type

In the last section, we looked at a collection of tools that would allow for the specification of what part of a hierarchy is to be selected when clicked in the Workspace. This next collection of tools work as a subset to the Hierarchy (Figure 1.16a), Objects (Figure 1.16b), and Components (Figure 1.16c) modes. This means there are several collections of tools that all occupy the same space. Depending on which mode you are in, the tools that relate to it are displayed. Figure 1.16 shows each collection of *Select by:* and the particular mode that the collection is attached to.

This particular collection of tools is extremely important as you work in Maya. In the next chapter, we will look closely at these tools in action but we will go over a quick theoretical discussion of them here. Before we get too deep, notice that the iconography of these tools (or any tool within Maya) can be deciphered quickly in two ways. The first is to move your mouse over any tool and leave it there for a bit. A screen hint will pop up (Figure 1.17) to identify the tool for you. The second is by keeping an eye out for the Help Line at the bottom-left corner of your default interface. When you mouse over a particular tool, the name of the tool will appear in the Help Line (Figure 1.17).

Select by Hierarchy:

This small collection of options (Figure 1.16a) is tied to the Hierarchy mode. The default tool is *Select by Hierarchy:Root*. This means that when you click on any object that exists within a group or other hierarchy, the hierarchy to which it belongs will be selected. Note that besides the default, the other two tools include *Select by Hierarchy:Leaf* and *Select by Hierarchy:Template*. These allow you to select parts, or *leaves*, of a hierarchy rather than the entire hierarchy or you may select Template objects.

FIGURE 1.16   (a-c) Select by Hierarchy, Object, or Component Type.

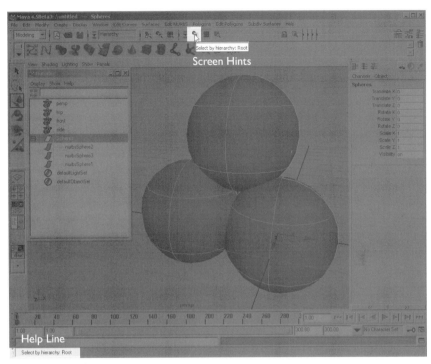

FIGURE 1.17   If you ever get confused over which tool is which, let Maya tell you with screen hints or in the Help Line.

We'll talk much more of templates later but the basic idea is that any object can be temporarily made into a Template object that doesn't render and usually isn't selectable. Template objects can be great as guides for animation or size reference. In any other mode, templates are not selectable.

In Figure 1.18a, you can see that the top sphere is shaded differently than the others. This wireframe, gray representation indicates that the object is a template. When Hierarchy mode is active, and *Select by Hierarchy:Template* is activated, templates can be selected as shown in Figure 1.18b.

Select by Object: Type

This is a much broader collection of tools as you can see back in Figure 1.16b. This collection allows you to decide what sorts of objects will be selectable. The options are Handles, Joints, Curves, Surfaces, Deformations, Dynamics, Rendering, and Miscellaneous. Notice that by default, all of these are activated, meaning that unless you deactivate items, when in Object mode, you can select any type of object within your Workspace. To turn off an item, simply LMB-click it.

FIGURE 1.18   (a-b) Templates cannot be selected except with the *Select by Hierarchy:Template* tool.

There are too many specifics for each of these to go into depth in this chapter. However, as we work, we'll occasionally turn these off and on to help us in different parts of our work process.

One important thing to note about this collection of tools before we move on: there are actually nested tools within these items. If you rest your mouse on any of the *Select by Object:* items, the screen hint (Figure 1.19a) will indicate *RMB for more info*. Indeed, if you RMB-click on any of these items, there will be a collection of sub-items that you can turn on or off (Figure 1.19b).

Select by Component: Type

As discussed earlier, objects are made up of, or can be edited by, various components. Of course, the specific components vary depending on the type of object. In general, if all the components were visible at one time in the Workspace, it would be difficult to see what you needed to find. The *Select by Component: Type* collection of items allow you to decide what types of components will be selectable (Figure 1.19b).

The components are grouped into the Points, Parm Points, Lines, Faces, Hulls, Pivots, Handles, and Miscellaneous buttons. Again, these are general

FIGURE 1.19   (a-b) Many of the *Select by Object Type* items are actually categories. The items within these categories are accessed with an RMB-click.

categories of components and most have a collection of specific components nested within them that are accessible through an RMB-click.

One note about this collection of tools: as with many aspects of Maya there is more than one way to skin this virtual cat. You can also access specific components of a given object while in Object mode. By RMB-clicking on an object (while in Object mode) you'll be given a marking menu that allows you to select a component of that object directly (Figure 1.20). Generally, I find that this method is preferable in most cases.

Lock Current Selection and Highlight Selection Mode

Lastly, before we move onto other parts of the Status Line, it is important to notice the two tools shown in Figure 1.21.

If you have selected a particular hierarchy, object, or component and you know that you wish to work with it for a prolonged period of time, you can lock it with the Lock Current Selection tool. Although this does prevent unintentional deselecting, it also prohibits you from selecting other objects, which can become very bothersome very quickly. In general, this tool is not of tremendous use, so leave it alone.

By default, when you select a hierarchy, object, or component in the Workspace, the item is highlighted. However, you may toggle this off with the Highlight Selection Mode button. Why exactly you would *need* to do this is a mystery, unless you have an incredibly large amount of items selected (more than you would ever want to have selected at once). However, if you want to remove highlighting from the items you select, this is where you toggle off that option.

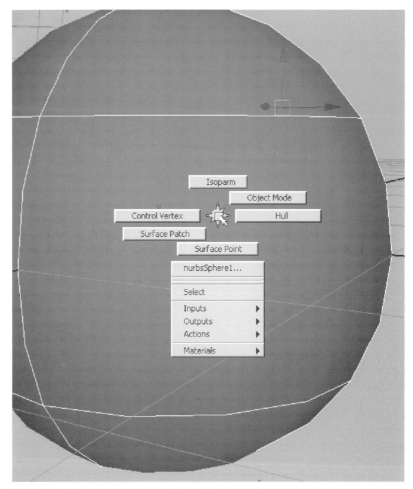

FIGURE 1.20   Select components while in Objects mode.

FIGURE 1.21   The Lock Current Selection and Highlight Selection Mode tools.

Snap to Grids, Curves, Points, View Planes, and Make the Selected Object Live

The next collection of tools (Figure 1.22) is great when you are interested in exact objects, component movements, or curve creation. The next four tools when toggled on allow you to snap the selected object or component to the active grid, curve, point, or view planes. We will be looking specifically at how to use these tools in later tutorials, but the general idea is illustrated in the following figure.

FIGURE 1.22   The Snap to Grids, Snap to Curves, Snap to Points, Snap to View Planes, and Make the Selected Object Live tools.

Figure 1.23 illustrates a very general example of how these tools work. Figure 1.23a shows a scene that includes a sphere and a curve. By selecting the sphere and moving it so that it sits at the end of the curve, we are telling Maya that there's going to be a relationship here (Figure 1.23b). Now, when Snap to Curves is toggled on (Figure 1.23c), the yellow box that was at the middle of the sphere's manipulator changes to a circle. When it is LMB-clicked and dragged, the sphere snaps to the curve (Figure 1.23d).

The notable variation of these tools is the last tool: Make the Selected Object Live. A *live* object is the object to which other objects or components will snap. So, if we wanted to create a curve that matched a particular surface, we would select the surface and click the Make the Selected

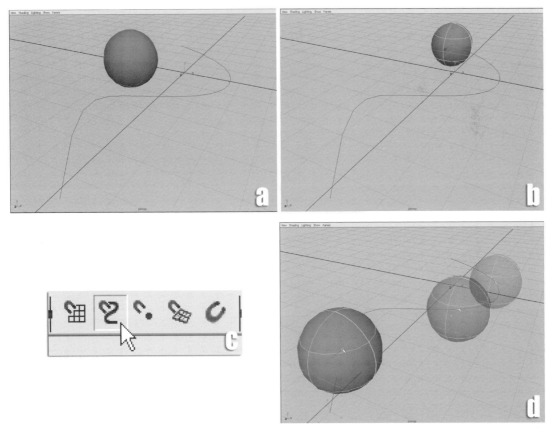

FIGURE 1.23   (a-d) An illustration of the Snap to Curve tool. The process is similar for all the Snap to tools.

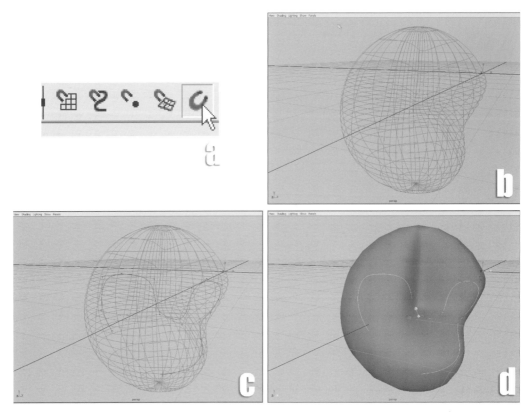

FIGURE 1.24   (a-d) You can use the Make the Selected Object Live tool to create curves on a surface.

Object Live tool (Figure 1.24a). The live object would then appear as a green wireframe (Figure 1.24b). At this point, when a curve is created (Figure 1.24c), all the points of the curve will snap to this live surface. When the curve is complete, and the Make the Selected Object Live tool is clicked once (which makes the Live object "unlive" again), the curve lays completely along the previously live surface (Figure 1.24d).

Similarly, when an object is live, any objects that are moved in the Workspace will snap to that surface automatically.

Operation Lists and Construction History

The next collection of tools (Figure 1.25) is part of Maya's use of the concept of *Construction History*. Construction History is an important part of the flexibility that Maya affords and is a vital part of understanding the concept of *nodes*. You can think of Construction History in a general sense as recorded Undos that are nested within each object of your scene. More accurately, Construction History keeps track of the Inputs and Outputs objects.

FIGURE 1.25   The Operation Lists tools and Construction History toggle.

Many objects in Maya are created from other objects. NURBS are a great example of this. A NURBS surface can be created from a collection of curves that provide some preliminary information on the desired 3D shape. For instance, Figure 1.26 shows a collection of circles that were used to make the three-dimensional, lofted surface next to it. The three-dimensional shape was created by selecting the four circles and choosing Modeling|>Surfaces>Loft. In this simple example the four curves are the inputs and the lofted surface is the output. The curves and the surface are linked via the Construction History stored in the surface.

The collection of tools shown in Figure 1.27 are used to help control and alter Construction History, inputs, and outputs.

Inputs to the Selected Object

The first tool is actually a collection of nested tools. When an object is selected in your Workspace, LMB-click and hold on to this tool and a collection of pop-up menus will appear (Figure 1.27). These allow you to

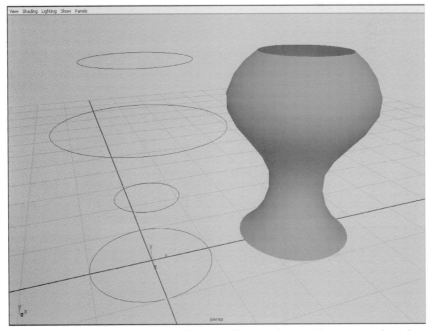

FIGURE 1.26   A lofted surface is created from a collection of curves. The curves at the right are the input that allows for the surface at the right (the output).

FIGURE 1.27   Select, Enable, and Disable all Inputs. This also allows you to make changes to the settings of any node used to create a shape.

select, enable, or disable inputs for a particular object. Figure 1.27 is for the lofted surface shown in Figure 1.26. As such, you can see that this also shows the node (loft) that was used to create the surface. You can select this node again here and make changes to the parameters that were set up to create the surface.

Outputs from the Selected Object

Next is the sister tool that allows you to Select, Enable, and Disable Outputs that might have been created using the element that is active (Figure 1.28). Again, be sure to LMB-click and hold to get this pop-up menu to appear.

Construction History On/Off

Although Construction History can be a tremendous help in modeling (we will look at how in Chapters 4 and 5), it can become a nuisance when it's time to animate. There are also other situations in which having a history attached to an object can cause some interesting problems. Although you can delete any objects of Construction History manually, some folks prefer to turn it off all together as they are performing certain functions.

FIGURE 1.28   Select, Enable, and Disable all Outputs.

This tool allows you to turn off or on the recording of Construction History. In general, you want to leave Construction History on, which is its default. Then, when you are sure your modeling is beautiful and complete, you can get rid of the history so you have a no-strings-attached form.

Now, this is probably the quickest discussion of inputs, outputs, nodes, and Construction History on record and it probably does not make a lot of sense at this point. Not to worry; these concepts are best explained when they are seen in action. We will illustrate again and again the benefits of these concepts through the course of the book. By the end of this volume, inputs, outputs, nodes, and Construction History will be second nature.

Render the Current Frame, IPR Render the Current Frame, and Display Render Globals Window

As discussed earlier, rendering is an important part of the 3D creation process. These next three tools give you access to Maya's rendering functions (Figure 1.29).

The first tool, Render the Current Frame, does just that using the settings defined by clicking on the last of the three buttons in this set. The second, IPR Render the Current Frame, makes use of a technology Maya uses called Interactive Photorealistic Renderer (IPR). We will talk much more of IPR in Chapters 8 and 9, but the basic idea is that IPR allows for quick adjustments in the rendering process at the expense of a little extra time up front. When you use IPR to render a scene, the render time is longer. However, then you can select interactive regions that automatically refresh as you make changes in your scene. Much more on this later.

The last tool of this set brings up the Render Globals Window (Figure 1.30). This allows you to define the parameters that Maya will use to render your scene. We will be looking at most all of these options in Chapter 9, "Rendering," so we won't spend much time on it here.

Numeric Input Tool

This tool is the last part of the Status Line and it contains two parts: a mode selection and an input field. It allows for quick direct entry of values and names (Figure 1.31).

Again, like many other tools, this is a collection of several others. LMB-click and hold where it says *sel* to see the Quick Selection, Quick Rename, Numeric Input: Absolute, and Numeric Input: Relative modes (Figure 1.32).

FIGURE 1.29   Maya's rendering functions can be activated and altered with these tools in the Status Line.

FIGURE 1.30   Render Globals Window.

FIGURE 1.31   Numeric Input tools.

FIGURE 1.32   These nested tools are within the Numeric Input tool.

Quick Selection

This allows you to enter a name in the input field and have Maya search all objects in the scene to find the name you have typed. Note that you may use wildcards. For instance *Loft searches for any objects that end in *Loft;" *Loft** searches for objects whose name begins with *Loft*; and *Loft* searches for objects whose name have *Loft* anywhere within it and selects it or them.

Quick Rename

Once you have selected objects, using Quick Rename a new name can be given to entire collections of objects or individual objects.

Numeric Input: Absolute

This allows you to enter values for any Translate, Rotate, or Scale value manually. For instance, Figure 1.33 shows the lofted surface that we've

FIGURE 1.33   (a-d) Numeric Input: Absolute allows you to enter values quickly where objects are to be placed, scaled, or rotated.

been looking at. It's currently at X=2.5 (Figure 1.33a). If we wish to center the lofted object back to X=0, we would follow these steps:

1. Select the surface.
2. Click on the X handle of the manipulator so that it appears yellow (Figure 1.33b).
3. In Numeric Input: Absolute mode, enter 0 in the input field (Figure 1.33c) and the lofted surface will be immediately moved to this absolute location (Figure 1.33d).

Numeric Input: Relative

This works exactly as do the previous tools except that the value entered in the input field is added or subtracted from the current value.

SHELF

The Shelf is a handy place on which to place the most often used tools. Maya has created by default a collection shown in Figure 1.34.

FIGURE 1.34   The Shelf is where Maya has placed tools that it thinks you will need.

To activate any of the items on the Shelf, simply LMB-click them. Of course, the Shelf can be organized in any way that you wish. See Appendix B, "Customizing the Maya User Interface," for details on how to organize this space to fit your work flow.

TOOLBOX

The Toolbox contains two main collection of tools: the QWERTY tools and a collection of tools that allow for quick customization of your interface (Figure 1.35).

QWERTY

QWERTY is often used as a label for these tools as they are accessed using the hotkeys **Q,W,E,R,T,** and **Y.**

- **Q** pulls up the top tool, the Select tool. This allows you to select a hierarchy, object, or component without altering it by clicking directly on the desired item, or marqueeing (clicking and dragging) around the desired item(s). The second tool down, the Lasso tool, has no default hotkey, but it can be used to draw a custom shape around the items that you desire to select.
- **W** brings up the Move tool, which allows you to move hierarchies, objects, or components.
- **E** launches the Rotate tool, allowing you to rotate items.
- **R** allows you to use the Scale tool, which—you guessed it—allows you to scale hierarchies, objects, or components.
- **T** pulls up the Show Manipulator tool. This tool allows you to show the manipulator (we will talk much more of this tool later) if it's hidden or gets hidden between tools.
- Finally, the **Y** hotkey brings up the last tool used, which occupies the last space of the Toolbox shown in Figure 1.35.

Quick Setup

The bottom half of the Toolbox contains a collection of quick setup options. One click and your interface is transformed with new collections of tools in new panels. The default setups are nice but remember you can create your

FIGURE 1.35 The Toolbox.

own. Be sure to see Appendix B, "Customizing the Maya User Interface," when you're ready to begin customizing these sorts of tools. For most of what we will do in this volume, the default setups are sufficient.

WORKSPACE

We've been referring to the Workspace throughout this chapter. Basically, the Workspace that Maya first shows is a sort of virtual window through which we're viewing the 3D world that we will alter (Figure 1.36).

Understandably, the Workspace is the largest chunk of screen real estate. It's so important that it has its own collection of pull-down menus to allow for quick alteration of the space. In upcoming chapters, we'll look at the details of how to maneuver within this space, and how to optimize and customize the Workspace for different steps in the production process.

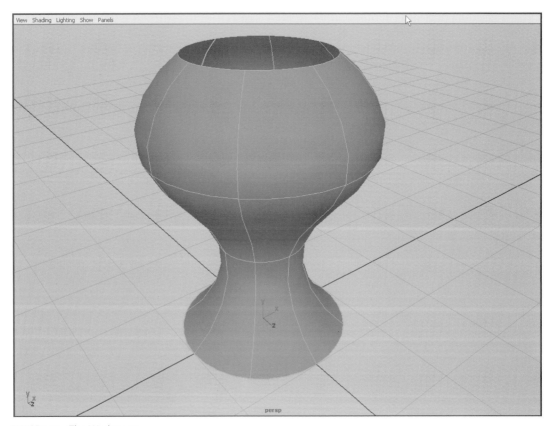

FIGURE 1.36 The Workspace.

CHANNEL/LAYER BOX/TOOL SETTINGS/ATTRIBUTE EDITOR

To the right of the Workspace is an area that can be used for a variety of purposes. The default setup uses this space to display the Channel box. The Channel box allows for the viewing and altering of many parameters of items within the scene (Figure 1.37a).

At the top of the Channel box are a collection of three small buttons that allow you to alter the default Channel box to show the Layer box,

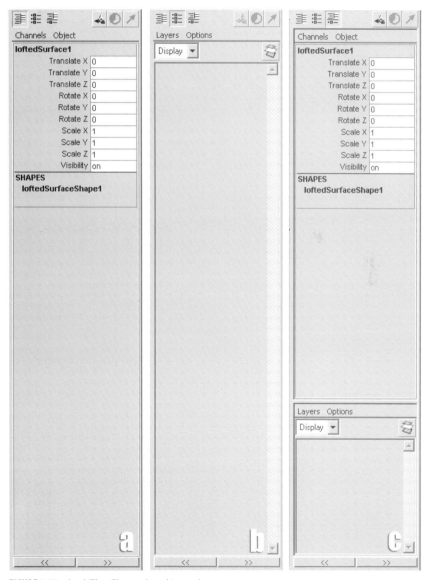

FIGURE 1.37   (a-c) The Channel and Layer boxes.

instead (Figure 1.37b), or both (Figure 1.37c). The Layer box allows you to create and alter layers that can contain collections of your scene. Later, the Layer box can allow you to render complex scenes by rendering chunks of data in your scene, rather than rendering everything at once.

Up at the top-right corner of the interface are three buttons (Figure 1.38a) that allow you to commandeer the space that the Channel/Layer boxes take up. This space can be used to display the Attribute Editor, which allows you to, well, edit the attributes of items within your scene (Figure 1.38b). You can also choose to see the active tool's settings (Figure 1.38c). The third button is the standard Channel/Layer box's use of the space.

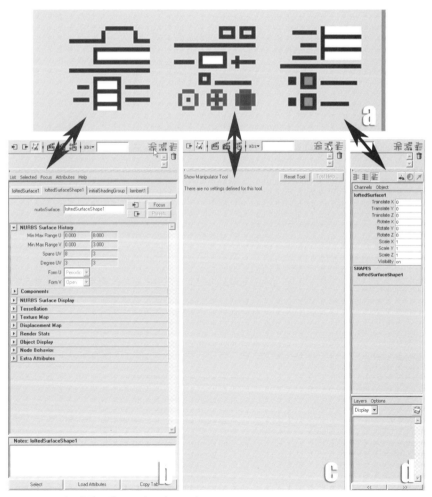

FIGURE 1.38   (a-d) The Channel and Layer boxes.

TIME AND RANGE SLIDER

Below the Workspace and running the length of the interface are Time and Range sliders (Figure 1.39). There are also some other animation tools that sit at the right-hand edge of these two sliders. These are exclusively animation tools, and because we'll explore them so extensively in Chapter 8, "Animation," we won't discuss these areas further here.

FIGURE 1.39   Time and Range slider.

COMMAND LINE AND HELP LINE

Below the Time and Range sliders is the command line. In this volume, we won't get to use much Mel Script or other high-end functions that would require the Command Line. However, the line below that, the Help Line, is of immense use. The left half of the Help Line can provide invaluable information on tools that you are unfamiliar with. The Help Line will list information indicating what tool your mouse is over, and then when a tool is active, the Help Line will provide details on what to do next within that tool. Watch this space closely when you are first learning Maya—it is a great aid (Figure 1.40).

FIGURE 1.40   The Command and Help Lines.

CONCLUSION

Pretty intense, eh? I know, kind of long and there is so much informaton here that it is impossible to retain it all. However, mastery of tools often depends on repetition of use or exposure to concepts. This chapter provides the first taste of where to find most collections of tools.

Remember that Maya allows for tremendous flexibility in how this interface is displayed and organized. Make sure that when you get comfortable with Maya and are at the point of streamlining your creation process, read Appendix B, "Customizing the Maya User Interface," to see how to make the Maya user interface a custom tool.

Throughout the rest of the book we will explore heavily how to use the collections that we have been introduced to in this chapter. That's where the fun begins.

So, no more overviews of collections. On to the specifics. On to the creation process.

GETTING STARTED WITH MODELING

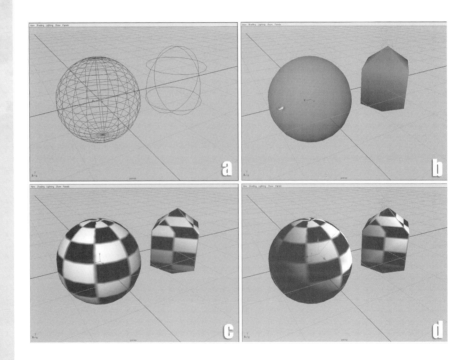

S o, we looked at where tools are organized within the Maya interface in Chapter 1. We've looked at a general sense of how projects
are realized with a rough idea of a work flow. This chapter will start
that work flow journey with modeling. Each of the chapters in the rest of
the book will begin with a bit of theory or general techniques. Then, we
will get to the good things and look at all the details—the specifics of how
projects get created. We will look at a wide variety of tools and how to
bend them to your creative will. At the end of this modeling chapter, we
will have created the room shown in Figure 2.1.

SETTING UP YOUR PROJECT

Before we start building or even maneuvering, we need to be sure and set
up a project where we can store our Maya information. Follow these
steps to do this:

1. With Maya open, select File>Project>New.
2. In the New Project window that pops up, enter **Room_Tutorial** in
   the Name input field and then choose a location where you'd like to
   save all the related files. Remember that Maya is very particular with

FIGURE 2.1   The completed room model created in this chapter will look like this.

*Although we cover things step-by-step in the tutorials of this and later chapters, if you
ever want to see the finished project, be sure and take a look at the included CD-ROM.
In the Tutorials folder, you will find folders for each chapter. Contained in those folders will be the Maya scene files for the tutorials with scene files in that chapter.*

its naming conventions and spaces or special characters are not acceptable. Be sure to have the underscore in the Name input field.

3. Hit the Use Defaults button at the bottom of the screen and then hit the Accept button.

You are ready to start creating a project in Maya. Be sure you remember that any changes you make to preferences or to the interface will be stored in this project.

MANEUVERING IN MAYA

Before we can get cranking building our room, it is important to know how to move around in our digital world. The default view of our virtual world shows us a grid that lies along the X, Z plane. In the middle of the plane is an indicator to let us know which directions Maya understands as the X, Y, and Z directions. Also notice the small axis at the bottom-left corner of the screen. This small axis always stays there so you can always get your bearings.

The **Alt** (the **Command** key on a Mac) key is critical to all movement. The other vital part of movement is a three-buttoned mouse. All movement through our virtual world will take place through some combination of these two elements.

Maneuvering through your space assumes that the Workspace is the view through a type of virtual camera. To move through the scene, you are moving the virtual camera to a new location. As such, all the names for different types of movement are traditional camera terms. Take a moment to try these combinations:

- *Tumble* (**Alt**-LMB): *Tumbling* can also be referred to as *rotating* your camera around the object and you'll use it often. Hold down the **Alt** key, then click and drag the LMB to tumble around the scene. Notice that you always tumble around the center of the Workspace.
- *Track* (**Alt**-RMB): *Tracking* is similar to moving your camera from side to side without turning it. This allows you to move what your camera is looking at and brings into play a new center of your Workspace. Once you've tracked to a new location, when you tumble, you'll tumble around the current center of the screen.
- *Dolly* (**Alt**-LMMB—that's left and middle mouse button): A *dolly move* is the equivalent of moving your camera closer to the center of the Workspace. It is important to notice that the camera's focal length doesn't

change (we don't get any more telephoto or fish eye), but the camera does get closer to the scene, and consequently the objects look bigger.

Get familiar with these combinations. Maya is amazingly snappy in its OpenGL implementation and you'll find yourself doing much more work in a perspective view than you may have done in your previous 3D experience. So it is important that you feel comfortable and in control of movement within the 3D perspective view.

Much modification of any item within Maya takes place via a *manipulator*. To better understand the manipulator, consider the following mini-tutorial.

TUTORIAL

2.1 EXPLORING THE MANIPULATOR

Step 1: Select Modeling │ Create>NURBS Primitives>Sphere.

Step 2: Dolly into the scene until the sphere appears a bit larger in the Workspace (Figure 2.2a).

Step 3: Hit **3** and then **5** on your keyboard. We will talk more about this in a minute. For now, suffice it to say it makes the geometry more intuitive (Figure 2.2b).

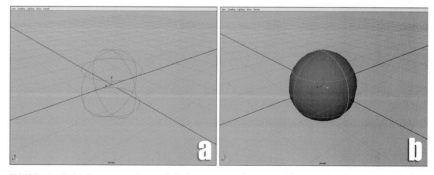

FIGURE 2.2 (a-b) Create a sphere, dolly in to see it closer, and have it displayed as a solid object.

Step 4: Activate the Move Tool from the Toolbox or hit **w** (make sure it is lowercase) on your keyboard to activate it. Immediately, you'll notice that in the middle of the sphere is a new icon for the manipulator (Figure 2.3a).

Step 5: Switch to the Rotate tool (**e**) (Figure 2.3b) and then to the Scale tool (**r**) (Figure 2.3c). Notice how the manipulator changes to match.

FIGURE 2.3   The manipulator appears at the geometric center of the selected object. (a) The Move manipulator, (b) The Rotate manipulator, (c) The Scale manipulator.

When you wish to move, rotate, or scale any element within your scene, the manipulator is the visual tool that allows you to do so. The manipulator is essentially a collection of handles that you can grab to make changes. The Move manipulator, for example, consists of four handles: X, Y, Z, and center (Figure 2.4a).

The way these handles work is simple. Just LMB drag any of the handles to move the selected item in the direction of the handle. So, to move the sphere in the X direction, simply grab the red X handle and drag (Figure 2.4b). Do the same for the Y and Z directions and handles (Figures 2.4c and 2.4d).

The center handle allows you to LMB drag the element in all directions. The center handle for the Move manipulator does have some other important qualities. Look closely at the center handle and you'll notice that it is a square (Figure 2.5a). No matter which direction you look at the manipulator from, that center handle remains a square. This square represents the *view plane*. The view plane is the imaginary plane that runs perpendicular to you the viewer. This means that when you grab this center handle and move the object (although it is moving absolutely in three dimensions), it is always sitting on the current view plane.

If you **Ctrl**-LMB any one of the X, Y, or Z handles, it turns off that direction handle. The center handle (previously a box) then becomes a plane that corresponds to the two directions that you can still move the object (Figure 2.5 b, c, and d).

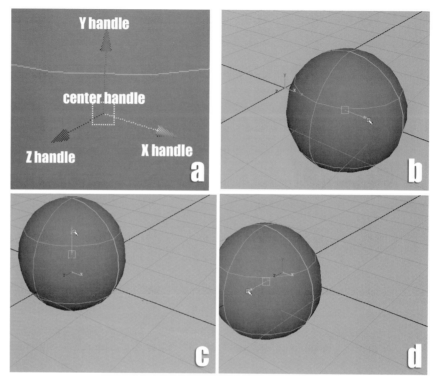

FIGURE 2.4   (a) Handle break down. (b) Moving object in X direction with the X handle. (c) Moving object in Y direction with Y handle. (d) Moving object in Z direction with Z handle.

FIGURE 2.5   (a-d) The center handle indicates the directions in which you can move an item in the Workspace. You can turn off potential directions by Ctrl-LMB-clicking them.

To return the Move manipulator's center handle to move along the view plane, simply **Ctrl**-LMB-click the center handle again.

The Rotate manipulator and Scale manipulator aren't quite as complicated. In each of these, LMB-dragging any of the directional handles rotates or scales exclusively in that one direction. LMB-dragging the center of the rotation handles, or the center scale handle, rotates or scales in all directions.

UNDERSTANDING STATES OF OBJECT DISPLAY

When we first created the sphere, it didn't look much like a sphere—it kind of looked like four circles that intersected each other at their poles. In the early days of 3D, the actual visual representation of your model wasn't much more than this view of the *Isoparms* that made up the shape. Isoparms are one of the components that make up NURBS shapes (more on what exactly NURBS are later in Chapters 4 and 5).

By default, Maya shows objects to you as simply as it can. In the case of a NURBS object, it does this by showing these circles that help define the shape. If we were looking at a polygonal sphere, the default view would show us a transparent view of all the polygons that make up that shape (Figure 2.6a). This view of objects that allows us to see through the object as though we were looking at a papier-maché piñata before the papier-maché was placed over the frame is called a *wireframe*.

Wireframe is a mode that your computer with its video card is able to draw quickly. It doesn't have to spend a lot of energy deciding which surfaces aren't going to be seen or thinking about how those surfaces react to the virtual light around them. However, wireframes can be a bit distracting. For one thing, displaying your model as a wireframe really doesn't look much like the actual object.

As computers have increased in power and complexity, they've become better able to show 3D objects in increasingly lifelike fashions. OpenGL is the technology that allows your video card to take the 3D information and process it into increasingly lifelike representations in real time. This means that instead of having to work with collections of lines, we can work with visual forms. Maya has one of the best OpenGL implementations in the industry.

To display your model as a smooth object, simply hit **5** on your keyboard. This brings up *Smooth Shade* (Figure 2.6b), which attempts to create a solid version of your model. Something to note about Smooth Shade is that it functions with the assumption that there's a flood light sitting atop your virtual camera. That's, no matter how you tumble,

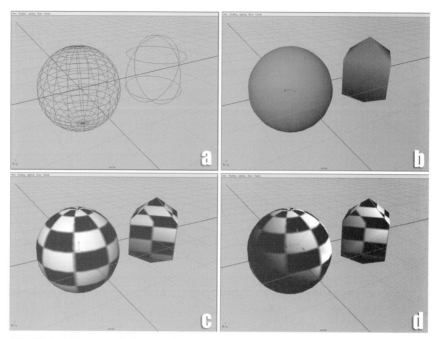

FIGURE 2.6   (a) Compare Polygon Sphere (left) and NURBS Sphere (right) using Wireframe, (b) Smooth Shade, (c) Smooth Shade with Hardware Texturing, and (d) Smooth Shade with Hardware Texturing and Lighting.

you'll never see the dark side of your object. Also, it doesn't show any textures or shaders that may have been applied.

To get a better idea of how light in a scene actually functions, hit **6** on your keyboard to bring up *Smooth Shade with Hardware Texturing* (Figure 2.6c). This tells Maya not only to show you the objects as solid shapes but also to show an approximation of any textures that may have been applied to the surface.

Hitting **7** on your keyboard adds the extra burden and help of attempting to calculate how the light in the scene would look, approximately (Figure 2.6d). Now of course, this quick hardware shading (the hardware refers primarily to your video card) isn't tremendously accurate. However, it can give you a very rough idea of where your lights are pointing and how the colors of the lights and the colors of the surfaces will interact.

Now, you'll notice that the NURBS sphere to the right in each of the examples shown in Figure 2.6 doesn't look much like a sphere. This is because NURBS can be displayed as rough, medium, or fine within the Workspace. To change the level of smoothness, simply hit **1, 2,** or **3** for rough, medium, or fine, respectively (Figure 2.7).

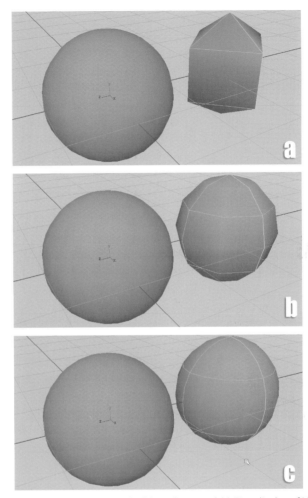

FIGURE 2.7   (a) Change the Rough, (b) Medium, and (c) Fine display of NURBS.
Note that the change has no effect on the polygonal sphere on the left.

In general, when you first start a scene, it is a habit to hit **3** and **5** or **6** quickly to get a vision of the 3D space you are working with that has solid shapes. Later, if things get complex and the interface begins to slow down, you can always reduce the smoothing, choose not to show textures, and so on. However, up front, it is nice to take advantage of that expensive video card in your machine and give it a bit of a workout for your benefit.

MOVING ON

So now we've talked about the manipulators and know how to do basic move, rotate, and scale functions; how to move around within our scene;

and how to can control how Maya displays our scene. Now it is time to start creating the scene. LMB-click on the sphere used for these examples to select it. Then delete it from your scene by hitting the **Backspace** or **Delete** keys and start on the next tutorial.

T U T O R I A L

2.2 PRIMITIVE ROOM FORMS

To start modeling this room, we're going to begin with 3D shapes that Maya makes automatically. Although you can make just about any shape imaginable in Maya, there's a small collection of shapes that Maya has built in; that are readily accessible through the Modeling module pull-down menus.

In this tutorial, we will look at how to create, scale, and position these primitives into position to rough out our room. At the end of this chapter, you should be comfortable with maneuvering within Maya's Workspace and feel confident in your knowledge of basic object manipulation.

Step 1: Activate the Modeling module.

Step 2: Create a floor with a NURBS plane. To begin with, we will work with both NURBS and polygonal objects. We will talk much more about when to use which later, but for this project, we will explore the placement and alteration of both.

Go to Modeling | Create>NURBS Primitives>Plane (Option) to bring up the NURBS Plane Options window. To be sure that you are not inheriting any earlier settings, use the Edit>Reset Settings (within the NURBS Plane Options window) to clear out everything. For now, simply hit the Create button to place the plane in the scene.

Step 3: Resize to 20 units by 35 units. Although we could just eyeball the size of this floor, since it will help define the shape of the entire rest of the room, it will be important that we create it with accurate dimensions.

In the Channels box, enter **25** in the Scale X input field and hit Enter. Then, enter **40** in the Scale Z input field and again hit Enter. This tells the previous 1 unit by 1 unit plane to become 25 by 40. For the sake of this tutorial, we will assume that the units here are feet.

Hit **3** and **5** on your keyboard to give yourself a solid look at the floor (Figure 2.8).

There are a few things to notice about this NURBS plane. First, it is truly two-dimensional. It has depth in the X and Z directions but it has no actual thickness. It is like a piece of paper lying in space though it is infinitely thinner.

The next thing that's important to notice about this step is that we resized the plane, but left it in place. This means that the plane's center is sitting at 0,0,0. The benefit of this is that the floor is indeed on the default ground plane.

FIGURE 2.8   Our 25 by 40 floor is made from a NURBS plane.

Step 4: Create the first wall with a Polygon Cube primitive. Choose Model-ing│Create>Polygon Primitives>Cube (Option). Again, this will open the op-tions box for the Cube, and again make sure to reset the settings to clear out any random settings that may already exist. Hit the Create button.

The cube that will be created will be small and sitting in the middle of your room. For this cube, we will resize and position it using the Channels box.

Without clicking anywhere in the Workspace, enter **40** in the Scale Z input field in the Channels box. We know that the floor is 40 feet long, so a side wall would also need to be this long. Also enter **2** in the Scale X input field to give this wall some extra thickness. Finally, enter **9** in the Scale Y input field.

The wall will still be sitting halfway into the floor. So, we need to place it so it rests on the floor. We know that the wall is 9 feet tall, and that the wall ex-panded up and down from the middle. So, we need to move the floor up 4.5 feet (half of the height of the wall). Again, in the Channels box, enter 4.5 into the Translate Y input field. This will move up the wall so that it sits on the floor.

Continuing on with the Channels box method, we know that the wall's center is sitting at halfway across the room (in the X direction). From the cur-rent position to the edge of the floor is 12.5 feet (half of the floor's 25 feet). But, the wall is 2 feet thick. If we just entered 12.5 in the Translate X input field, the wall would be hanging halfway off the floor. So, we need to subtract 1 foot (half of the 2 foot thickness of the wall) from the direction it needs to move. So,

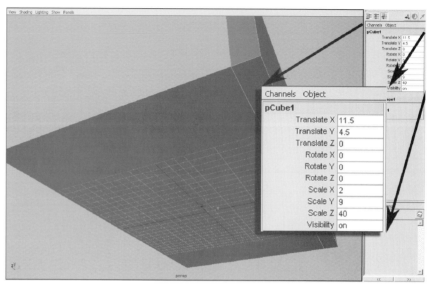

FIGURE 2.9   Placed wall and resulting Channels box with defined values.

enter **11.5 feet** into the Translate X input field to move the wall so that the outer edge of the wall perfectly lines up with the edge of the floor (Figure 2.9).

Step 5: Create a second wall through duplication. To create the wall on the opposite side of the room we could simply repeat the process outlines in Step 4. However, to save time, we will take this perfectly good wall and make a duplicate of it.

Select Edit>Duplicate (Option). Again, because this is the first time we've used the tool, select Edit>Reset Settings in the Duplicate Options window to clear any past settings. Hit the Duplicate button.

In the Workspace, there won't seem to have been any change. This is because the new duplicated wall is sitting in exactly the same space as the original one. Open the Outliner (Window>Outliner) and see for yourself that there are two pCube objects in the scene.

Step 6: Use Maya's Align tool to align the new wall to the opposite end of the room. We could simply work with another collection of values in the Channels box to position this wall on the opposite end. However, though that method is exact, it isn't necessarily the most wieldy or intuitive. For this step, we will use a new function in Maya 4.5—the Align tool.

Select Modify>Snap Align Objects>Align Tool. This will make your mouse change from an arrow to a small cross and some small grayed out icons appear around your wall. The reason they are grayed out is that the Align tool needs at least two objects to work with. So, hold down the **Shift** key and click on the

FIGURE 2.10   When two objects are selected, the Align tool will present icons that allow you to pick how you wish to align your objects.

floor. All of a sudden, you'll get a collection of gray and blue icons surrounding objects in your scene (Figure 2.10).

These icons are fairly intuitive but let's look at a few for just a minute (Figure 2.11). There are some conventions that are important to know. The first is that the initial object that you select (of the two that must be selected to align) will be the object that moves. Further, this first object (the one that moves) is represented by the hollowed-out box. The solid blue box is the second object selected and it remains stationary. So, in this case, the wall was selected first, so it will be doing the moving and is represented in the Align tool by the hollow box. So, if the middle icon shown in Figure 2.11 is pressed, the wall will be moved so that its horizontal (X) center matches the center of the center of our floor.

Similarly, on the far left are two icons. The top icon represents moving the wall so that it is inner edge lines up with the outer edge of the floor. The bottom icon is the one we want as we want the outer edge of the wall to match the outer edge of the floor (Figure 2.11b).

To exit out of the Align tool, just select any other tool.

Step 7: Rename the elements created thus far. Before we get going too far, it is important that we take control of the scene in terms of nomenclature.

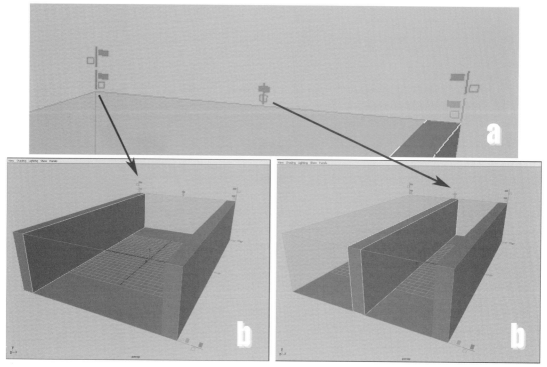

FIGURE 2.11 (a-b) Take a quick look at the Align tool. Remember that the first object selected will move and that it is represented by the hollow blue box.

Terms such as pCube1, pCube2, and nurbsPlane1 do nothing for us as we try to organize our scene. For now, it may not seem like any big deal that we are not giving objects more indicative names, but when there are 200 or 300 objects and hierarchies in a scene, it is vitally important.

There are a few ways to name objects or rename objects that have already been created. The easiest is through the Outliner, which is a window that outlines objects within your scene. It can be pulled up through the Window>Outliner pull-down menu, or viewed by pulling up one of the premade panel organizations.

In the Toolbox at the left edge of the UI (user interface), select the Persp/Outliner preset (Figure 2.12). This will change your interface to look like Figure 2.12.

The Outliner, of course, is the new box on the left of the Workspace with a list of objects. Some of these objects are invisible to you presently (such as the defaultLightSet, defaultObjectSet, and the four cameras), but don't worry about them for now. What's important is that we've created the three objects now. To rename an object, double-LMB-click its name in the Outliner. The name will highlight and you can change it to whatever you wish.

FIGURE 2.12   Take some time to bring the Outliner into your panel layout. The premade Persp/Outline setting will do the trick.

Rename nurbsPlane1 to **Floor**; rename the wall that's to the left (-X) direction **WallNorth**; and rename the wall to the right (+X) **WallSouth**. The directions aren't arbitrary because the final image will make use of lights coming in through the window and we want to make sure that's facing east. Plus, it becomes easier to refer to walls by their north, south, east, and west bearings.

Step 8: Create WallEast and WallWest by duplicating existing walls and put them into position with the Align tool. Select **WallNorth** and hit **Ctrl-D** (the keyboard shortcut for Duplicate). We can just use the keyboard shortcut because we can remember that the settings are all clear since we reset them earlier.

A new wall called WallNorth1 will appear in the Outliner. Again, there will be little visible difference as the new wall is in the same space as the old one. We want to rotate this wall 90 degrees of its present heading. The easiest way to keep track of how Maya rotates objects is to decide along which axis the object would need to turn. In this case, to rotate the wall so that it is at a right angle to the other walls, we would need to rotate the wall around its Y axis. So, enter **90** into the Rotate Y input field (Figure 2.13a).

We know that the floor is 25 feet wide. For the floor, this is the X measurement. However, because we've rotated the wall, remember that the length of the wall is its Z scale measurement. Change the existing setting (40) to the new 25 in the Scale Z input field of the Channels box (Figure 2.13b).

Now, activate the Align tool (Modify>Snap Align Objects>Align Tool) and first align the wall to the middle of the floor in the X direction (Figure 2.13c). Then align it so that its outer edge matches the inner edge of the floor (Figure 2.13d). Notice that to do this, we used icons that resided along different planes of the gray align box that the Align tool creates to assist.

Rename this new wall to **WallEast**.

Duplicate WallEast and use the Align tool to place it on the opposite end of the room. Rename this new wall to **WallWest**.

FIGURE 2.13   (a-d) Duplicate an extant wall, rotate it, and resize it to match the floor. Figures c and d show the results of the Align tool and which icons to use.

Step 9: Create a placeholder wall. Later, in Chapter 4, we're going to create the arched wall seen in the final rendering of this room. However, for now, to help with spacing, we're going to just place a primitive polygonal cube in the middle of the room to help us as we create the beamwork in the ceiling. To do this, select **WallEast**, duplicate it (**Ctrl-D**), and change its Translate Y to 0 and its Scale X to .3. This puts a wall in the middle of the room with a thickness of about 4 inches. Again, this will go away but it will be important for us in future steps. Rename this wall **WallMiddlePH**.

Step 10: Create and position the first beam. The first beam that we're going to create will rest right up against the placeholder wall that we've created. Although you could copy and paste walls that exist, for practice, create a new cube polygon primitive. Resize this polygon primitive so that it is 25 units in X (Scale X = 25); .5 units in Y (Scale Y=0.5); and .1 units in Z (Scale Z=0.1). This makes a beam that's 25 feet long, 6 inches tall, and a bit over 1 inch thick.

Use the Align tool to align this new beam to the top of the placeholder wall. Now activate the Move tool (hot key **w**) and move this beam along its Z axis just far enough so that you can see it without it being inside of the placeholder wall (Figure 2.14). We will place this beam much more accurately later, of course, but for now, we just need to see it.

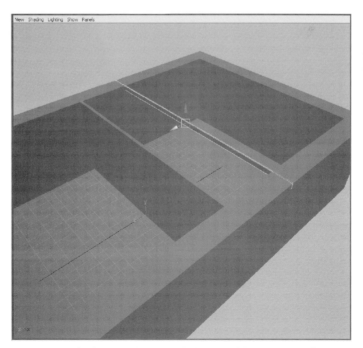

FIGURE 2.14   The beam is aligned with the top of the walls and offset from the middle placeholder wall.

Now we could figure out mathematically where this beam would need to be so that it butted up against the middle wall, but let's take a minute to examine some other methods of moving and aligning objects.

While your mouse is inside the Workspace, press and hold the **Spacebar** until you get the Marking menu shown in Figure 2.15. Click in the middle of the Marking menu and select Top View. The Workspace will shift into an orthographic Top view. *Orthographic* means that you can only see and manipulate two dimensions. In this Top view, you can see and alter objects in the X and Z direction.

Hit **4** on your keyboard to display the scene as a wireframe. Otherwise, everything is a flat gray and it is impossible to differentiate where one shape ends and the next one begins. Assuming that the Move tool is still active, you'll see the manipulator for the beam sitting in the middle of the beam in both the X and Z directions (Figure 2.16a). We're going to shift this manipulator so that it rests on one of the corners of the beam. Then, once it is sitting right on the corner, we can snap that corner to other parts of our model.

To do this, hit the Insert button on your keyboard. The manipulator will change immediately to an icon similar to the one shown in Figure 2.16b. Be sure to notice the inset image in Figure 2.16b to get a better idea of what this looks like.

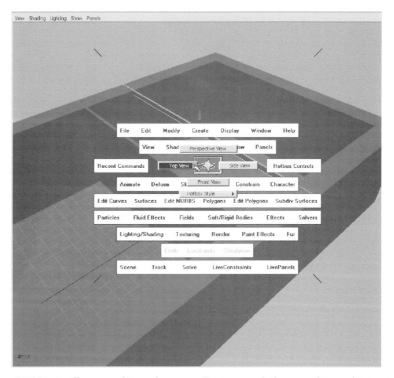

FIGURE 2.15 Changing the Workspace to Top view with the Spacebar Marking menu.

FIGURE 2.16   (a-c) Manipulate the position of the manipulator. In this case, there's special care to make sure that the manipulator is snapped to the corner of the beam.

This new manipulator allows us to change the position of the manipulator for the Move, Scale, and Rotate tools. In situations where you are rotating an object, this is especially important as the geometric middle of an object such as a door isn't the place where you want the door to rotate. You can move this manipulator by LMB-clicking and dragging in the middle of the yellow box, or by dragging any of the manipulator handles represented by simple lines.

In this case, we want to get the manipulator to be right at the corner of the beam. To do this, we will snap the manipulator to the point (or vertex) that exists at the corner of the beam. You can activate Snap to Points in the Status Line, or hold down the **v** hotkey. Either way, the manipulator's yellow square will change to a yellow circle. LMB-click and drag the manipulator to the bottom-right corner of the beam (Figure 2.16c). Release the mouse before releasing the **v** on your keyboard. You may need to dolly in to see closer where the manipulator is sitting. You should be able to feel it snap into position. Hit the Insert button again to tell Maya that you are done changing the position of the manipulator.

Still in Top view, take a moment to dolly out until you can see both the beam and the box that represent the placeholder wall. Again, using the Move tool, we can snap this beam right up against the placeholder wall by again holding down the **v** hotkey and LMB-dragging the blue (Z) manipulator handle down until it snaps into place against the wall.

Press and hold the **Spacebar** and select Perspective view again by clicking in the middle of the marking menu. In Perspective view, tumble around so that you can see how the beam lines up against the placeholder wall (Figure 2.17). Rename the beam to **Beam**.

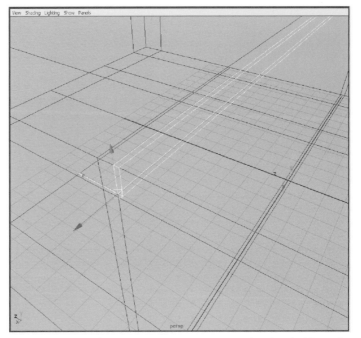

FIGURE 2.17   View of the beam snapped up against the place holder wall.

Step 11: Duplicate and place another beam against WallEast. Hit **Ctrl-D** to duplicate Beam. This will create a new object called Beam1 automatically. To get it butted up against WallEast, we could change the position of the manipulator as we did earlier. But in the interest of exploring various methods, we will make use of the Numeric Input Tool in the Status Line (far right).

Using the Move tool, hold down the **v** key to indicate that you wish to Snap to Points. Then LMB-click and drag the Z handle of Beam1's manipulator so that it snaps against the inside vertex of the WallEast (Figure 2.18). Now, remember that because the manipulator is on the inside corner of the beam, this newly placed beam is inside the wall.

However, we know that this beam is exactly .1 units thick. So, you can double-check this in the Channels box while Beam1 is selected. This is important as this means that the beam is exactly 0.1 foot into the wall.

In the Status Line, at the far right, change the Numeric Input tool to Numeric Input: Relative (Figure 2.19a). To refresh your memory from the last chapter, this change will allow us to enter a value that will be added to the active value. Right now, by default, there's no active value; we need to activate one in the Channels box. Because we want to move Beam1 out of the wall, we need to make the adjustment in the Z direction. So, click on the words *Translate Z* in the Channels box (*not* the input field). It should highlight.

FIGURE 2.18   The newly placed Beam1 is actually 0.1 foot inside the wall.

Now, in the Numeric Input tool's input field, enter **0.1** (Figure 2.19b). When you hit Enter, Beam1 will shift in the Z direction 0.1 units. The new value for Translate Z, 17.95, should be reflected in the Channels box.

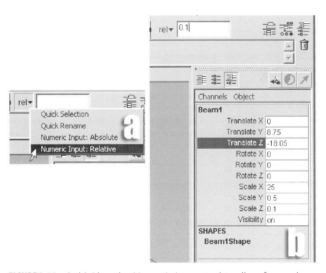

FIGURE 2.19   (a-b) Alter the Numeric Input tool to allow for a value that adds to the one in the Channels box.

Step 12: Hide extraneous objects and measure the distance between Beam and Beam1. We're going to need to put some additional beams between Beam and Beam1. To make sure that they are appropriately spaced, it is important that we know exactly how far apart the extant beams are from each other.

Maya has some nifty measuring tools, but if there are too many objects in the scene, it can become tricky to indicate which distances you really want to measure. So, we will hide objects that would be in the way. Select **Floor**, and then hold down the **Shift** key, and add all the walls to the selection. You can do this in either the Workspace or in the Outliner (the Outliner is probably slightly easier).

Once all of these objects are selected, hit **Ctrl-h**. The pull-down menu for this command is Display>Hide>Hide Selection. The result should be Beam and Beam1 visible in the Workspace.

Change the Workspace to Top view (Spacebar, Marking menu, click in the center, Top view). This will give you a clear view of the distance between the beams.

Select Create>Measure Tool>Distance Tool. Your mouse will change to a sort of crosshairs. These crosshairs allow you to plot points between which Maya will measure the distance. In our case, we want to know the distance from the inside corner of Beam to the inside corner of Beam1 (or in this view, the bottom corners of each). To get exact measurements, we also want to make sure that as we're plotting these points to measure between that we snap right to the corner. So, hold **v** down and LMB-click on the bottom corner of Beam in the Workspace.

A large green cross should appear and a new object called locator1 will appear in the Outliner. Now, while still holding down the **v** key, click on the bottom corner of Beam1. A whole slew of things happen at this point. Two new objects appear in the Outliner: the second locator (locator2) and the actual distance (distanceDimension1). In the Workspace, the measurement should read 17.75 (Figure 2.20).

FIGURE 2.20   Here you have the results of taking a measurement.

Step 13: Duplicate three new beams directly into place. Because the design calls for five beams, that means we will have four spaces between beams. A quick calculation (one-fourth of 17.75=4.4375) gives us the distance that the next three beams should be from each other to give us five beams that are equal distances apart. However, instead of duplicating and placing each beam individually, we will have Maya do it with the Duplicate function.

Select **Beam** in the Workspace and choose Edit>Duplicate (Option). Figure 2.21 shows the Duplicate Options dialog box. The three columns connected to the rows—Translate, Rotate, and Scale—although unlabeled, represent X, Y, and Z values, respectively. This window allows us to do things such as move (Translate), rotate, and scale duplicates. So, in our case, we know that we want each duplicate to be 4.4375 feet from the beam before it. Specifically, we need the duplicate beams to be moving in the –Z direction. So, by entering this value in the Z column of the Translate row, we're telling Maya to move each duplicate –4.375 units from the original object *or the last duplicate*. Up to now, we've been making single duplicates but notice that there's an area to define the number of copies. In our case, we would like three.

Click the Duplicate button, and voilà! Three new beams called Beam2, Beam3, and Beam4 appear and they are each –4.375 feet from the last beam and right in between the two beams created and positioned earlier (Figure 2.22).

One caveat to remember now. Because we changed the values in the Duplicate Options window, if we now hit **Ctrl-D**, whatever object is selected will be duplicated three times and moved –4.375 units from its present location. Be sure to remember that the settings have been changed and reset them before duplicating again.

FIGURE 2.21   The Duplicate Options window with altered Z Translate input field and Number of Copies.

FIGURE 2.22 Results of duplication.

Step 14: Clean up. Cleaning as you go is important as your projects increase in complexity. In this case, we will clean in a couple ways. First of all, in the Outliner, select **locator1**, **locator2**, and **distanceDimension1**, and delete them. The measurement is important to remember for a few steps in the future but its nice to clean out those things as you go.

Second, select all the beams in either the Workspace or the Outliner (marquee around them or hold down the Shift key to add to selections) and hit **Ctrl-g** to group them together. In the Outliner, you'll notice that a new hierarchy called *group* will have appeared. If you expand the hierarchy, you'll see all the beams sitting within it. Rename the group BeamsNS (for beams north and south).

Step 15: Duplicate BeamsNS to the other side of the room. To do this, first we need to see the rest of the room. Select Display>Show>All to bring back all the objects you had hidden before. Or, if you've not hidden anything since we hid the walls you could use the hotkey combination **Ctrl-Shift-h** to Show Last Hidden.

Hit **4** on your keyboard to make sure you are viewing the scene as a wireframe. For an exercise, click anywhere in your scene that there's not an object. This effectively selects nothing and deselects any active objects. Now, click on any of the beams in the Workspace. Notice that the beam will highlight in both the Workspace and the Outliner. But what if you wish to select the entire group of beams? Well, you could try and marquee around them in the Workspace, but that would also likely select a bunch of other elements in the scene that you didn't mean to select. Some better methods include selecting directly the group BeamsNS in the Outliner, or choosing any one beam in the Workspace, and hitting the Up Arrow key. Doing this selects up in any hierarchy to the next parent level. Now, the group BeamsNS is selected and highlighted in both the Outliner and Workspace.

Your manipulator for the group BeamsNS is likely in the geometric middle of the group of beams. To get a duplicated group of beams into the other side of the room we could figure it out mathematically, or simply move the manipulator so that it rested on one of the outer corners of the outer beams.

Figure 2.23a shows the manipulator snapped onto the bottom corner of the bottom beam. As a quick review, remember to move the manipulator, hit Insert, and then activate the Move Tool (**w**). Hold down **v** (to snap to point/ vertex) and then click and drag the manipulator into the desired position. You

FIGURE 2.23   (a-b) Adjust the manipulator for the newly created BeamsNS1 and move the new group into position (snapped to the WallWest).

may need to dolly in close enough to make sure that you snap to the edge of the beam and not some other vertex that might be close by. Finally, hit Insert again to lock the manipulator into position.

Now, select Edit>Duplicate (Option) and reset the settings (Edit>Reset Settings) before hitting the Duplicate button. This will create a new group in the Outliner called BeamsNS1 and a new collection of beams that is sitting at the same place in space.

Still with the Move tool active, hold **v** down and click and drag the group BeamNS1's Z manipulator handle down so that it snaps into place on the west wall (WallWest) as shown in Figure 2.23b.

Step 16: Create new beams that run the length of the room. As the final rendering shows, this room includes another set of beams that run the length of the room. To do this, use the same sorts of methods to start out. Create a new polygonal primitive cube (Modeling⎮Create>Polygon Primitives> Cube). We know that the room is 40 feet long (Z), so change the Scale Z in the Channels box to read **40**. These beams also happen to be 0.3 foot by 0.3 foot, so change the values in the Scale X and Scale Y to 0.3.

Now, use the Align tool to get it aligned to the tops of the walls (select the new cube. Shift-select one of the walls, and choose Modify>Snap Align Objects>Align Tool). After aligning, hit Enter to exit out of the Align tool. The results should look close to Figure 2.24. Be sure to rename this beam CrossBeam in the Outliner.

FIGURE 2.24 Newly created and aligned CrossBeam.

Click anywhere in the scene where there's no object to deselect both your new CrossBeam and whatever wall you used to align it, and then select **CrossBeam**. Make four duplicates of the CrossBeam, each 2 feet in the positive X direction (Edit>Duplicate (Option). Be sure to enter **2** in the X column of Translate and the number of copies to 4).

Again, select just CrossBeam and duplicate four copies again, only this time make them all −2′ from the last. Select all the CrossBeams in the Outliner and group them together (**Ctrl-g).** Rename the group CrossBeams. The result should look like Figure 2.25.

Step 17: Create a ceiling. You can create the ceiling either by creating another NURBS plane (Modeling | Create>NURBS Primitives>Plane) and changing the Channel box's Scale X and Scale Z to 25 and 40 respectively; or by selecting the Floor and duplicating it (be sure to reset the Duplicate Options settings). Either way, be sure to either enter 9 for the Translate Y setting or snap the new plane to the top of the walls. Also, rename the object to Ceiling.

Step 18: Organize layers. In the never-ending battle of properly organizing your project, let's take a minute to organize parts of the creation into layers. Layers in Maya aren't like layers in Photoshop, Illustrator, or other 2D-based applications. Don't think of layers as resting one on top of another but rather as

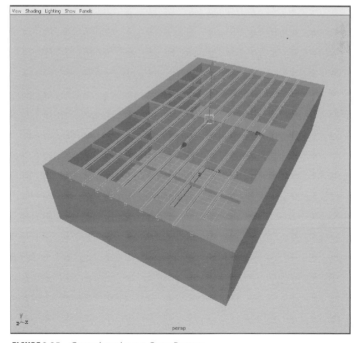

FIGURE 2.25   Completed new CrossBeams.

FIGURE 2.26   Display the Layers
Editor and create a new layer.

collections of objects. Part of the reason we want to do this is to be able to hide collections of objects quickly. Right now, we're looking at an entirely enclosed box that makes it fairly awkward to do anything inside the room.

At the top of the Channels box are three buttons (Show Channel Box, Show Layer Editor, and Show Channels Box and Layer Editor). Click the one to the far right that will show both the Channels box and the Layer Editor in this space to the right.

The Layers Editor will appear below the Channel box (Figure 2.26). There are several ways to create a new layer but the quickest is to click the button that the mouse is resting on in Figure 2.26.

Once you've created a new layer (Figure 2.27a), double-LMB-click the name to rename it. The new dialog box that appears will allow you both to re-name a layer and assign colors to it. For now, simply rename this layer **Ceil-ing_Floor** and click the Save button (Figure 2.27b).

Now, in the Outliner, select the groups **BeamsNS**, **BeamsNS1**, **Cross-Beams**, and the objects, **Floor** and **Ceiling**. Remember that holding down the

FIGURE 2.27   (a-b) Rename layers.

Shift button will add to a selection in much the same way as does Microsoft Explorer, including selecting everything between two selections. **Ctrl** will allow you to add to the selection without choosing objects in between on the list. Once all of these groups and objects are selected, RMB-click the layer, Ceiling_Floor in the Layers Editor and select Add Selected Objects from the pop-up menu. Notice that the Ceiling_Floor layer has three boxes to the left of the layer's name. We will discuss other uses of these boxes but for now, the box of interest is the one to the far left with a *V* in it. The V stands for visible and once you've added objects to a layer, you can click the V to make that layer invisible in the display. For now, click this V and you should be able to see the room with just the walls.

Step 19: Save and take a break. If you've not done so already be sure to save your scene (File>Save Scene). You may want to name it something like Room. Then take a break; we've covered a lot of different methods and have the basic shape of our room to show for it. However, we still have lots more to do to make this room the beautiful creation as it is designed.

CONCLUSION

We've covered in this chapter how to create some basic primitive shapes. We've discussed how to scale them, move them, place them, and rotate them. We've looked at how to align objects so that they butt up exactly against one another. We've looked at how to measure objects and distances so that we can make exact calculations in our creations. In projects of the future, we won't get so precise in all our measurements; most of the time we will simply eyeball the shapes to get them about right. However, in areas such architecture, being this exact is important.

ON THE CD

Remember that if you want to check your work against this tutorial, you can open the results on the CD-ROM (Tutorials/Chapter02). Also remember that if there are slight variations—no sweat. Feel free to improvise and change things as you see aesthetically fit.

In the next chapter, we will learn how to begin cutting holes in objects and changing the shapes of these primitives that we've begun to create. After all, not everything is perfectly square or flat. Being able to tweak shapes is what makes Maya a powerful modeling tool. So read on, the modeling that's most fun is yet to come.

NURBS AND COMPONENT-
LEVEL EDITING

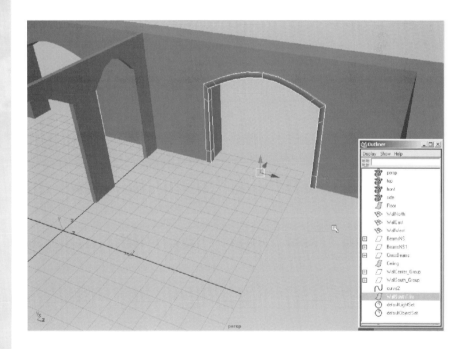

n the last chapter, we looked very quickly at how to create, scale, rotate, and move basic shapes. Primarily, we dealt with polygonal cubes. Polygons are one of the various ways to model within Maya; however, for most forms, it is not the most effective.

NURBS (non-uniform rational b-splines) represent a very dynamic method of modeling almost any shape imaginable. NURBS are especially good for smooth surfaces and organic forms. Now before we go to far, it is important to point out that while you can use NURBS to create forms in Maya, eventually, Maya must convert those NURBS into polygons to render. This process is called *tessellation* and we will talk much more about it later. So, you may ask, why bother modeling in NURBS when they end up as polygons anyway? Well, for several reasons, the first of which is tessellation is no picnic. When Maya takes the nice curved surfaces possible with NURBS and creates collections of polygons to simulate that curve, it has to do so with quite a few triangles. Without enough triangles, the model looks blocky. If you were building your shape with polygons, it would be incredibly painful and a waste of time to have to go in and modify all of the thousands of polygons.

Figure 3.1a shows a section of a NURBS surface. Figure 3.1b shows the same surface with the tessellation visible. Notice the sheer volume of polygons needed to create this type of surface.

FIGURE 3.1 (a-b) Tessellation of NURBS surface.

It is usually easier to allow Maya to take the information you have provided in NURBS and do all the hard work by determining how the polygons need to be arranged.

Now, there are some cases where pure old, grab-a-polygon-and-move-it is the method to use. Games, for instance, are typically limited on the number of polygons that can be displayed at any one time. So, economical use of polygons is key; thus, being able to control each polygon becomes tremendously important.

SubD (subdivision) surfaces is another place where being able to control the polygons directly is important. Although we will talk much more about subD surfaces later, the basic idea is that you make a low-poly proxy of a particular shape. There are comparatively few polygons to have to deal with on this proxy, thus you can quickly get general shapes roughed out. Maya then takes every polygon, subdivides it into smaller polygons, and rotates each polygon to create a smoother, rounded, and more complex shape.

Because these two instances are both important situations in which modeling with polygons is important, we will be talking more about polygon modeling in Chapters 4 and 5.

But for now, NURBS will rule this chapter. NURBS are great tools and offer some flexibility that polygonal modeling does not. Although many shapes that we will create in this chapter could be created with either NURBS or polygons, we will be using NURBS in an effort to understand this powerful modeling tool.

CURVES

Before we can really get into effective NURBS creation and editing, we need to talk for a second about how to create and manipulate curves. *Curves* are the splines that NURBS surfaces use to define the three-dimensional shape. Although ultimately, NURBS surfaces can exist completely independent of the curves that created them, effectively manipulating curves before creating the surfaces can get you started on the right foot, and make your modeling job much easier.

Before we start in on the steps, it is important to know that there are two main types of curves in Maya: EP (Edit Point) curves and CV (Control Vertex) curves. Both have their uses and some folks prefer different curves for different situations. In general, CV curves are a more easily controlled and more easily predictable method of creating curves. However, we will still look at how EP curves work before taking an in-depth look at CV curves.

3.1 GETTING STARTED WITH CURVES

Step 1: Start with a clean slate. To explore curves, we want to start off with an empty scene without having to worry about messing up the boxy room we created in the last chapter. So, make sure and save the work you have done on the room and exit out of Maya (File>Exit).

Start Maya up again and you will have an empty scene. You should have an interface where you are back to a single panel for your Workspace with a Perspective view. If you do not, be sure to select Single Perspective View from the Toolbox.

Move your mouse over the Workspace and quickly click the **Spacebar**. This will swap the view into the four-paneled view.

Step 2: Create a curvilinear (Cubic) EP curve. Select Modeling | Create>EP Curve Tool (Options). Unlike other tool's options, the EP curve's options may appear at the right where the Channels box was. There are a couple of things to notice here before tearing into creating curves with the EP Curve tool (Figure 3.2).

The first is the Curve Degree setting. This value indicates how smooth the curve will be between the Edit Points that you will define. The default—3 Cubic—is usually a pretty good setting for curvy curves while 1 Linear works great for more straight curves.

For now, leave the default 3 Cubic as the setting for Curve Degree. In the Top view, LMB-click and place the first Edit Point. Move to another space (still in Top view, of course) and LMB-click again. Technically, you could end this curve right now, as an EP curve only needs two Edit Points to define it. But, for now, move to another place and LMB to create a third Edit Point; here is where you begin to see the curve part of EP curve emerge.

Click in several other places and play with how the position of each Edit Point controls how the curve develops. Notice that if you LMB-click and hold, you can create a new Edit Point and drag it around the space to see how the curve is affected.

EP Curve Tool		Reset Tool	Tool Help...
▼ **EP Curve Settings**			
Curve Degree	⦿ 1 Linear	○ 2	
	○ 3 Cubic	○ 5	
	○ 7		
Knot Spacing	⦿ Uniform	○ Chord Length	

FIGURE 3.2 The EP Curve Tool Options box.

FIGURE 3.3   Completed EP curve.

When you are done, or have created enough Edit Points for you to get the idea, hit **Enter** to tell Maya that you are done creating this curve (Figure 3.3).

Select this curve and delete it.

Step 3: Create a curvilinear (Cubic) EP curve in three-dimensions. The curve we created in the last step was all drawn in the Top view. This means that the curve and all its Edit Points laid flat along the XZ plane. However, you can also create curves in three-dimensions on the fly.

Select the EP Curve tool again but this time simply select the tool on the Shelf (Figure 3.4).

Now, create three or four Edit Points in the Top view. When you get ready to place the next Edit Point, instead of placing it in the Top view, do so in the Front view. Notice that this new Edit Point now brings the curve into a new dimension other than the XZ plane. Place a couple more Edit Points in the Front view and then place a few in the Side view. Next, go up to the Perspective view and place still more Edit Points. Finally, hit **Enter** to finish off with the EP Curve tool.

Notice that you probably have a very bizarre curve that exists in all three dimensions (Figure 3.5). The point of this little exercise is that curves can be built in any view or any combinations of views to create any sort of shape you wish.

Select this crazy curve and delete it.

FIGURE 3.4   Activating the EP Curve tool on the Shelf.

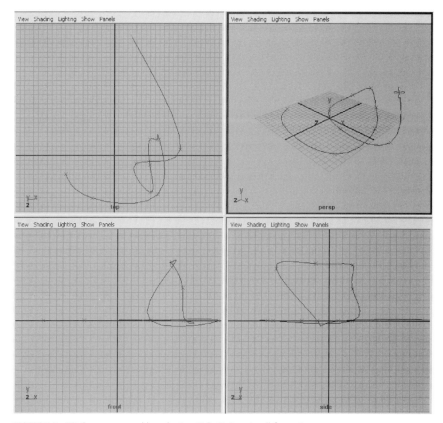

FIGURE 3.5   EP Curve created by placing Edit Points in all four views.

Step 4: Create a straight (linear) EP curve. Select Modeling│Create>EP Curve Tool (Option). In the Options for the tool (shown at the right of the UI), change the Curve Degree to 1 Linear. Again, in any view you please, LMB-click several Edit Points into place. Notice that the result is a curve that is straight—linear. This works great for creating profiles of stairs or other man-made shapes. Remember that holding down the **x**, **c**, or **v** keys while creating a curve will snap the Edit Points to the grid, curve, or vertex (Figure 3.6).

Delete this linear curve.

Step 5: Create a curvilinear CV curve. When we created EP curves, we created Edit Points through which the curve ran. When we create CV curves, we are creating control vertices that act like magnets on a wire. When we created EP curves, we only needed two Edit Points to create a complete curve. With CV curves, you must have at least four.

The first- and the last-placed CVs will indicate where the curve is to begin and end. The other points help to define the general curvature of the curve.

FIGURE 3.6   Creating an EP curve with a 1 Linear Curve Degree setting.

The CV Curve tool takes a bit of getting used to before you can control curves exactly like you want them. However, once you get the hang of it, you can truly make any shaped curve you can imagine.

To get started, select Create>CV Curve Tool (Option). This will display the options for the tools on the right of the UI. Because we have already talked about Curve Degrees, we will not cover them again for the CV Curve tool, but do notice that you can change the degree to include things like linear lines. Also note that like the EP Curve tool, 3 Cubic is usually just right for most curves.

In the Top view, create four CVs by LMB-clicking and releasing at any four points (Figure 3.7a). Notice that the only points that the CV curve actually touches are the first and the last. Hit **Enter** to complete the curve and exit the CV Curve tool.

To understand this a bit better, select the Move tool. RMB-click-and-hold on the curve in the Top view and select Control Vertex from the Marking menu that pops up (Figure 3.7b). This will show the CVs that you created earlier as little purple dots. Using the Move tool, select one, and LMB-click-drag the point to a new location and see how the curve changes (Figure 3.7c).

FIGURE 3.7   (a-c) Creating and editing a basic curvilinear CV curve.

Remember also that, like the EP Curve tool, this tool can be used to create CVs for a curve in any window. Delete this curve before moving onto the next step (RMB-click-and-hold off the curve and select Select All from the marking menu. Then hit **Delete**).

Step 6: Create curvilinear/linear combinations. If we continue on with the idea of CVs as magnets that control the curve that is a wire, it makes sense that if you cluster magnets (CVs), then the wire (curve) will hug tighter to that cluster.

Consider the following examples. Figure 3.8 shows four examples of CVs or clusters of CVs in the exact same locations. The difference between each sub-figure is that some curves include two CVs placed at the exact same place. The result of this mini-cluster is a line that hugs the CVs closer or determines the path of the curve as it moves away from the cluster.

Increasing the number of CVs causes the curve to hug that cluster even closer. In most cases, three CVs in the same place makes for a sharp corner (Figure 3.9). This can make for combinations of linear and curvilinear curves.

The caveat to this is that you want to make sure the CVs are in exactly the same place. Often, the best strategy to do this is by snapping to the grid

FIGURE 3.8   (a-d) Results of clustering CVs.

FIGURE 3.9   By placing three CVs in one location, there is no "pulling away" of the curve from the placed CVs.

(**x** hotkey) so that as you place subsequent CVs, you know that they are all snapping to the same spot.

Step 7: Close a curve. Up to now, we have been creating curves that are *open*. That is, the curves are lines that do not encompass a shape. It will be important as we work in the future that we know the difference between open (Figure 3.10a) and closed (Figure 3.10b) curves, and can close off open curves.

Many 3D applications allow you to create closed curves on the fly. Maya does not. However, it is fairly easy to create an open curve and then to close it off. Begin by using the CV Curve tool to create an open curve (Figure 3.11a); the exact shape does not matter. Hit **Enter** to exit the CV Curve tool.

To close the curve, select Modeling│Edit Curves>Open/Close Curve (Option). The Options window (shown in Figure 3.11 b, c, and d) allows you to determine how Maya will close the selected curve. The Shape option tells Maya what sort of shape it is to create as it attempts to create the needed CVs or

FIGURE 3.10   (a) Shows an open curve—one that does not completely encompass a shape; (b) shows a closed curve.

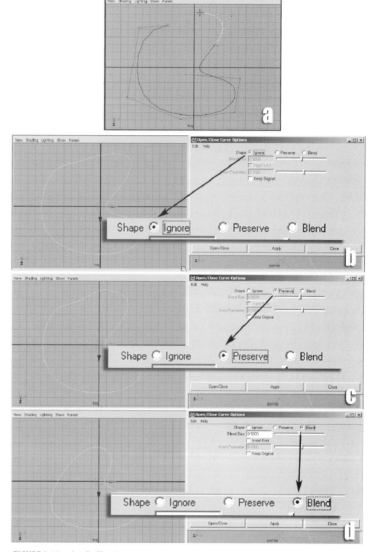

FIGURE 3.11 (a-d) Closing curves.

weld together the extant CVs to create the closed shape. We will not go into too much depth here on these options as it is beyond the scope of the book; however, note that in most cases, the Preserve option is a good setting. Delete this closed curve, when you are done exploring this tool.

Step 8: Edit existing curves. Use the CV Curve tool to create a new open curve (Figure 3.12a). Hit **Enter** to exit the tool.

FIGURE 3.12   (a) Creating an open curve. (b) Telling Maya to show you a curve's control vertices. (c) Moving the position of a CV.

There are several things that we can do with this curve:

- Select the entire curve and move, rotate, or scale it similar to any other three-dimensional shape.
- In Component mode, or by RMB-clicking and holding (Figure 3.12b), you can tell Maya to display the control vertices of the curve. You can then select a CV and move it to adjust the shape of the curve (Figure 3.12c). Remember that you can select more than one CV at a time.
- Extend a curve with Modeling│Edit Curves>Add Points Tool. This will display your curve as though you were creating it with the CV Curve tool. Your mouse will also turn to the thick white cross. Just LMB-click where you would like to add new CVs to the end of your existing curve. Hit **Enter** to exit the Add Points tool.
- Change the shape of the curve through the Curve Editing tool. Access this tool through Modeling│Edit Curves>Curve Editing Tool. This tool will appear on the surface of the selected curve (Figure 3.13a). There are several different tools all nested within this tool. The first is the blue box that sits on the curve itself. LMB-click-drag that box to move that particular point of the curve to a new location (Figure 3.13b). The little blue diamond immediately above it (that turns yellow when clicked) allows you to shift the tool to a new point on the curve (Figure 3.13c). Off of these tools is a black line that represents a tangent to the curve. The blue box along this line allows you to change the tangent (and thus the shape of the curve) as shown in Figure 3.13d. The blue diamond at the end of the line allows you to shorten the tangent (Figure 3.13e).

Notice that in the Modeling│Edit Curves pull-down menu there are many more options that we have not covered. Later, we will look more closely at some of the other tools here. Unfortunately, we haven't the room to cover everything

FIGURE 3.13   (a-e) The Edit Curve tool.

in this volume. However, if you have the control covered earlier in this chaper when creating the curves, many of the Edit Curves options will not be necessary.

NURBS

Non-uniform rational b-splines (NURBS), despite the name, are actually best thought of as surfaces. We have looked briefly at creating NURBS primitives in the last chapter's tutorials. The Sphere, Cube, Cylinder, Cone, Plane, Torus, Circle, and Square are all NURBS primitives. These are NURBS surfaces that Maya creates for you. As our tutorials progress, we will be creating custom surfaces. For now, let's look a bit at the anatomy of a NURBS surface.

Figure 3.14 shows a primitive NURBS sphere. By RM- clicking-and-holding, we are presented with a Marking menu that allows us to select components of this surface object. These are some of the basic anatomical parts of a NURBS surface.

- **Control Vertices (CVs)**: These are represented in the Workspace as small purple dots that can be selected by marqueeing around a collection of them, or by selecting and **Shift**-clicking to add to the selection. Once a collection of CVs are selected, they can be moved (Figure 3.15b), rotated (Figure 3.15c), or scaled (Figure 3.15d). We will do much more work with manipulating CVs as we go along.

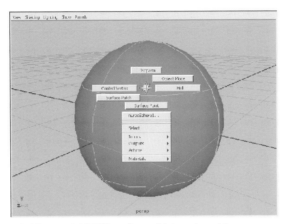

FIGURE 3.14   A NURBS surface with its selectable components.

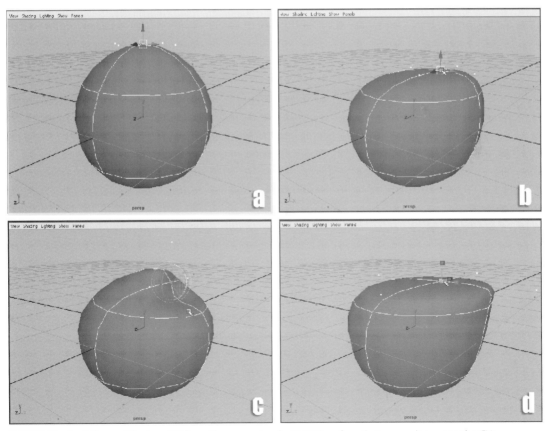

FIGURE 3.15   (a-d) Control Vertices (CVs) are the magnets of a NURBS surface that are analogous to the CVs discussed in curves.

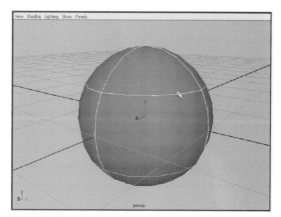

FIGURE 3.16 Isoparms are a visual indication of a surface topology. Although they themselves are not editable, they accompany CVs and Hulls, which are.

- **Isoparms**: These are visual lines across the surface of a NURBS surface that give an indication of the organization of the NURBS topology (Figure 3.16). By adding isoparms to a surface (more on how to do this later) you add CVs as well. Although you cannot move or otherwise alter isoparms, the accompanying CVs and hulls related to an isoparm can be edited.
- **Hulls**: If you were to take some CVs and connect them in rows (both horizontally and vertically), you would get hulls. You can move, rotate, or scale a selected hull. This works well for manipulating a surface in multiple directions at once (Figure 3.17).
- **Surface Points and Surface Patches**: We will look more at these later in more detail. For now, suffice it to say that these are visual representations of points along the surface (Figure 3.18a) or patches between collections of isoparms (Figure 3.18b). Neither may be directly moved, rotated, or scaled.

Alrighty. Enough theory. To get to know how to build NURBS from curves that we have created, we are going to get right into a tutorial to continue working on our room. Over the course of the next tutorial or two we will be creating a multitude of NURBS surfaces to add new visual interest to our room.

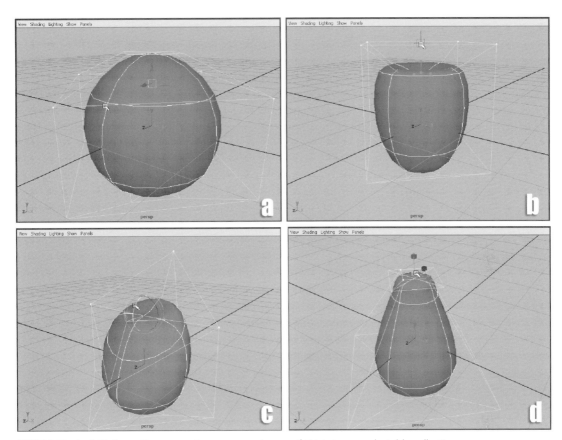

FIGURE 3.17   (a-d) Hulls are like connecting rows or columns of CVs into one selectable collection.

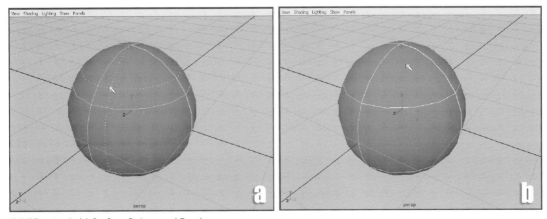

FIGURE 3.18   (a-b) Surface Points and Patches.

TUTORIAL

3.2 NURBS MODELING IN "THE ROOM"

To continue building the room, make sure you open the room that we were using in the last chapter—it is probably named Room. You can do this by either selecting File>Open Scene or going to wherever you saved the Room_Tutorial project. Open the Scenes folder and double-click the scene, Room, from there. Remember that you can see the results of this tutorial on the CD-ROM (Tutorials/Chapter03/).

ON THE CD

Step 1: Make sure to have your Workspace set up similar to Figure 3.19. It probably is already. However, it will be important for our modeling steps for a while that you have the standard four-view panel layout with the Outliner available as a separate floating window.

FIGURE 3.19 Layout needed for the modeling in this tutorial.

CREATING ARCHED WALLS

Step 2: Create center arched wall curve. In our earlier tutorials, we created a wall called `WallMiddlePH` with the *PH* standing for *place holder*. In this step, we will replace this wall. To do this, we will create two curves and create two types of NURBS surfaces—Loft and Planar.

Before we can create the NURBS surfaces, we need to create the curves that will be used to create them. Move your mouse over the Front view and hit your **Spacebar**. This will maximize this view in your Workspace.

Select Modeling | Create>CV Curves Tool (Options). Make sure that your Curve Degree is set to 3 Cubic.

Now, in the Workspace, we want to make sure that we are using a combination of the grid and the `WallMiddlePH` to act as guides in creating this curve. Hold **v** (to snap to points, or in this case, vertices) and click three times on the vertex at the bottom-left corner of the `WallMiddlePH` (Figure 3.20a). Still holding down the **v** key, move up and click three times on the top-left corner (Figure 3.20b). Continue holding down the **v** and click three times on the top-right corner (Figure 3.20c). Because we have carefully put three CVs right atop one another at every point, we should have nice crisp corners so far. Continue down to the bottom-right corner and again, holding down the **v**, LMB-click three times to create another corner (Figure 3.20d).

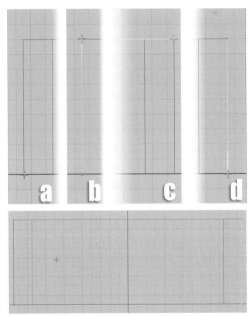

FIGURE 3.20   (a-d) Creating the hard corners for the bottom and tops of the wall. No arches have been created yet. Each corner was snapped to point (v).

This is where things get interesting. For the arches in the middle of the wall, we really do not want to snap to any point on the wall itself. We have already snapped to all the vertices we can see from the Front view. However, snapping is still an important thing to do because we want to be able to place multiple CVs atop one another.

The solution will be to snap to the grid. Hold down **x** and LMB-click on a grid point about three-and-a-half units from the outside of the wall (Figure 3.21a). Still holding down the **x**, place two more points on the same spot so that we get a crisp corner here.

Still holding down the **x**, move up six feet (or six units, each represented with a box on the grid) and place three more CVs in that spot (Figure 3.21b). Now, move over two units and up one (still with the **x** down) and place *one* CV here (Figure 3.21c). We want this CV to define a gentle curve, so one will suffice. Do not worry that it is looking awfully linear here; it will round off in a bit. Continuing on (still with the **x** button depressed) move over two units and down one, and place three CVs here (Figure 3.21d). Finally, place three more CVs straight down from the last at ground level (Figure 3.21e).

Move over two units and place three CVs, up six units, place three more CVs, and then for this middle arch, move over three units and up one to place one CV. Continue over three units and down one, and place three CVs. Now, move down to the floor level and place three more (Figure 3.22).

FIGURE 3.21   (a-e) Creating our first arch.

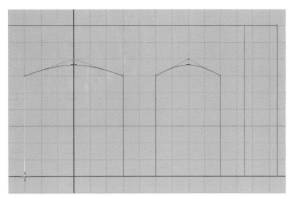

FIGURE 3.22   Creating the middle arch in much the same way.

Move over two units and repeat the first arch created (Figure 3.23). When you get to the bottom of the arch (where you will have created three CVs), *do not* attempt to close the curve by going back to the very first CV we created. Instead, hit **Enter** to finish the CV creation process and exit out of the CV Curve tool.

To close the curve select Modeling | Edit Curves>Open/Close Curves. This should close the curve off so you have the completed curve.

Step 3: Adjust the manipulator to the bottom corner of the curve. Hit the **Spacebar** quickly so that you can see a four-view panel. Notice that the curve you have just created is sitting flush against the west wall while your manipulator is sitting back at 0,0,0 (Figure 3.24). This happened because as we were snapping in the Front view, Maya assumed we were snapping to the nearest object to the view plane (which was the west wall). This could have been prevented by hiding all the walls except the middle one, but because we want to adjust the location of the manipulator, there was no need.

FIGURE 3.23   Completed arches.

FIGURE 3.24 Curve exists on the west wall, but manipulator is back at 0,0,0.

We want to be able to snap this curve (and a copy of this curve) to the front and back of the middle wall. Because we will be snapping to the wall, we want to be able to snap to the wall's vertices, which sit on the corners of the wall. So, on the curve, we want the manipulator to be sitting on its corner also.

Hit the **Insert** key to indicate to Maya that you wish to reposition the manipulator. Press the **v** key to tell Maya you want to snap to points, and then move the manipulator so that it snaps into the bottom-right corner of the curve (Figure 3.25).

Hit **Insert** again to lock the manipulator into place in this new location.

Step 4: Position `curve1` at the front of `WallMiddlePH`. We will now use `WallMiddlePH` as what it was meant to be used. With the Move tool and the **v** key held down (to snap to point/vertex), move our curve (`curve1` in the Outliner) so that it snaps back to the front of `WallMiddlePH` by LMB-click-dragging the Z (blue) manipulator handle (Figure 3.26).

Step 5: Duplicate and place another curve on the opposite side of `WallMiddlePH`. Remember to reset your Duplicate settings if you cannot remember exactly what they are and then duplicate our curve. You should now have two curves listed in your Outliner (`curve1` and `curve2`). With `curve2` still selected, snap to points (**v**) and move this new curve so that it snaps to the back end of the `WallMiddlePH` (Figure 3.27).

FIGURE 3.25   Repositioned manipulator.

FIGURE 3.26   Placed `curve1` at front of `WallMiddlePH`.

Step 6: Delete `WallMiddlePH`. Now that our curves are created and placed, `WallMiddlePH` is no longer needed. Select it in the Workspace or Outliner and delete it.

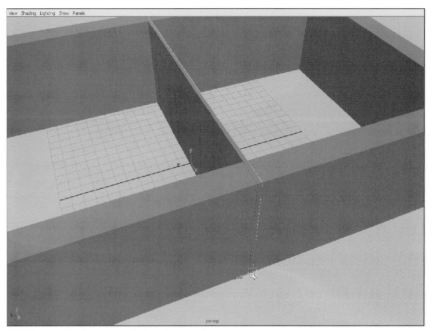

FIGURE 3.27 Duplicated and placed second curve.

Step 7: Loft `curve1` and `curve2` to create a NURBS surface. As we discussed in theory earlier in this chapter, NURBS surfaces can be created through primitives or we can create them ourselves through curves. In earlier steps, we have created two curves that we will use to create a wall.

To create a NURBS surface, you must first select the curves that will be involved in its creation. The order in which you select these curves is often very important, especially if there are more than two curves involved. In this case, because there are only two, it is less important.

Select `curve1` and then hold down the **Shift** key and select `curve2`. Both will appear highlighted in the Outliner and Workspace. In the Workspace, one will appear white (the first one selected) and the other will appear green.

With both curves selected, go to Modeling│Surfaces>Loft (Option). Once you have the Loft Options window open, make sure and reset the settings. Notice, however, that among the options here (Figure 3.28) is the ability to choose things like the Section Spans (how many spans, and thus isoparms will be created on the new surface), and the Output Geometry (allowing you to choose to create a NURBS surface, Polygonal, Subdivision, or Bezier). We will not be delving too deeply now into each of these options as the default setting works just great. Hit the **Loft** button.

The results of the Loft function displayed in Figure 3.29 show that a new surface has been created between the two curves. Notice also that in the Outliner a

FIGURE 3.28   The Loft Options window.

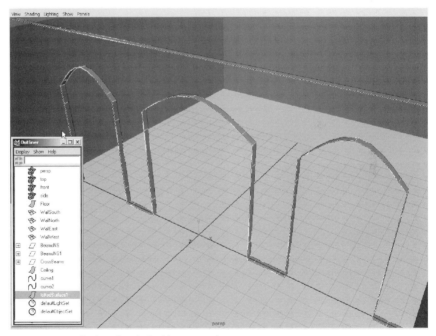

FIGURE 3.29   Lofted surface lofted between the two curves.

new object called `loftedSurface1` has been created. If the surface seems to "pull away" from the curves, it is because this new surface is being displayed at too low a resolution display. Make sure and hit **3** to display it smoothly.

Now, this is a nice start, but it is obvious that there is something missing in this wall. To make this wall so that it actually appears solid, we will be creating another NURBS surface.

Step 8: Create a new planar NURBS surface from each of the two curves, `curve1` and `curve2`. When we created the lofted surface in the last step, the two curves we used to create the surface remained intact. This is important as we will need these to create the solid part of the wall. Planar NURBS surfaces can be created from just one curve.

First, select `curve1` and go to Modeling│Surfaces>Planar (Option). Again, make sure and reset the settings for this tool and hit the **Planar Trim** button. The result should be a new surface seen both in the Outliner (`planarTrimmedSurface1`) and in the Workspace (Figure 3.30).

Tumble around to see the other side of this wall, and you will see that you are still missing another planar surface. Select `curve2` and again select Modeling>Surfaces>Planar. This will create a new surface that completes the wall.

FIGURE 3.30   Planar surface.

Step 9: Clean up. Through these last few steps we have not taken time to re-name objects or get rid of objects that we no longer needed. Now would be a good time to do so. First, select `loftedSurface1`, `planarTrimmedSurface1`, and `planarTrimmedSurface2` in the Outliner and hit **Ctrl-g** to group them together. The Outliner will show a new object called `group1`. Rename this group as `WallCenter_Group`.

Right now, `curve1` and `curve2` are linked to all three of the NURBS surfaces contained in the group `WallCenter_Group`. As an example of the

FIGURE 3.31   (a-c) Because Construction History has been active, if we now choose to reshape the curves, the surfaces that were created from them will be updated.

benefits of this, select `WallCenter_Group` and hit **Ctrl-h** to hide this group. This will leave just the curves visible. Move your mouse over the Front view and hit your **Spacebar** to maximize that view in your Workspace.

Select both `curve1` and `curve2` in the Outliner (Figure 3.31a). Then in the Status Line, change to Component mode and make sure that the Points mask is on (Figure 3.31b). This will display the CVs of those two curves in the Workspace. Select the points that make up the top of the curves by marquee-ing around them, and with the Move tool and snapping to grid (**x**), move them up a couple units (Figure 3.31c). You may choose to do some further reshaping of the curves if you wish.

Hit **Ctrl-Shift-h** to unhide the last hidden (which in this case is `WallCen-ter_Group`). You can see that the changes we made in the curves have translated into the surfaces (Figure 3.32).

Because we are sure we like this wall, we will further clean up some things. Make sure to return to Object mode in the Status Line. Next, select `curve1` and `curve2` (in the Outliner is probably easiest) and delete them as they are no longer needed.

Step 10: Repeat this process (Steps 2-9) for a new `WallSouth`. The idea here is to create a new wall like that shown in Figure 3.34 that has two arched doorways into the room. Remember to position both curves on the front and back of the old `WallSouth` so that the thickness of the wall is correct.

In this case, you probably will find that creating the curve from the Side view is a better method than the Front view. Remember to create the curve with the CV Curve tool and place the appropriate amount of CVs (three on each corner) to create sharp corners where they should be (Figure 3.33a). Close the curve (Modeling>Edit Curves>Open/Close Curves and move the manipulator so that it sits on a corner of the curve (Figure 3.33b).

FIGURE 3.32   Altered surfaces.

FIGURE 3.33   (a-b) Creating the curve and aligning the manipulator into place.

Duplicate the curve and make sure that it sits on the other side of Wall-
South (Figure 3.34a). Select WallSouth and delete it as it is no longer
needed (Figure 3.34b).

FIGURE 3.34   (a-b) Duplicating curve and placing in new location. Deleted unnecessary wall.

FIGURE 3.35   Lofted surface from two curves. Two Planar surfaces created from each curve.

Now, create the Loft NURBS surface between the two curves and create Planar surfaces from each of the two curves (Figure 3.35).

Finally, group the newly created surfaces into a new group called `Wall-South_Group`. The results of all this hard work should look like Figure 3.36.

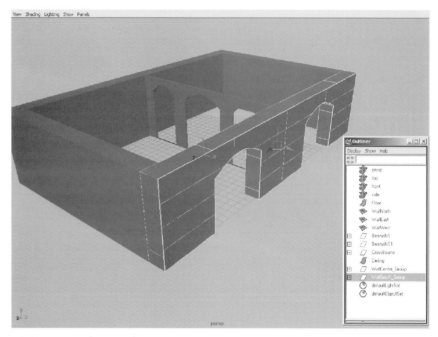

FIGURE 3.36   Newly created `WallSouth_Group`.

CREATING TRIM FOR DOORWAYS

To do this, we will be creating an Extrude NURBS surface. An Extrude NURBS surface requires two curves. One curve is the shape that is to be extruded—think of this as the profile. The second curve is the curve along which this profile is to be extruded.

Because we want to create trim around a doorway, we will need to create a curve that is the shape of the doorway. Because we created the wall with two arches very carefully by snapping to the grid, we can use this to our advantage in creating our new curve.

Step 11: Create curve for the profile to follow. View your model from the Side view. Zoom in on one of the arches in `WallSouth_Group`. Modeling|Create>CV Curve tool activates the tool we need. Snap to grid (**x**) and create a new curve by placing CVs (and clusters of CVs) where we did when creating the curve that made this wall (Figure 3.37). Make sure to hit **Enter** to exit the CV Curve tool.

Step 12: Center the pivot point. Notice that as soon as you exit from creating this new curve, the curve will appear green in the Workspace. However, as soon as you select the Move tool, the manipulator will be back at 0,0,0. In the past, we have been moving the manipulator manually so that it was closer to

FIGURE 3.37   Creating new curve for use with an Extrude NURBS surface.

the actual object it represented. Maya actually has a function that helps make this a bit easier. Select Modify>Center Pivot. Your manipulator for this newly created curve will now be in the middle of the curve.

Step 13: Create the profile to be extruded. Now that we have the curve that our profile will be created along, we need to create the profile itself. We will want to create this from the Top view.

The profile we wish to create will be in an *L* shape that has two sides that are four inches long, each about one inch thick. To do this, we will create it at first as 4 *feet* long by 1 *foot* thick. This makes it easy to create nice straight lines as we snap to grid from the Top view.

Because this shape is going to have all straight edges, there is no need to create three CVs on each corner. Instead, select Modeling│Create>CV Curve Tool (Options) and change the Curve Degree setting to 1 Linear. Hold down the **x** key to snap to grid and make a shape similar to that in Figure 3.38. Remember to leave the curve open and close it with the Open/Close Curve command. Also make sure to move the manipulator so that it matches Figure 3.38.

Step 14: Arrange our two newly created curves. The two curves just created in Perspective view will look something like Figure 3.39a. Move curve2 (our profile shape) so that it snaps to the bottom of curve1 (our path to follow) as in Figure 3.39b.

Step 15: Resize the profile to around the actual size. Now resize curve2 (our profile shape) to about 1/10th its current size. The easiest way to do this is activate your Channels box (with the rightmost button at the top-right of the UI), and enter 0.1 in the Scale X and Scale Z input fields.

FIGURE 3.38   Large profile made with a linear CV Curve tool while snapping to grid.

FIGURE 3.39   (a-b) Arranged curves.

Step 16: Extrude the curve2 along curve1 to create a new surface. Extrude NURBS surfaces is one of those cases in which the order that you select curves makes a big difference. The way to think of Extrude surfaces is: "Take this curve (the profile curve, in this case, `curve2`) and extrude it along this curve (the path curve, in this case, `curve1`)." So, in this case, select `curve2` first, then hold down the **Shift** key, and add to the selection `curve1`.

Now, select Modeling | Surfaces>Extrude (Option). As this is the first time we have used this tool, make sure and reset the settings and hit the **Extrude** button. The default settings have all the things set as we need them. The results should look like Figure 3.40. To finish this off, move the manipulator (pivot) so that it sits in a more appropriate place. Then move this newly created `extrudedSurface1` (as it appears in the Outliner) into place (Figure 3.41). Finally, rename the extrudedSurface1 to `WallSouthTrim`.

FIGURE 3.40   Newly created Extrude NURBS surface.

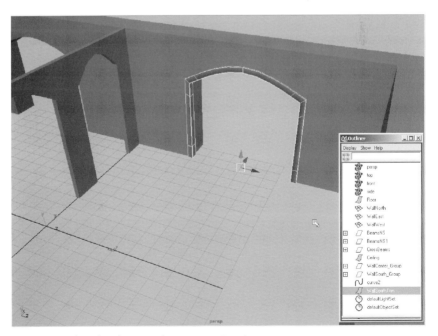

FIGURE 3.41   Placed and renamed `WallSouthTrim`.

Step 17: Clean up by deleting `curve1`. `Curve1`, which is the curve that defined the shape of the archway, is no longer needed, so delete it. However, the profile will be useful for the other arches in the room, so leave `curve2` alone.

Step 18: Duplicate `WallSouthTrim`, **and place the new** `Wall-SouthTrim1`. Edit>Duplicate will create a new piece of trim in the same spot as the old one. Use the Move tool and move the new `WallSouthTrim1` along its Z axis (use the blue manipulator handle) so that it sits in the second hole on `WallSouth`. You can eyeball this or hold down the **x** key to find the exact center (Figure 3.42).

FIGURE 3.42   Creating a duplicate and finding the exact center.

Step 19: Organize. We already have a `WallSouth_Group`. Currently, this group only includes the surfaces that make up the wall. Select `Wall-SouthTrim` and `WallSouthTrim1` in the Outliner and MMB-drag them onto `WallSouth_Group`. This will add these two surfaces as children to the group, `WallSouth_Group`.

Step 20: Repeat the process for the arches in `WallCenter`. From the Front view, create a new CV curve (remember to set the Curve Degree back to 3 `Cubic`) that matches one of the arches (Figure 3.43a). This curve will be listed in the Outliner as `curve3`. Center the pivot (Modify>Center Pivot) and move it away from the wall (snapping to grid) to get a better look at it. Because you snapped this surface, you can now move the profile shape (`curve2`) while snapping to grid so that it aligns perfectly with the bottom of `curve3` (Figure 3.43b).

Again, select `curve2` first (the profile) and then **Shift**-select `curve3` (the curve to be extruded along), and select Modeling│Surfaces>Extrude. Center the pivot and move this new `extrudedSurface1` back into position (Figure 3.44). Rename it to `WallCenterTrim`.

Duplicate this `WallCenterTrim` and place the new `WallCenter-Trim1` into the other arch. Again, delete `curve3` (our path that the profile `curve2` was extruded along) as it is no longer needed.

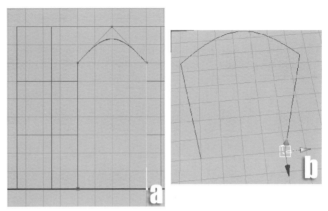

FIGURE 3.43   (a-b) Creating curve and arranging curves in preparation of Extrude surfaces.

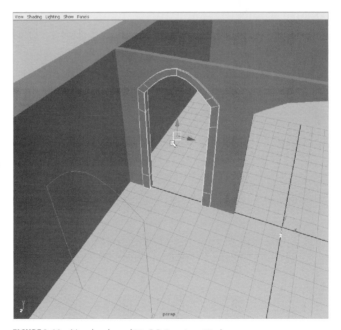

FIGURE 3.44   Newly placed `WallCenterTrim`.

From the Front view, create another CV curve for the center arch. Again, organize the new `curve3` and the old `curve2`, create the new Extruded surface, and place the new surface into place. Rename it `WallCentreTrim-Center`. Now, delete `curve2` and `curve3`.

Finally, select all three and group them (**Ctrl-g**). Rename the group to `WallCenterTrim_Group`. Select this group and duplicate it. In the Channels box, enter `180` in the Rotate Y input field so that you can place this group of trim on the other side as well. Adjust the position of this new `WallCen-terTrim_Group1` as appropriate.

The room should look like Figure 3.45.

FIGURE 3.45   All the trim in place.

Step 21: Make `WallCenterTrim_Group` and `WallCenterTrim_Group1` children of `WallCenter_Group`. Do this by selecting them and MMB-dragging them onto the group, `WallCenter_Group`.

CONCLUSION

Hopefully, through the course of this chapter, you have gotten a good idea of the theory behind NURBS surfaces and the technique of building them. There are still more NURBS surfaces yet to come. In the next chapter, we will continue on with NURBS surfaces and build the furniture that will live in this room. We will explore other surfaces and how they are created and modified.

ON THE CD

Remember to take a look at the completed file on the CD-ROM in the Tutorials folder if you have any questions over what things should look like at the end of Tutorial 3.2.

After that, we will look at some methods of creating complex forms through Boolean functions. Finally, we will look at how to use the ever-powerful subdivision surfaces.

4

NURBS CONTINUED

B y now, hopefully, you have the general gist of how NURBS surfaces are created. In this chapter, we are going to continue looking at new surfaces and how to create them. By the end of this chapter, you will be a NURBS creation master.

4.1 NURBS SURFACES CONTINUED

In this tutorial, we will continue our work from the last chapter. Our room will continue to take shape as we begin to add things like furniture, lamps, doors, and windows. We will use a variety of surface creation techniques and do some basic editing of these surfaces.

ON THE CD

As always, the results of this Tutorial can be found on the included CD-ROM. So, take a look if you are having problems getting any of the results you are looking for.

Step 1: Open the `Room` **tutorial that you have created to this point.**

Step 2: Create a new layer and name it `Walls`**.** Make sure that you can see the Layer Editor beneath the Channels box and select Layers>Create Layer from the pull-down menus within the Layers Editor. Double-click the layer and name this new layer `Walls`. Hit the **Save** button.

Step 3: Add all the walls (except `WallCenter_Group`**) to this layer and make it not visible.** In the Outliner, select `WallNorth`, `WallEast`, `Wall-West`, and the `WallSouth_Group` (**Ctrl**-LMB). RMB-click on the Walls layer within the Layers Editor and select Add Selected Objects from the pop-up menu. Lastly, in the Visibility column, click the **v** to turn off the visibility of this layer. This will hide all the walls except for the group, `WallCenter_Group`. We are leaving this wall so that you have an idea of scale.

Step 4: Begin making a vase by creating a profile curve. We are going to create a vase using a Revolve surface. This is much like a Lathe surface in most other 3D applications and is based on the old idea of a wooden lathe. Basically, a wood lathe takes a block of wood and spins it very quickly. The craftsman then can use a blade that when held up to the block of spinning wood, cuts in nice round curves. Lathes or Revolves are surfaces that are made by creating the desired profile of the object desired, and then spinning the curve around to create a three-dimensional surface.

　To create the curve we want, first take a minute to organize your Workspace. For now, we will create the lamp on the floor. Again, to make sure that we create a clean surface, we are going to make use of the grid for snapping and create a lamp that is too big. Later we will scale the lamp to size.

FIGURE 4.1   Zooming into about the center of the 3D space allows for quick creation of curves and shapes without having to worry above adjusting manipulators/pivots later.

Maximize the Front view and zoom in on 0,0,0 in 3D space (Figure 4.1).

Create a CV curve using the CV Curve tool with a Curve Degree of 3 Cubic that approximately matches Figure 4.2. Notice in Figure 4.2 the number of CVs are listed to show how the curve was created on the fly. There is no need for this curve to match exactly—make adjustments as you see fit.

FIGURE 4.2   CV curve listing the number of CVs.

There are a couple of things that are important though. The revolved surface is going to be revolved around the Y axis. So, to make sure that this lamp base is closed at the bottom and the top, make sure that those two points are snapped to grid (**x**).

Hit **Enter** to exit the CV Curve tool. Remember that as you are creating the curve, if you place a CV that you dislike, immediately hit **Ctrl-z** and the CV will be undone, while still leaving you in the CV Curve tool. Also remember that when all is done and you have exited the CV Curve tool, you can use the Move tool and RMB-click on the curve, select Control Vertex from the Marking menu, and then select the CVs you have created and adjust them.

Step 5: Create the three-dimensional lamp from this CV curve. Make sure that this newly created curve is selected and then go to Modeling│Surfaces> Revolve (Options). For now, make sure you reset the settings as the defaults are great for what we are doing. Before moving on, notice that within this Revolve Options window, you can choose what axis to revolve the curve around; you can choose to revolve in straight segments with the Surface Degree setting; and you can even choose not to revolve all the way around. Using the Start and End Sweep Angle settings, you can choose to create half a form, or a quarter, or whatever you would like. Notice that you can decide how many segments to create as Maya revolves this curve around. The default (8) is usually sufficient for basic shapes like lamp bases. Finally, notice that you can choose to make the surface you are going to create NURBS, polygons, subdivision surfaces, or Bezier.

For now, just hit the **Revolve** button and get back to Perspective view to see the results (Figure 4.3).

Rename the new `revolvedSurface1` to `LampBase`.

Step 6: Use Construction History to your advantage to change the shape of the lamp base. This new surface, `LampBase`, has some linkages. Because we used what is called `curve1` in the Outliner to create this surface, this is the primary linkage. This is important because of how Maya uses Construction History.

Select `curve1` in the Outliner. This, of course, is the CV curve we created to define the curvature of the `LampBase`. This will highlight the curve in green that is clearly seen in the Front view. RMB-click and hold the curve (in the Front view) and select Control Vertex from the resulting Marking menu (Figure 4.4a). Select any one of the control vertices and use the Move tool to change the position of that vertex; do this from the Front view (Figure 4.4b). Notice that as you change the position of the control vertex of the *curve*, the *revolved surface* that the curve created is updated in real time to match (Figure 4.4c).

Now, this is not to say that the surface cannot be altered without the curve that created it. It is quite easy to edit a NURBS surface and we will talk more about it later. So, keeping a curve around is not necessary. Further, a huge col-

FIGURE 4.3   Revolved lamp base.

lection of curves can become visually distracting in the Workspace and confusing in the Outliner.

In general, when creating a surface and making the general adjustments, the curve is great to have around. However, once you are fairly comfortable with the shape, go ahead and delete the curve. Of course, with complex surfaces (like some of the faces we are going to create in later tutorials), you may want to keep these curves around a lot longer and simply hide them. Making decisions as to when to get rid of what will develop as your comfort level with your own work flow increases.

For now, and for this tutorial, go ahead and delete `curve1`.

FIGURE 4.4   (a-c) Because Construction History is active, when the curve is adjusted, the surface updates as well.

FIGURE 4.5 (a-c) Creating the lampshade also with a revolve surface.

Step 7: Create the lamp shade using a Revolve surface. Repeat the process outlined above by created a CV curve in the shape of the lamp shade you would like (Figure 4.5a). With the curve selected, create a new revolved surface (Modeling│Surfaces>Revolve) (Figure 4.5b). Make any adjustments to the shape via the curve used to create the Revolve surface (Figure 4.5c) and then delete the curve. Rename this new surface to LampShade.

Step 8: Do some organizing. First, select LampShade in the Outliner and **Ctrl-**LMB-click LampBase. Hit **Ctrl-g** to group them together. Name the new group Lamp. Now, for a simple but effective trick: with the group Lamp selected, hit **Ctrl-g** again. It will appear that you just relabeled Lamp to group1. Not to fear. Expand the group group1 and you will see that the group Lamp has just been placed as a child to a new group—group1. Rename this group1 to Furniture_Group. We will be placing other furniture in this group later.

Finally, in the Layers Editor, create a new layer called Furniture, add Furniture_Group to it, and make the layer invisible. While you are there, make the layer Walls visible again.

Step 9: Create curves for the floorboard. The plan here is to create a lofted surface for the floorboards that is able to turn corners. To get started on this process, we need to create a curve that is a profile section of the floorboard. Rather than trying to create this at exactly the right size to begin with, we will create it really large, and then resize it to the right scale.

In the Front view, move off to the left of your walls, and create a curve that matches either Figure 4.6a or the floorboard in the room where you are now working. Make sure to close the curve. Also, as you create, make sure to snap the CVs at the bottom of the curve to the ground plane.

Center the pivot to get it in the general region of your curve, and then snap it into position at the bottom corner (Figure 4.6b). We want to make sure that we are snapping with this point to get these curves right into the corners of the room, and we want to resize from here so that we make sure that the curve stays sitting on the ground.

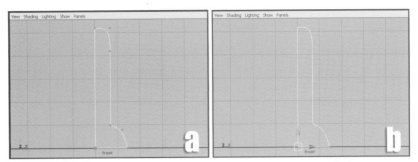

FIGURE 4.6   (a-b) Create the floorboard curve and position its pivot to the bottom corner.

Step 10: Using snap to points, move this curve into the northwest corner of the room. An easy way to do this is hold down the **v** hotkey and in the Front view, slide the curve into position for the inside of the wall (Figure 4.7a). Then, still with the **v** hotkey down, in the Side view, slide the curve back into place from the center of the room (Figure 4.7b). The result in the Perspective view (after you have tumbled around to see the northwest corner) will look like Figure 4.7c.

FIGURE 4.7   (a-c) Placed floorboard curve.

Step 11: Resize and rotate this curve into place. Because this curve was not created with any particular attention to size, we will just be eyeballing the resizing process. Using the Scale tool, LMB-drag the center of the manipulator (the yellow box) to resize the curve in all directions at once. Resize it to that it is about 1/3rd the height of one of the grid units (Figure 4.8a). This will make the floorboard about 4 inches tall.

We also want to make sure that this floorboard is a consistent width all through the room, so we want to make sure that it is turned in 45 degrees. In the Channels box, enter 45 in the Rotate Y input field (Figure 4.8b).

FIGURE 4.8 (a-b) Resized and rotated curve.

Step 12: Duplicate and place the new `curve2` into the next corner. Duplicate curve1 (**Ctrl-d**). Then in the Top view with the Move tool, move the curve along the Z axis to the corner of `WallNorth` and `WallCenter_Group`. Be sure to dolly in so that you can see that the curve is really sitting in the corner. We want the curve facing into the room, so change the Rotate Y input field of the Channels box to −45. The approximate placement is shown in Figure 4.9.

FIGURE 4.9 Second curve placed in the next corner and rotated to face the center of the room.

Step 13: Duplicate and place the next three curves to go around the center wall. Again, duplicate, move, and change the Rotate Y values so that you have curves at each corner of the center wall archway. `Curve3` should remain at −45 degrees, `curve4` will be at 45, and `curve5` will also be at 45 degrees. The curves should approximately match Figure 4.10.

FIGURE 4.10 Duplicated and placed curves to allow the floorboard to go around the inset wall.

Step 14: Continue to duplicate and place curves for all corners of the room. Continue to duplicate, move, and rotate each curve for each corner of the room. For now, do not worry about the archways in the `WallSouth_Group`. Figure 4.11 shows a breakdown of the location of each of the needed curves.

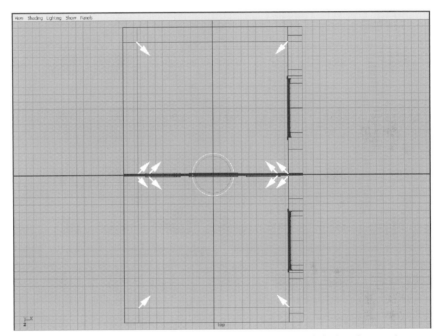

FIGURE 4.11 Breakdown of needed curves for floorboard using a lofted surface. Each arrow represents a curve in the direction it should be facing.

Step 15: Loft `curve1` through `curve2` into a new surface. Select `curve1` through `curve12` in the Outliner. Select Modeling | Surfaces>Loft (Options). By default, the settings for the Loft Options windows are set to create a nice organic looking lofted surface. However, in this case, we want to have crisp corner and straight lines—very inorganic.

To fix this, change the Surface Degree from Cubic to Linear. This will give us the straight surface we are looking for. Also, because we want this floorboard to go all the way around the room—including from the last curve back to the first—click on the Close option. Maya will then close the surface by extending it from `curve12` back to the first `curve1`. Hit the **Loft** button.

Take a minute to inspect the new surface that runs all around the room. Check to make sure that it really squeezes into every corner and does the things you need it to. If not, remember that this surface is tied to all those

FIGURE 4.12   The Loft Options window with appropriate settings for our clean, crisp floorboard.

curves you place. If you need to adjust things you can do so quickly with the curves.

Once you are happy with this new surface, rename it `Floorboard` and delete `curve1` through `curve12`.

Step 16: Build crown molding using an extruded surface. We are now going to add crown molding to the room. Although we could certainly do this using a lofted surface, we are going to instead use an extruded surface. As a review, this will consist of two surfaces—the profile that we are going to extrude and the path along which it will extrude.

Start by creating a curve that will represent the profile of the crown molding. A suggested shape is shown in Figure 4.13a. Make sure to close the curve (Figure 4.13b) and place the pivot/manipulator at the top corner of the curve. Move the curve to the top corner in the Front view and then in the Top view,

FIGURE 4.13   (a) Create the curve using the CV Curve tool. (b) Close the curve and place the pivot at the top corner. (c) Place and scale this curve into the northwest corner of the room.

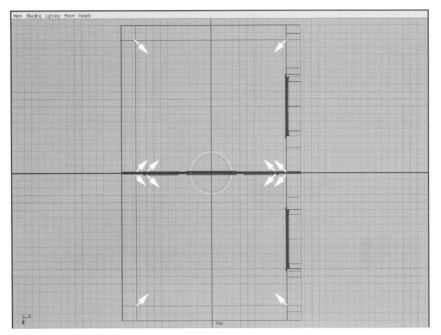

FIGURE 4.14   Creating the curve that the profile will follow.

make sure that it is in the northwest corner of the room (Figure 4.13c). Finally, resize the curve so that it matches the size it should be for the room (the exact size is not important—eyeball it).

Now, in the Top view, select Modeling│Create>CV Curve Tool (Options). Within the CV curve settings, change the Curve Degree to 1 Linear. We are creating a curve that will represent the overall shape of the room, so we need sharp corners. Create a curve with CVs in each of the corners. Remember to leave the curve open and use Edit Modeling│Curves>Close Curves to close off the shape (Figure 4.14).

Snap to grid and snap this curve to the top of the room. You will need to switch to Front, Side, or Perspective view to do this (Figure 4.15).

Now, select `curve1` in the Outliner and **Shift**-select `curve2` (selecting the profile first and then selecting the curve to extrude the profile along). Select Modeling│Surfaces>Extrude. Violà! Your new crown molding will be created (Figure 4.16). Rename the new `extrudedSurface1` to `Crown-Molding`, and delete `curve1` and `curve2`.

With `CrownMolding` selected, RMB-click the layer `Ceiling_Floor` in the Layers Editor and select Add Selected Objects from the pop-up menu. Because the layer `Ceiling_Floor` is not visible, `CrownMolding` will immediately disappear.

FIGURE 4.15 Curve snapped to top of the walls.

FIGURE 4.16 Finished CrownMolding.

For fun, make the `Ceiling_Floor` visible again by clicking on the Visibility column. If your view from the Perspective view is outside the room, this will close off your view of the room. Dolly into the inside of the room and take a bit of a look around to get a feel for what you have created. Hopefully, it all looks like Figure 4.17.

FIGURE 4.17 The room so far.

Step 17: Make a lofted surface to create a picture frame. Again, in the Front view, create a profile for the frame using the CV Curve tool. Make sure that the Curve Degree is set to 3 Cubic. Figure 4.18a shows a suggested shape.

Center the pivot and then snap it to the bottom corner (Figure 4.18b). Enter 45 into the Rotate Y input field of the Channels box. In the top view, duplicate and rotate three more so that you have a setup similar to Figure 4.18c.

Again, do not worry much about the scale of this frame. Use the grid to make sure that you are snapping each of the curves into position so that they are really straight across from the necessary curves. We will resize this frame when it is all done.

FIGURE 4.18   (a-c) Preparing a lofted surface for a picture frame.

Now, select all of the curves one at a time to define the order in which Maya is to loft together these curves. Select Modeling⏐Surfaces>Loft (Options). Make sure that the Surface Degree is set to 1 Linear. Hit the **Loft** button and you should have a frame similar to Figure 4.19a. Rename it to Frame.

This time, **do not** delete the curves. We are going to use these same curves to create some other frames. However, because we are going to use the curve on other frames, we want to make sure and break the connection between the surface and the curves. With Frame selected, choose Edit>Delete by Type>

FIGURE 4.19   (a-b) Creating the surface and final frame for pictures.

History. This will erase all of the construction history for the frame, thus freeing it from any ties to the curves.

Create a new NURBS plane Modeling│Create>NURBS Primitives>Plane (Figure 4.19a). Then, scale and move it into position on the bottom of the frame (Figure 4.19b). Finally, group together this new plane and frame, and re-name the group to `Picture`. With this picture selected, move, scale, and ro-tate into position on one of the walls in your room. It is up to you.

Step 18: Use curves to create an alternately proportioned frame. So, if we want to make a frame that is square, or very long, why not just take the old frame and use the Scale tool to lengthen it? Well, Figure 4.20 shows the frame created in the last step that has been rescaled. Notice that the thickness of the frame at the top and bottom becomes incredibly large, while the width along the sides remains constant.

Clearly, rescaling this type of surface is not the key. Instead, we will create a new surface from the curves created earlier but we will reposition the curves, first. Select `curve1`, `curve2`, `curve3`, and `curve4` in the Outliner. Make sure you have a standard `Four View panel` setup, move your mouse over the Perspective view, and hit **f** on your keyboard. This frames the selected curves in the middle of the panel. Now move your mouse over the Top view and hit **f** again. Now, we can see the four curves and alter them easily.

Select the top two curves by marqueeing around them in the Top view. Activate the Move tool, hold down **x** to snap to grid, and move them in the Z direction (blue manipulator handle) until you have set up a fairly square con-figuration (Figure 4.21a).

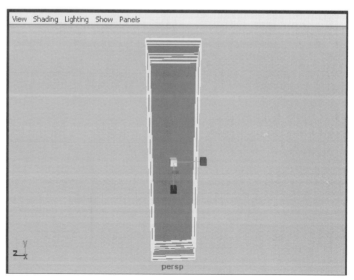

FIGURE 4.20 Rescaled frame. Notice the thick tops and bottoms with the thin sides.

FIGURE 4.21   (a-b) New square frame created from the same curves as in Step 17.

Again, select `curve1`, then `curve2`, then `curve3`, and finally, `curve4`. Create a lofted surface by clicking on the **Loft** button in the S helf or bselecting Modeling│Surfaces>Loft (Figure 4.21b). Because we will continue to create shapes, select this new surface and delete its history (Edit>Delete by Type> History). Create a new NURBS plane primitive and put it on the back of this new frame. Group together the plane and surface and name the group `PictureSquare`. Rotate, scale, and place this new frame into your room.

Step 19: Using these same curves or new combinations of curves, create various other frames. Figure 4.22 shows a variety of different frames created from variations of the original frame curve. Some frames use various curve placements, while others use more than the standard four curves. Notice

FIGURE 4.22   (a-d) Variety of lofted surfaces for frames.

the last example is round. This was accomplished by laying out the curves in a diamond shape and selecting Modeling | Surfaces>Loft (Options) and changing the Surface Degree setting to Cubic.

When you have explored the lofted surface enough, be sure to delete the curves.

Step 20: Duplicate, place, and organize (in the Layers Editor and Outliner) a variety of frames into your room. Scale, move, and rotate away until you have a load of pictures and frames placed through your room. When you are happy with your placements, create a new layer in the Layers Editor called `WallHangings`. Add all the Picture objects to this layer. This will allow you to hide them when necessary.

Finally, you will notice that with a lot of duplicated frames, your Outliner is getting a bit unwieldy with all the objects in it. Select all your pictures in the Outliner and hit **Ctrl-g** to place them all into a group that you will name `Pictures_Group`. This keeps your Outliner tidy as well.

Step 21: Create windows through a collection of loft and extrude surfaces. Figure 4.23 (a-c) shows the lofted surface created from two CV curves. Make sure to organize the curves from the Top View (assuming that the curve was created in the Front View) so that you make sure that they remain straight. After you have lofted the two surfaces, go ahead and delete the curves.

FIGURE 4.23   (a-c) The beginnings of the transoms and mullions of the window.

Figure 4.24(a-b) shows the lofted surface being duplicated and rotated into place to create the woodwork that will lie between the glass. Remember to use the Channels box to rotate things exactly 90 degrees. You may find it helpful to snap to grid and simply count the units you snap to make sure that each of the units remains a constant distance from the unit just duplicated.

When all the transoms and mullions are created, group them together and name the new group `Transoms`.

When you are comfortable with this woodwork, it will be time to make the frame for the window. To do this, we will also use a lofted surface. Create a CV

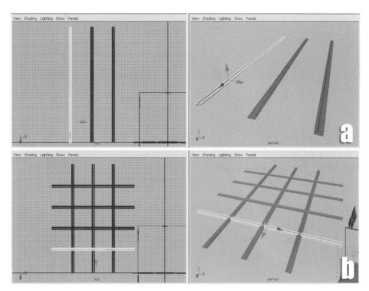

FIGURE 4.24   (a-b) Creating all the inner transoms and mullions. All are duplicates of the original lofted surface.

curve and be sure to rotate each curve to point toward the center (45-degree angles). Make sure to change the options for the loft back to linear for the Surface Degree and then loft together these curves (Figure 4.25a-c).

FIGURE 4.25   (a-c) Creating the lofted surface that is the window frame.

At this point, the window looks too stumpy. So, select the two curves that are the top of the window and use the Move tool to move them up to a new location. The lofted surface that is the window frame will reshape to match. Resize the vertical units of the Transoms group to fit and add new units as necessary.

Figure 4.26 shows the completed window that includes a new NURBS plane placed in the window. Later, this plane will be textured to represent glass and will become transparent but we must have the geography there to do that.

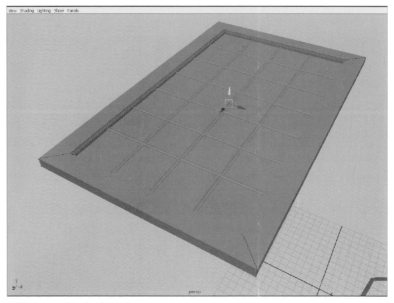

FIGURE 4.26 Finished window.

Finally, make sure to group all the elements for the window into a group that you rename `Window_Group`.

Step 21: Place windows in the room and organize. If your window matches the preceding figures, it is probably entirely too large. Resize the window, rotate, and place it into position in the room on `WallEast`. Duplicate the window and place the new duplicated window a bit to the south.

Duplicate and place three more windows so that they match Figure 4.27(a-b). Notice that these windows are placed about flush with the outside of

FIGURE 4.27 (a-b) Placed windows. Notice in b that we have changed the view to Wireframe in order to see the positions of the windows.

the walls. Although this seems a little strange, it will make more sense in a bit when we cut the holes for these windows to sit in.

Now, to keep our scene clean, select all the windows and group them into a new group called `Windows_All`. Also create a new layer called `Windows` and add all the windows to it.

Step 22: Add columns (polygonal cubes) with ornate tops (lofted surfaces).
Create a polygonal cube and resize it so that it is positioned between the arches of the center wall. Figure 4.28 (a-b) shows the curves and how they are organized atop the cube to create the trim. Be sure to get close so that these curves are placed appropriately. Loft the trim on top, get rid of the curves. Then, group the polygonal cube and both lofted surfaces into a new group called `Column`. Duplicate the column and place it between the other arch and between the two side arches and the wall. Finally, select all the columns and group them into a new group called `Column_Group` (Figure 4.29).

FIGURE 4.28   (a-b) Creating the tops of columns.

FIGURE 4.29   Final placed duplicated columns.

Step 23: Make the layer `Ceiling_Floor` **active and make adjustments to accommodate it.** Click the Visibility column in the Layers Editor and dolly into the room so that you can see how the columns look with the room in place. It probably looks like Figure 4.30 with the beams smacking right into the middle of the columns. This will never do.

FIGURE 4.30   Because we built the columns without the ceiling visible, we can see that there are problems with how the beams intersect the tops of the columns.

In the Outliner, expand the group `Column_Group` and expand each of the columns so you can see the objects in each group. **Ctrl**-LMB-click each of the lofted surfaces in all of the columns (Figure 4.31a). This selects all of the trim for all of the columns without selecting the center part of the column. Now, with the Move tool, move these down their Y Axes (green manipulator handle) so that the trim lines up with the bottom of the beam sitting at `WallMiddle_Group` (Figure 4.31b). When you are satisfied with the new placement, make sure to collapse all the groups in the Outliner to keep that space clean.

FIGURE 4.31   (a-b) Fixing the tops of the columns to be appropriate to the ceiling.

Step 24: Save and take a break before moving onto the next step. The next step includes a lot of things that we will not cover step-by-step as it is mostly information that we have covered already. However, it is all quite a bit of work and could be frustrating if you need to go back and review some steps.

Step 25: Create and place all the tables in the room. The furniture in the room is not particularly complex. However, there is a lot, so take some time to create the tables and objects on them using primitive, or make surfaces to create the forms that you need. This will undoubtedly include resizing the lamp you made earlier. Remember to hide different parts of your room if they are in your way as you work. You can do this through the Layers Editor or through **Ctrl-h**.

Do not worry about too many "props" right now—just create the major pieces. The tables should look something like Figure 4.32.

FIGURE 4.32 The room with the tables, and odds and ends, created and placed.

Make sure and place all of these tables in the `Furniture` layer. Be sure to also group as you go within the Outliner in ways that will make sense to you.

CONCLUSION

We are getting ever so close. By now, you should feel comfortable with moving objects around, creating and modifying curves, and creating and modifying surfaces. We have looked at creating loft, extrude, revolve, and planar surfaces. These are not all, and we have not really explored how to edit those surfaces. Not to worry—much more on that later.

Coming up in the next chapter, we are going to be wrapping up a lot of loose modeling ends. We will look at how to edit on a component level including altering extant surfaces. We will look at other ways to take control of the Duplicate tool, and finally, we will look at the powerful tool of Boolean operations to cut out the holes for our windows.

At the end of the next chapter, our room will be completely modeled. After that, we will look at some methods of subdivision modeling and do a bit of organic work. Next, we get to move on to making our room not quite so—well, gray. We get to work on creating textures, colors, and lights.

5

COMPONENT LEVEL EDITING AND BOOLEANS

We can start to see the room really coming together now. It is starting to feel like we might even know a bit of what we are doing. In this chapter, we will solidify that feeling by getting down into the minutiae of the editing process. Up to now, we have been focusing generally on creating and editing objects—entire objects. In this chapter, we will look at taking these objects and making the tweaks that turn basic shapes into dynamic and sophisticated forms.

We will also look at how to subtract shapes from each other. We will look at how to add shapes. We will look at ways to break up surfaces that we have already constructed. Finally, we will look at how to "glue" together surfaces.

Although this is by no means an exhaustive treatment of Maya modeling techniques, at the end of this chapter, you will have had a good look at a wide variety of the core tools. In Chapter 6, we will look at the specialty subdivision surface editing and then move on to texturing.

ON THE CD *Again, be sure to note that the results from tutorial 5.2 can be found and referenced on the included CD-ROM. There is a lot to learn from a finished file, so feel free to pull the file out and dig into it.*

POWER OF THE DUPLICATION TOOL

Up to now, we have been looking at duplication as just a shortcut for the ol' Copy and Paste routine. It turns out that there is quite a bit more to this tool. To understand this tool, consider the following tutorial.

TUTORIAL

5.1 EXPLORING THE DUPLICATE TOOL

Step 1: Create a new scene. Select File>New Scene. Do not worry about where this file is in terms of projects—you won't save it.

Step 2: Create and resize a polygon cube primitive so that it is 5 units in X, .5 units in Y, and 1 unit in Z. Selecting Modeling│Create>Polygon Primitives Cube will create the cube. Then, enter 5, 0.5 and 1 on the Scale X, Scale Y, Scale Z input fields. The cube should be something like Figure 5.1.

Step 3: Duplicate a translated cube. Open the Duplicate Options window by selecting the Edit>Duplicate (Options) pull-down menu. Assuming that all settings are set at the default, all the values in the Translate, Rotate, and Scale input fields should read "0." Because of this, when we have been duplicating objects,

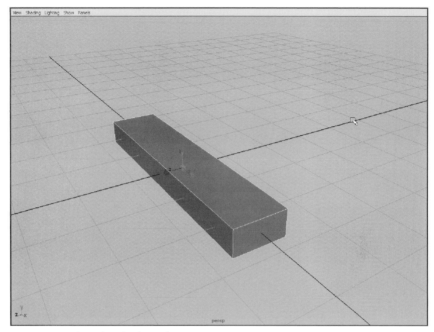

FIGURE 5.1   Cube to be duplicated.

the new object is resting at exactly the same position as the original. However, we can have Maya move, rotate, or scale each of the duplicates.

For instance, we know that his cube is 1 unit deep in the Z direction. Enter 1 in the Z column of the Translate row (Z is the third column over). Click the Apply button. Notice that first of all, your Duplicate Options window stays around. Second, notice that the new pCube2 (as it appears in the Outliner) is created and translated 1 unit in the positive Z direction from the original (Figure 5.2).

LMB-click anywhere in the Workspace and hit **Ctrl-z** to undo the duplicate.

Step 4: Create a set of stairs. If we wanted to create some basic stairs from this block, we just need each duplicate to be translated 1 unit in the Z direction, and up 0.5 units in the Y direction. To make sure that we can see things a bit better, enter 0.5 in the Y column and −1 in the Z so that the new duplicate is moved up 0.5 units, but *back* 1 unit. Hit the Apply button (Figure 5.3).

Click in the Workspace and undo the duplication.

This is a good start, but it would require multiple duplications to create a lot of steps. One of the nice things about the Duplicate Option window is the Number of Copies slider. Change this to 10. So, now you are telling Maya, "Create 10 duplicates, and move each successive duplicated shape up 0.5 units and back 1 unit." Hit the Apply button. The result should look like Figure 5.4.

Undo this duplication.

FIGURE 5.2 Duplicated cube translated 1 unit in the positive Z direction.

FIGURE 5.3 Duplicated step translated back and up.

FIGURE 5.4   Duplicating multiple copies.

Step 5: Create a spiral staircase. This time, we do not only want to duplicate and move (translate) many duplicates, but we also want each of the duplicates to be slightly rotated. For this one, let's put a little bit more space between duplicates; change the Translate Y column to 1 and the Z column to –1.5. In the Rotate row, change the Y column to 15, meaning that each duplicate will be rotated 15 degrees on the Y axis from the duplicate before. Lastly, change the number of copies to 50 and hit the Apply Button (Figure 5.5).

FIGURE 5.5   Spiral staircase created from manipulating the Duplicate Options window.

Step 6: Create spiral stalk. So, that always makes for a nifty demo to show an insta-spiral staircase but you really do not make a spiral staircase all that often. In this step, we will look at a quick alternate use.

Start by creating a primitive NURBS circle (Modeling│Create>NURBS Primitives>Circle). Select it and open the Duplicate Options window. What we want to do here is create a spiral of these circle curves. Enter 2 in Y Translate and –5 in Z Translate. Enter 30 in the Y Rotate and .95 in the X and Z Scale. Change the Number of Copies to 50. What this will do is create 50 copies of this circle;

each will be .95 the size of the last and each will be moved up 2 units, 5 units back, and be rotated 30 degrees. Hit the Duplicate button (Figure 5.6).

Now, in the Outliner, select nurbsCircle1 and **Shift**-select nurbsCircle51. This will select all the circle curves in the scene. Now, loft them together and the result will be something like Figure 5.7—a spiraling surface that becomes smaller as it raises. Pretty cool, eh?

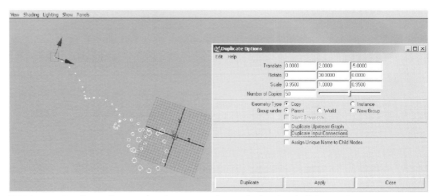

FIGURE 5.6   Duplicated curves. Each curve is also scaled to be slightly smaller than the last.

FIGURE 5.7   Lofted duplicated circles.

The Duplicate tool can really be used for an incredible variety of things. In fact, in future tutorials, we will use it to help us quickly create the backs of furniture.

TUTORIAL

5.2 FINISHING THE ROOM

Well, we have been working on this room long enough. In this tutorial we will finish up by creating the missing furniture pieces and cutting holes in the walls for windows. When we are done, we will be ready to texture.

Step 1: Open the project. Make sure you have the room file open from wherever you have saved it. Assuming you have not changed projects, the project setting should be all good. If not, make sure to set the project so Maya knows where to save things as you work.

Step 2: Make all layers not visible. Turn off all the "V's" in the Layers Editor. This should leave you with the middle wall (because it has not been assigned to any layer) and perhaps a few extraneous things like floorboards.

As we build the furniture, it can become rather dicey when there are just too many other things in the scene.

Step 3: Create the frame for the couch from anything you would like (although primitive polygon cubes work well). The exact size is not really important; just eyeball what you think works well proportionally. The piece in Figure 5.8 is about 2 feet deep and about 6 feet long. From the floor to the top of the backrest is about 3 feet. When I constructed this, the grid was relied

FIGURE 5.8 Framework of the couch.

upon heavily to give a good estimate of what size the piece would become. One thing to notice is that the two end pieces of the back are made as lofted surfaces to give them a bit of a curve. This was done by creating curves (that were 0.25 feet, or 3 inches, wide in the X direction) on the ground plane, one at the level of the seat, and a third above and behind the seat.

Step 4: Organize your Workspace to begin duplication. To create the back slats of the couch back, we will begin by using one of the back frame ends. As discussed in the last step, this was created with a lofted surface. To get a better visual handle on what will be happening, we will alter the Workspace a bit.

In Figure 5.9, you can see the loftedSurface fairly easily. To view your scene like this in the Workspace window, first hit **4** to display the window as wireframe, and then select the Shading>Smooth Shade Selected Items pull-down menu that is in the Workspace panel.

FIGURE 5.9 Displaying the scene as a Wireframe with Smooth Shade Selected Items.

Step 5: Duplicate one of the back ends to create one of the middle slats. Select one of the back frame ends. Choose Edit>Duplicate (Options). To make sure you are starting with a clean slate and not the crazy stuff we did in earlier tutorials, reset the settings.

It so happens that this slat is about 3 inches thick or 0.25 feet. If you do not know how thick your slat is, use the measurement tool to find out (Modeling|Create>Measure Tool>Distance Tool). The thickness of the slat is important so we know how far to distance each duplicate.

If your slat is indeed 0.25 feet thick then 6 inches will provide a nice spacing between (3 inches). So, in the Translate row in the X column, change the value to 0.5. Hit the Apply button (Figure 5.10) to leave the Duplicate Options window open because we will need to keep using it.

Step 6: Duplicate the slat to create all of the middle slats. It so happens that as the images show, and discussed above, the couch is about 6 feet long. So, if

FIGURE 5.10   Duplicated frame to be used as a slat.

we have 3-inch slats with 3 inches between each, then 10 copies of this original slat will do the trick. Change the Number of Copies input field to 10.

Finally, do one other thing. Change the Geometry Type to Instance. By default, this is set as Copy, meaning that when you duplicate, it creates an unrelated copy of the geometry. An *instance* is an entirely separate beast.

When Maya creates 10 instances, what it is actually doing is showing you the original object 10 times. There are not really 10 copies of the slat but rather Maya is showing the same slat 10 times just in different places. The real benefit of this is if you change anything about the original slat, then all the instances are instantly updated. Hit the Duplicate button (Figure 5.11).

FIGURE 5.11   The settings and results of creating duplicated slats.

Step 7: Alter the original back slat and watch the instance magic unfold.
Right now, all the back slats go clear to the floor. Although this is an interesting design choice, it is not the choice for this project. What we want to do is quickly make them all so that they end at the base of the couch.

Select the original back slat (not the original frame but the slat) (Figure 5.12a). We will edit this object at a component level by moving the control vertices (CVs) that make up this surface. To make the CVs visible and selectable,

FIGURE 5.12 (a-c) Getting to the component level of the original back slat.

RMB-click and hold the slat (Figure 5.12b). Then, select Control Vertex from the Marking menu. You will then be able to see the purple CVs of the surface (Figure 5.12c).

Marquee around the bottom four set of CVs (5.13a). Do this in any view that makes these CVs easy to see (Figure 5.13a shows the front view). As soon as you do this, the selected CVs will change from purple to yellow (Figure 5.13b). But not only do they change to yellow on the original back slat, but all of the bottom four CVs are also selected on all the instances as well. Now, with the Move tool, move these selected CVs up in the Y direction (green manipulator handle) so that the bottom of the slat is within the seat slat (Figure 5.13c). Make sure to take a look at views like the Side view as you do this to get a good idea of where you are actually placing these.

FIGURE 5.13 (a-c) Selecting and moving the CVs of one object with dynamically updated instances.

When all is said and done, your couch should appear something like Figure 5.14.

When you are happy with the shape, be sure to group all the objects that were used to make the couch into one group and call it Couch.

FIGURE 5.14   Completed couch woodwork.

Step 8: Repeat a similar process to create two loveseats and two chairs of similar styles. Again, the exact sizes are unimportant here but do repeat the same sorts of techniques so that your new loveseats and chairs are similar in style (Figure 5.15). Make sure to group and label each of the furniture pieces appropriately so that they are easy to work with and find.

Notice that the loveseats and chairs have arms. These arms were created using simple lofts and planar surfaces. To give the correct visual weight, the front legs were beefed up a bit (Figure 5.16 a-b).

FIGURE 5.15   Completed furniture woodwork.

FIGURE 5.16 (a-b) Creating arms with custom curves lofted and then created with a planar surface.

Here's a trick to modeling symmetrical objects (like the arms): first, model one arm. Duplicate the arm and then in the Channels box, enter −1 in the Scale input field in the direction you want Maya to create the mirrored duplicate. Even quicker is to change the Scale row in the Duplicate Options window to −1 in the appropriate column.

Step 9: Take a minute to organize. Take all the chairs, loveseats, and the sofa and in the Outliner, MMB-click and drag them into the `Furniture_ Group`. Because `Furniture_Group` is part of the layer, Furniture (which is not visible),when new objects become part of `Furniture_Group`, they will immediately become invisible as well.

COMPONENT LEVEL EDITING

Step 10: Create curves for cushions. One of the complaints that is always voiced about Maya is how it is impossible to create a cube with filleted edges. Filleted edges are just rounded off.

For the cushions in this room, filleted cubes would indeed be of value. So, we will look at how to create such a shape and how to really get down and dirty on a component level to make the shape what we need.

Begin by hiding any extraneous objects that are visible in the scene. This frees up the middle of the Workspace where we can create the curves we need. Figure 5.17 shows a CV curve created with the CV Curve tool with one CV at each point shown. Snapping to grid helps keep lines straight.

It is important to make sure that the first and last CVs are placed on the Y Axis as this is the axis that we will have this curve revolved around. So be sure to be snapping to grid when you place these two CVs.

Step 11: Revolve the curve. With just a curve, we have no surface. To create a surface from our curve, select Modeling | Surfaces>Revolve (Options). The only

FIGURE 5.17 Creating curve for cushions.

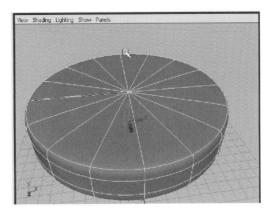

FIGURE 5.18 Revolved curve.

option we really need to change is the Segment input field. We want to have enough segments to be able to construct "corners" from the cylindrical shape that is going to be created. We want three rows of CVs for each corner for a total of 12, plus a row of CVs for each of the edges. So, we need 16, total. Enter `16` in the Segments input field and hit the Revolve button. (Figure 5.18).

Seems odd and far from a square cushion but do not lose hope.

Step 12: Adjust the Move tool to allow for CVs to maintain their space. Double-click the Move tool in the Toolbox. This will open the settings for the Move tool at the right of your interface. In the Move Snap Settings area, make sure to check Retain Component Spacing. We are going to snap collections of components to the grid in a second, and with this turned off, when we snap the group to the grid, all of the individual components would snap together to the same spot. This would destroy the soft edges we are working toward. With this turned on, we will be able to snap the manipulator of a collection of components to the grid, but each of the components still maintains their relative distance from the others.

Step 13: Rough out the cushion by altering "corner" collections of CVs. In the Top view, we need to alter the component CVs of this surface. To make these visible and selectable, RMB-click and hold on the surface until the Marking menu comes up that allows you to select Control Vertex (Figure 5.19a). When you have done so, you will be able to see all the purple CVs for this surface.

Notice that at each of the poles (as in North, South, East, and West), the CVs come to rest on a grid intersection because we snapped the curve as we were building it. What we want to do is take the collection of CVs for each of the corners (that do not exist yet) and snap them up to the same level or corner as the corner of a cube shape would exist.

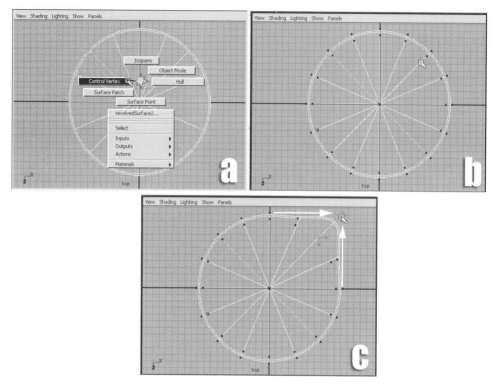

FIGURE 5.19 (a-c) Roughing out the rounded square shape.

For instance, Figure 5.19b shows the selection of the desired CVs. Figure 5.19c shows using the Move tool (while snapping to grid (**x**)) to move this collection of CVs to the place where the two poles would meet.

Step 14: Create all the corners. Repeat this process to create all four rough corners (Figure 5.20).

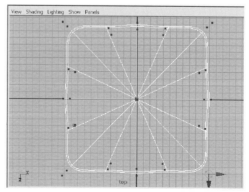

FIGURE 5.20 Created rough corners.

Step 15: Tighten the corners by moving additional collections of CVs closer to the new corners. Do this by again grabbing collections of CVs and snapping them a couple of units over or a couple of units down from the collection of CVs that make a corner. Figure 5.21a shows the breakdown of selecting the next set of CVs down, and moving them into place. By Figure 5.21b, you will have all the CVs in position to give nice soft corners to the shape.

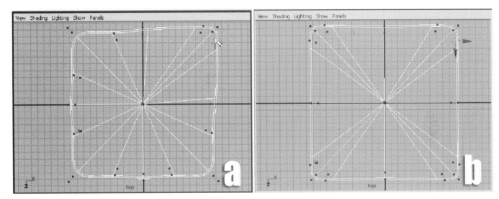

FIGURE 5.21   (a-b) Creating rounded corners by taking control of CVs.

So, the closer the collections of CVs on the corners, the tighter the corner. Move them further apart and the corner will be softer.

Step 16: Beat up the cushion a bit. First, take a second and turn off the Retain Component Spacing in the Move tool settings. Then, grab CVs and move them around—bend things up and make things less perfect. Remember that because we have kept our segments reasonably low, some ugly faceting will result if you pull things too far, but you can give things a little more interesting look by manipulating CVs (Figure 5.22).

FIGURE 5.22   The "beat up" cushion.

Step 17: Show the furniture and place these new cushions into place.
Scale, move, and rotate the cushions into place. If you need to reposition furniture, do so; make it all look something like Figure 5.23. Make sure to group your cushions with the piece of furniture they sit upon. Remember you can do this by MMB-dragging the cushions onto the group that is the piece of furniture; this makes the cushions children of that group.

FIGURE 5.23 Placed cushions.

Step 18: Take a look at everything in the scene. Make all the layers active to get an idea of where you are (Figure 5.24).

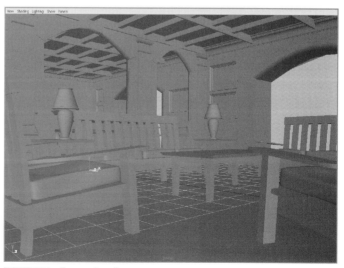

FIGURE 5.24 Scene thus far.

WORKING WITH ISOPARMS

Step 19: Rotate around until you can see the arches that lead you out of the room. Notice that we have a problem here (Figure 5.25). The floorboard that we brilliantly created goes right across the opening. Because this would lead to many tripped visitors, and a house would never really be built this way, we need to clean this up.

FIGURE 5.25   Problem spot of floorboard across door opening.

Step 20: Add isoparms in places to cut. Display your scene as Wireframe with Smooth Shade Selected Items (both within the Shading pull-down menu of the Workspace panel). Select the floorboard. If you look at the selection, you will see long green lines. These are visual clues as to what the organization of the objects. These green lines are called *isoparms*.

Isoparms themselves are not directly editable. You cannot take an isoparm and move it, scale it, or rotate it. As such, at first glance, they do not have much use in controlling a surface. However, isoparms are correlated to a lot of things, such as surface patches, CVs (which we have seen are very useful to editing a surface), and hulls, to name a few. However, besides being indicators of where other components are, we can use isoparms to help define where things are going to happen.

In this case, notice that there are lots of isoparms running horizontally but very few running vertically. We basically have isoparms in the corners of the room where the surface makes a turn. We need to get rid of the part of the surface that is sitting across the arch. To do this, we will create isoparms on both sides of the arch to mark where we are going to get rid of surface topology.

First, we need to be able to see and manipulate isoparms. So, RMB-click and hold on the Floorboard object and select Isoparm from the resulting Marking menu. All the green isoparms will now turn blue indicating that you can select them.

Dolly into the corner and for fun, click on one of the blue lines. When you first begin to click, the isoparm that Maya thinks you are trying to select will turn red. When you release the mouse, it will highlight yellow to indicate that you have selected it. Notice that if you click an existing isoparm and drag, you will get a red line indicating a potential location of an isoparm (Figure 5.26). When you release the mouse after such an action, you get a yellow dotted line. This indicates that an isoparm can be potentially placed here.

FIGURE 5.26 Clicking and dragging an extant isoparm will show potential placements of new isoparms.

For now, click on the vertical isoparm in the corner and drag the new potential isoparm so that it sits in the middle of the trim around the archway. When you release your mouse, the tell-tale yellow dotted line will appear (Figure 5.27).

FIGURE 5.27 Mapping out the location where the new isoparm is to be placed.

To add an isoparm here, select Modeling | Edit Nurbs>Insert Isoparms (Options). Notice that within this options window, you can choose to do things like add multiple isoparms by changing the Multiplicity setting. If you have two isoparms selected, you can add isoparms between the selected isoparms. However, in our case, we want to have our Insert Location set to At Selection because we have just pointed out to Maya exactly where we want an isoparm to be placed. Click the Insert button (Figure 5.28).

FIGURE 5.28   Newly created isoparm shows up in green at the location we defined earlier.

Repeat this process and place an additional isoparm on the other side of the arch.

Step 21: Detach the surface. Because we have two isoparms newly defined on the surface, we can have Maya think of the space between the isoparms as its own unique surface. This means we can also detach it from the parent surface (the floorboard) and thus delete it.

To do this, select and then **Shift**-select the isoparms on both sides of the arch (Figure 5.29a). Select Modeling | Edit Nurbs>Detach Surfaces. The results (Figure 5.29b) do not look incredibly different than before, but notice the Outliner. There will now be not only the floorboard, but also two new surfaces called `FloorboarddetachedSurface`.

Now, select the newly created surface in the middle of the arch and delete it (Figure 5.29c).

Step 22: Repeat the detach surface process for the other arch. Mark the isoparms, add the isoparms, and detach the surface so you have two archways that are easy to walk through (Figure 5.30).

Remember that any NURBS surface has isoparms. You can change the shape of these isoparms by altering the CVs or the hull. With any surface, you can use isoparms to detach sections of the surface. You can work these detached sections or delete them altogether. There is a huge multitude of options to working further with NURBS surfaces that would occupy its own book, so we cannot cover them here. However, take plenty of time to play with them and become the master of NURBS and NURBS surfaces.

FIGURE 5.29 (a-c) Ridding ourselves of sections of a surface by detaching them and deleting.

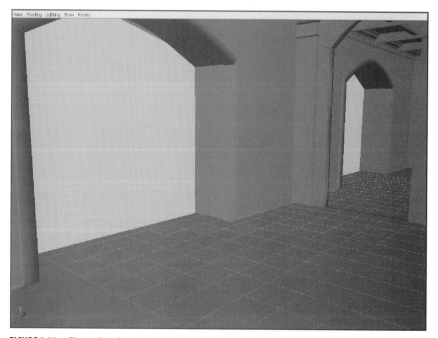

FIGURE 5.30 Cleared archways.

Boolean Functions

If you have used a library search engine or even many Internet search engines, you are probably familiar with *Boolean* functions. If you want pages about black cougars, you could enter "Cougar + black – cars." This would look for sites and books that had both *cougar* and *black* in the page, but not *cars*.

In 3D, Boolean functions allow you to subtract shapes from other shapes. They also allow you to add shapes and even find intersections where different forms meet. In these next few steps, we are going to use Boolean functions to cut out the windows and some of the doors in our room.

Step 23: Hide all layers except Walls and Windows.

Step 24: Create the "hole" shape. The first sort of Boolean function we will be performing is a *Difference*. That is, we will be finding the difference of two shapes, or subtracting one shape from another. We already have the walls that we are going to subtract *from* but we need the shapes that are going to be doing the subtracting. In this case, the forms will be elongated cubes to make the tall rectangular windows.

The walls are polygonal shapes (not NURBS) so we will want to create the hole forms from polygons as well. Create a new polygonal primitive cube and resize it so that it is about Scale X = 4, Scale Y = 6.5, and Scale Z = 4. The exact size is not overly important; what is important is that this shape looks something like Figure 5.31.

View your scene as Wireframe (**4**), so you can see where exactly you are placing this "hole." Notice in Figure 5.31 that the cube has been positioned so that it is above the ground and completely penetrates `WallEast`. If this hole object did now go all the way through the wall, the Boolean result would not be a complete hole. Position this hole object (with the Move tool) to about the position of Figure 5.31. Notice that this box sits right where our previously created window sits. Notice also that it should be about the size of the window; if it is not, resize.

Before you get much further, be sure and label this cube `WindowHole`.

Step 25: Duplicate and position other WindowHole objects. Duplicate this `WindowHole` and in the Top view, position this new `WindowHole1` into position for the other windows in the room. Moving `WindowHole1` from the top ensures that you do not move this hole up or down in the Y direction. Thus, your windows will be the same height on the wall (Figure 5.32).

Step 26: Create a Boolean Difference from `WallNorth` and `WindowHolex` (whichever `WindowHole` object that sits inside `WallNorth`). Maya decides which shape to subtract from which shape by the order that you select them. Maya keeps the object that is selected first and subtracts the second

FIGURE 5.31 First "hole" object created, sized, and placed within the wall. Notice that the hold object is big enough and placed in a location to allow for a clean cut to take place through the entire wall.

FIGURE 5.32 Duplicated `WindowHoles` positioned.

object from it. In this case, we want to keep `WallNorth`, so select `Wall-North` in the Workspace or Outliner. Hold down the **Shift** key and select the `WindowHole` in the Workspace (or hold down the **Ctrl** key and select `Window-Hole2` in the Outliner) that intersects `WallNorth`. `WallNorth` will be high-lighted white in the Workspace and `WindowHole2` will be highlighted green.

Once both are highlighted, select Modeling|Polygons>Boolean>Differ-ence. The result (Figure 5.33) should be fairly quick and should show a nice hole in the middle of the wall.

FIGURE 5.33   Result of a polygonal Boolean Difference.

Let's look for a minute at what has happened. Take careful notice of the Outliner. PolySurface1 is the result of the Boolean operation. Notice that the two originally involved parties (`WallNorth` and `WindowHole2`) are now actually hierarchies that contain a transform node. It is important to note that you can no longer see these two objects, although they are still integral to the shape, `polySurface1`. Here's why.

Because Construction History is (by default) turned on, the object poly-Surface1 is linked to the two objects `WallNorth` and `WindowHolex`. To see this relationship, select `WindowHolex` in the Outliner and activate the Move tool. In the Workspace, the move manipulator will appear right in the hole of the wall (Figure 5.34a). Grab hold of the Z handle of the manipulator and move it (Figure 5.34b). The "hole" will move!

FIGURE 5.34 (a-b) Because construction history is active, a Boolean Difference leaves the objects used in the function, which can be adjusted to change dynamically the result of the Boolean Difference.

The real benefit of this is that Boolean functions are not irreversible. In fact, 50 steps later, if you decide you want to move the window hole, you can do so by moving `WindowHolex`. The problem with this is that you begin to grow the number of objects in your Outliner. With a lot of Boolean functions, you can quickly find the number of objects in your Outliner out of control. Also, in certain animation cases, construction history can cause some funny problems. So, usually, if you know that your hole is where you want it, take a minute to clean out the object's history. To do this, select polySurface1 and choose Edit>Delete by Type>History. This cleans the object from any relations it might have due to construction history. Notice that `WallNorth` and `Window-Hole2` are gone from the Outliner.

Finally, rename `polySurface1` to `WallNorth_Window`.

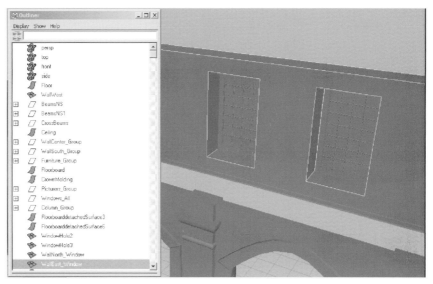

FIGURE 5.35   Results of double-Boolean Difference. This gives us two holes in one wall. Each hole has to be subtracted individually.

Step 27: Create a Boolean Difference and subtract `WindowHole` from `WallEast`. Select `WallEast` and add `WindowHole` to the selection; again, choose Modeling|Polygons>Boolean>Difference. While the new `poly-Surface1` that is created from this function is still selected, go to Edit>Delete by Type>History.

Step 28: Create a Boolean Difference to subtract `WindowHole1` from `polySurface1`. Before we bother renaming the wall, go ahead and **Shift**-LMB-click `WindowHole1` in the Workspace (or **Ctrl**-select in the Outliner) and select Polygons>Boolean>Difference. Again, delete the history for this object. Finally, rename what is now `polySurface2` to `WallEast_Window`. The results of all of this should look something like Figure 5.37.

Step 29: Repeat the process for `WallWest`. Create the Boolean difference shapes and be sure to name the final wall `WallWest_Window`.

Step 30: Create a hole for a doorway in `WallNorth_Window`. Do this by creating a new polygon primitive cube. Resize it (Scale tool) it so that it looks close to Figure 5.36 (the box here is X=3, Y=7, Z=4). Select `WallNorth_Window`, then **Shift**-select this new cube and choose Polygons>Boolean>Difference. Delete the history of the new polysurface and rename it `WallNorth_Window_Door`.

FIGURE 5.36 (a-b) Creating the hole for the doorway.

Step 31: Do some cleanup. This includes putting trim around all the newly created holes in the walls. It includes getting rid of the floorboard in front of the new doorway. After all that, make sure everything is visible and organize things so that everything fits where it should. All in all, your model should look something like Figure 5.37.

FIGURE 5.37 Room with mostly finished modeling.

CONCLUSION

Thus, we wrap up the modeling of the room. Of course, there are lots of props and other elements that could be added to the room to make it feel more "lived in." You probably will want to create those types of props to get the practice of using all the techniques we have covered so far. But for now, we will leave the tutorial discussion of modeling this room.

In Chapter 6, we will look at subdivision modeling since it is available in Maya 4.5 Complete and Unlimited. Then, in Chapter 7, we will return to this room and learn how to bring it to life with color and textures. So hang in there—the best eye candy is still to come.

6

SUBDIVISION MODELING

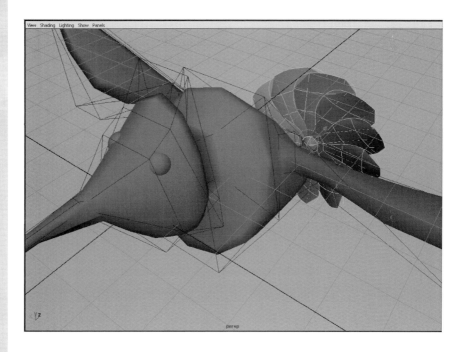

S o, we have looked at some basic Polygon modeling and some basic NURBS modeling. Although there is still much to be discussed in those two areas, you have the tools to move in a variety of different directions with those two ideas. The big area we have left to discuss is subdivision surfaces.

Think of subdivision surfaces as an interesting combination between NURBS and Polygon modeling. More accurately, think of subdivision surfaces as NURBS surfaces that can be altered like polygonal ones. This is what makes this chapter so valuable. The techniques we will be working with here are a little bit NURBS based and a little bit polygonal based. You will be able to use these techniques and ideas in other realms of modeling.

THE STATES OF A SUBDIVISION SURFACE

To get a better idea of how to work with subdivision surfaces, create one. Select Create>Subdiv Primitives>Cube (Figure 6.1).

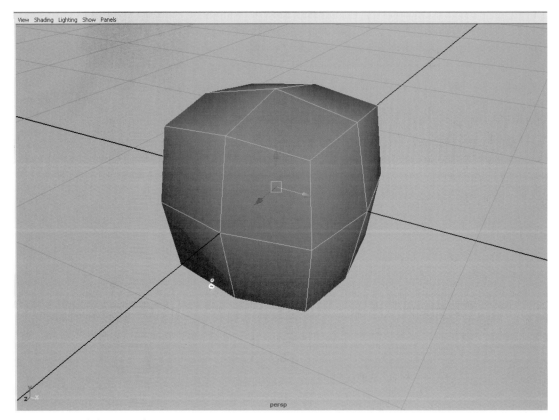

FIGURE 6.1   A subdivision cube.

This cube can be manipulated much like any other object—with the Move, Rotate, and Scale tools, you can manipulate the entire object. More important are the components that make up the surface.

Like other surfaces we have discussed, RMB-holding on an object brings up a hotbox with a collection of components to select from along with other choices (Figure 6.2).

By default, there are a few important components of note. First, the subdivision surface is in Standard mode. Notice that at the bottom right, you can change to Polygon (more on this later).

Standard Mode

While in standard mode, there are some interesting components that can be selected and manipulated. Figure 6.3a shows what happens when Vertex is selection. These are very similar to CVs of a NURBS surface; when

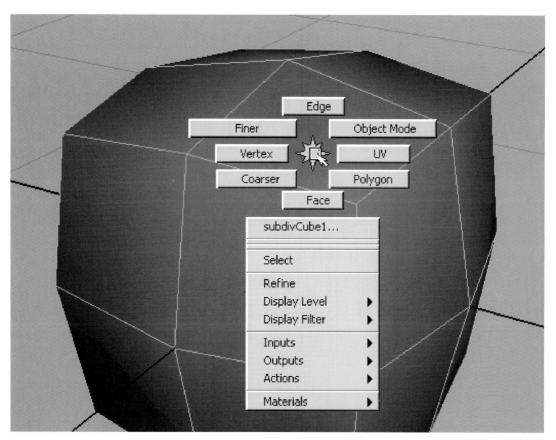

FIGURE 6.2   Subdivision surfaces' components can be selected with a RMB-click-hold.

they are selected, you can gently pull at the surface to change the shape in very organic ways. Similarly, you can select Face and you will be presented with a sort of cage (Figure 6.3b) that looks much like collections of Hulls from a NURBS surface. The only difference is that instead of just being able to select rings of CVs as you do with hulls, you can select the imaginary face that rests between the vertices. These faces can be pulled or pushed, also changing the shape of the subdivision surface.

You can also select an Edge (just one side of a face) to be maneuvered as you wish.

Polygon Mode

However, with all of these fancy handles and slightly different ways to change the NURBS-like surface, the real power comes when you are able to maneuver the cage in true Polygon-like ways.

To see how this works, RMB-click-hold on the subdivision cube and select Polygon from the hotbox. The immediate change may seem rather subtle; the purple/orange color scheme used to indicated NURBS changes to the green of polygonal shapes. You can still see the green cage and see the isoparms of the surface.

Just like in standard mode, you can use the hotbox to select a Vertex, Edge, or Face. However, different than standard mode is your ability to manipulate these vertices, edges, and faces like polygons.

RMB-click-hold on the subdivision cube and select Face from the hotbox. Now, select any of the faces of the resulting cage (Figure 6.4).

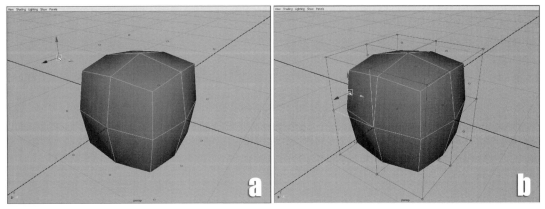

FIGURE 6.3 (a) Selecting Vertex from the hotbox. (b) Select Face from the hotbox. In both cases, you can change the shape of the subdivision surface through the manipulation of these components.

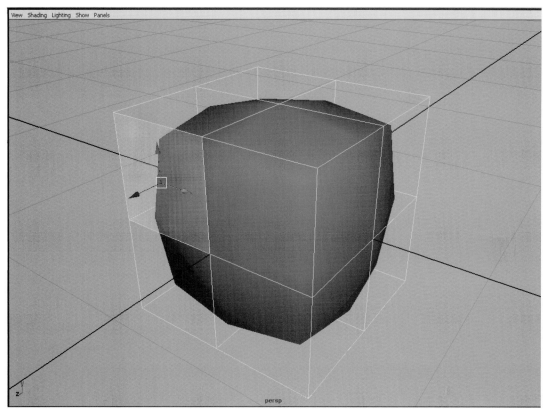

FIGURE 6.4   Selecting a face of the subdivision cage while in Polygon mode.

You can move, rotate, or scale this face. More important, you can extrude a new face off of it. Select Modeling|Edit Polygons>Extrude Face (Option). When the Extrude Face Options window comes up, make sure and reset the settings. Then hit the **Extrude Face** button. Figure 6.5 shows the result of this. What has actually happened is that a new face has been created right on the surface of the old face. The new manipulator is interesting in that it allows you to move and scale this new face, directly. Notice that with this new face created, the corner of the subdivision surface has become crisper. This is because there is actually a whole new bunch of geometry all packed together.

To use this new manipulator, grab the move handle that allows you to pull away from the surface (in the case of Figure 6.6, this is the Z handle) and pull away the newly extruded face.

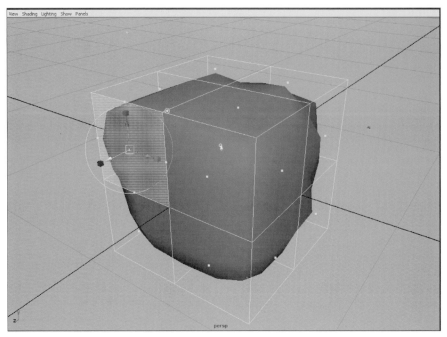

FIGURE 6.5   Extruded face still sitting on the surface of the old face.

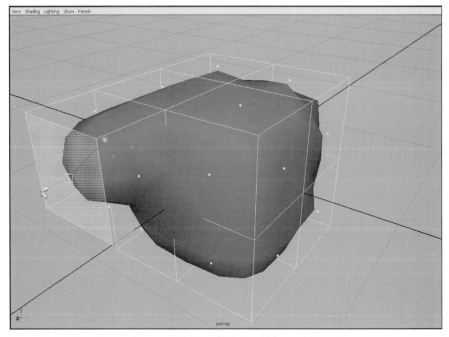

FIGURE 6.6   Pulling the newly extruded face off of the old face to show all new geometry.

What is happening here is more than just adjusting the extant geometry. By creating a new face, you have also created faces on all four sides of that face. When you pull out the new face, you are stretching the new geometry created by adding a new face.

Now, there are several different variations of how to use this tool. For instance, undo back until you have no extruded faces. Now, select two faces that are right next to each other; select one and then **Shift**-select the other (Figure 6.7a). Select Modeling│Edit Polygons>Extrude Face. Use the new manipulator to pull out the new faces that have been created (Figure 6.7b).

Notice that the new face, and the new faces that surround the new face, cause a cleft to appear between the two faces. This is because there is a face running perpendicular to the extruded faces between the new surfaces.

In certain cases, this can be very effective; you can have new faces extruding out in multiple directions, all independent of the faces that are adjacent to them. However, in more cases, when you select more than one face, you want them to extrude as one mass. There are a couple ways to do this. To see how, undo back to the point where two faces are selected but not extruded.

Go to Modeling│Polygons>Tool Options>Keep Faces Together. This is essentially telling Maya that as you make adjustments—such as extruding faces—you don't want it to be creating new faces between collections of extruded faces. Now, select Modeling│Edit Polygons>Extrude Faces. Again, use the manipulator to pull out the new faces (Figure 6.8). Notice that now these two faces come out together with no faces between them.

So, there are the basics. To get a better feel for the process, let's quickly create a little hummingbird creature that we can use later in the book.

FIGURE 6.7   (a-b) Extruding two faces.

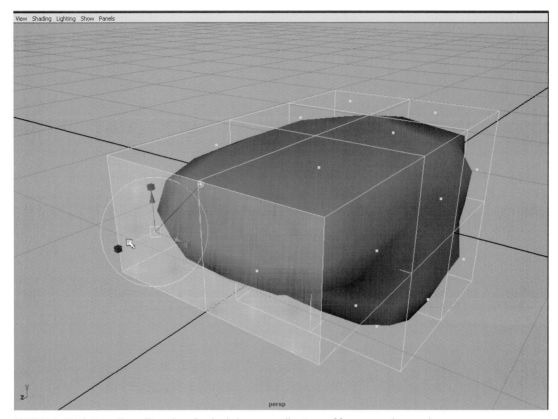

FIGURE 6.8   With Keep Faces Together checked, the new collections of faces extrude together en masse.

T U T O R I A L

6.1 CREATING A HUMMINGBIRD

The little creature we want to create is shown in Figure 6.9.

Because it is essentially a round character, we can save ourselves some time by starting out with a round subdivision primitive.

Step 1: Create a subdivision cylinder. Select Create>Subdiv Primitives> Cylinder.

Step 2: Rotate the cylinder so that it is laying down. Select the entire cylinder and rotate it 90 degrees along the X axis. You can do this manually with the Rotate tool or via the Channels box (Figure 6.10).

Step 3: View the subdiv surface in Polygon mode. RMB-click-hold and select Polygon from the hotbox. This will give you the cage that we can manipulate as polygons.

FIGURE 6.9   The hummingbird created from subdivision methods.

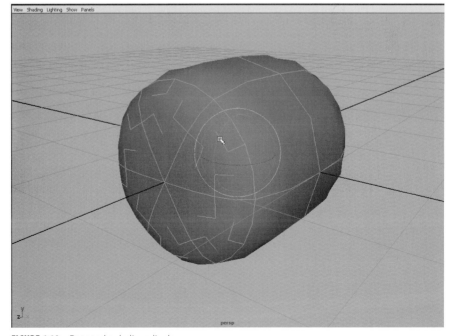

FIGURE 6.10   Rotated subdiv cylinder.

Step 4: Select the faces on the front of the cylinder. Tumble around to the other side of the cylinder and RMB-click-hold on the cylinder again to bring up the hotbox. Select Face. Now, LMB-click the faces on the front end (**Shift**-LMB to add to the selection). Make sure that as you selected, you didn't accidentally select faces on the sides (Figure 6.11).

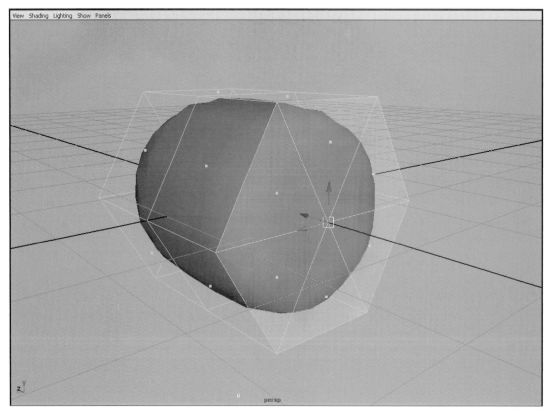

FIGURE 6.11 Selected faces on the front of cylinder.

Step 5: Resize faces to match Figure 6.12. This is going to be the front of the face that the hummingbird's long, thin beak comes out of. We want to taper the head a bit before bringing out the long beak. Use the Scale tool (keystroke **r**) and scale them down.

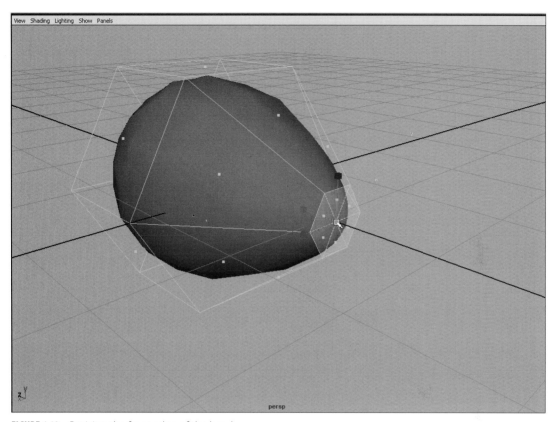

FIGURE 6.12   Resizing the front edge of the head.

Step 6: Move up these faces to match Figure 6.13. Use the Move tool to move up the already selected faces.

Step 7: Extrude these faces out to form the start of the beak. First, make sure that the faces will stay together (Modeling│Polygons>Tool Options>Keep Faces Together). Then, select Modeling│Edit Polygons> Extrude Face. With the new manipulator, extrude out just a little bit (Figure 6.14a), and then with the Scale tool, LMB-click-drag the center of the manipulator to resize these new faces also (Figure 6.14b).

We want to make this short extrusion to keep the transition from the head to the beak crisp. The farther away each ring of faces is from another, the softer the bend.

FIGURE 6.13 Moved faces.

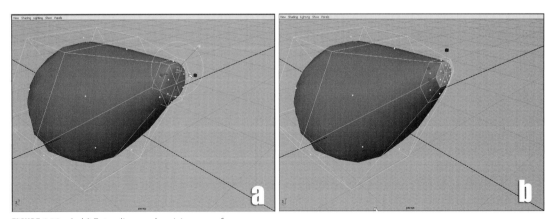

FIGURE 6.14 (a-b) Extruding and resizing new faces.

Step 8: Extrude the same faces way out for the beak and resize them.
Choose Extrude Face again and drag the new manipulator way out to create
the long beak. When the faces are pulled out (the exact distance doesn't matter), resize them to come to a point (Figure 6.15).

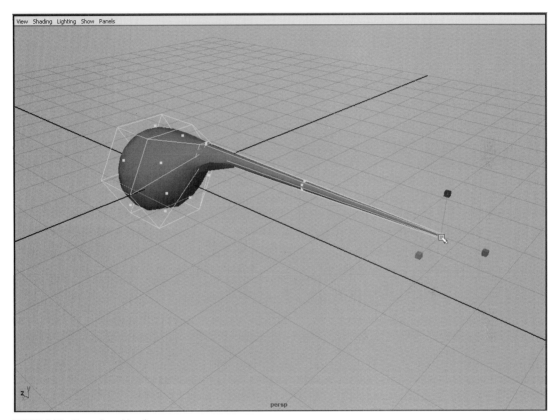

FIGURE 6.15   Completed beak.

Step 9: Reshape the head by adjusting the faces. Come back to the head
and select the face that sits right on top of the head. Move it up (Figure 6.16) to
give the head a more interesting shape.

**Step 10: Create a neck with a new set of extruded faces that stay on the
surface.** Select the faces that sit on the back of the head. Choose the Extrude
Face command, and this time, instead of pulling them out with the manipulator, use the cubes on the very edge of the manipulators to resize the new faces
without pulling them off the surface (Figure 6.17).

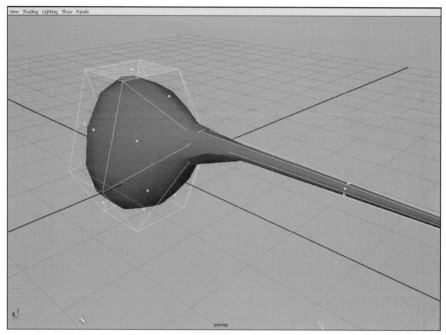

FIGURE 6.16 Altering the head shape by simply moving faces.

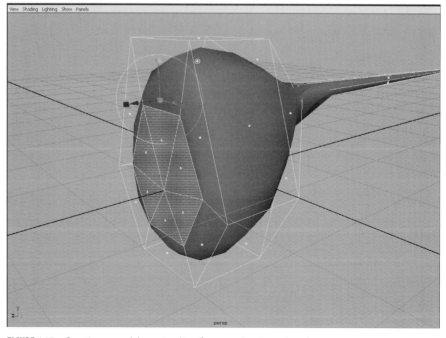

FIGURE 6.17 Creating a neck by extruding faces and not moving them away.

Step 11: Continue with the neck by extruding another set of faces, and moving and rotating these new faces. With the same set of faces selected, choose the Extrude Face command and pull away the faces a little. Hit **e** to activate the Rotate tool and rotate this new set of faces down in anticipation of the body (Figure 6.18).

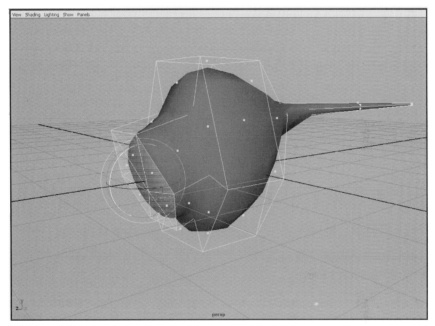

FIGURE 6.18   Creating the neck by extruding again and rotating the new faces.

Step 12: Create the body with three sets of extruded faces. Each time, with the same set of faces selected, choose the Extrude Face command and then pull out and resize the new faces to match Figure 6.19. Make sure to rotate the last set so that the tail part can emerge perpendicular to the ground plane.

FIGURE 6.19   (a-c) Extruding and resizing each of the new set of faces for the body shape.

Step 13: Create the tail with four extruded sets of faces. The extrusions are shown in Figure 6.20 a-d.

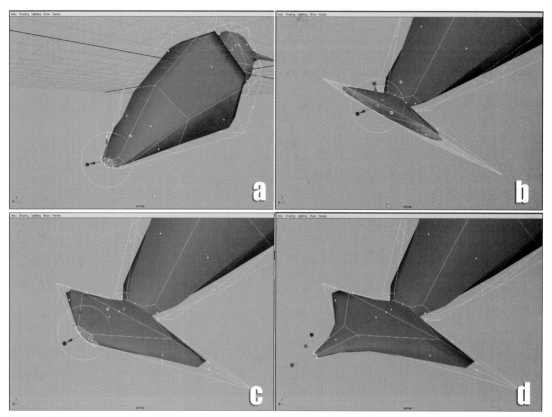

FIGURE 6.20 (a-d) Creating the tail through extrusions.

Step 14: Create the wings. We will create both wings at once. To do this, start out by selecting the Polygons shown in Figure 6.21. Figures 6.22-6.26 show the series of extruding the face, resizing and moving, and then repeating.

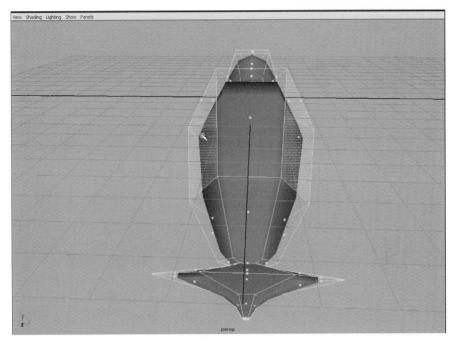

FIGURE 6.21   Start the wings by selecting faces on both sides.

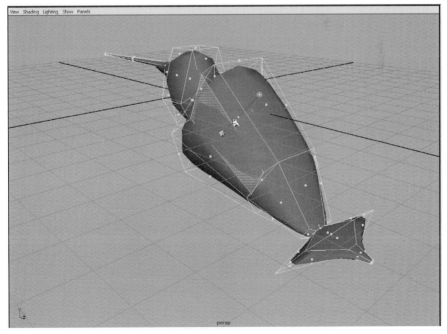

FIGURE 6.22   Extrude faces and then resize the faces immediately using the Extrude Face manipulator in the Y direction.

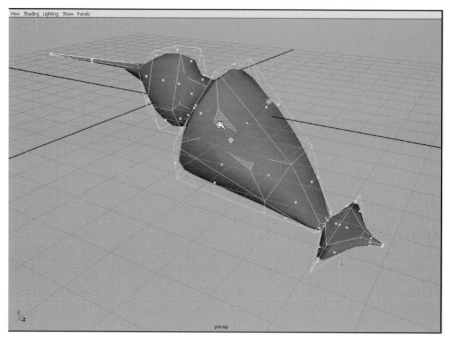

FIGURE 6.23 Still with the same tool and without extruding again, resize in the Z direction.

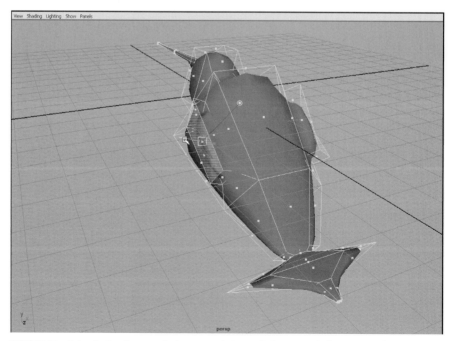

FIGURE 6.24 Extrude the Face again but extrude just a little way to help create a sharper distinction between the wings and body.

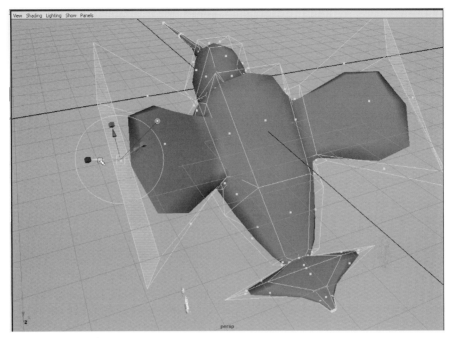

FIGURE 6.25   Extrude Face again. Resize as necessary.

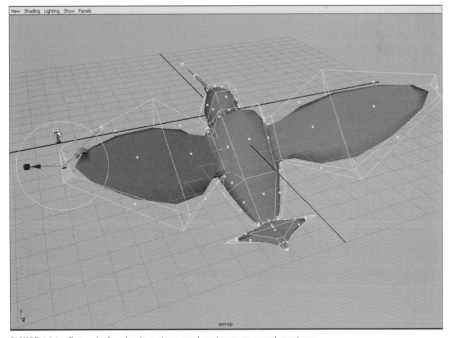

FIGURE 6.26   Extrude for the last time and resize to taper the wings.

Step 15: Refine the shape of the wings on the Vertex level. RMB-click-hold on the bird and select Vertex from the hotbox. Select the vertices that make up the middle and edge rings of each wing. Move, scale, and rotate these vertices to match Figure 6.27 (approximately).

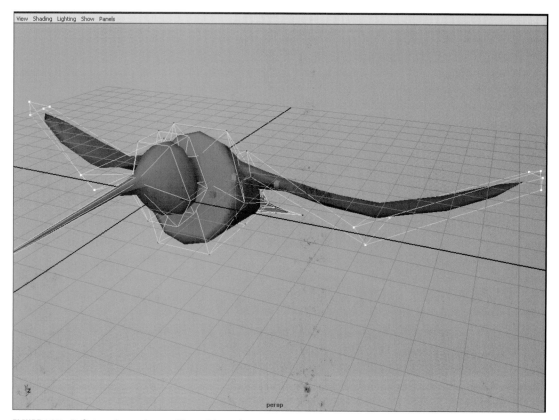

FIGURE 6.27   Refining shapes by working with vertices.

Step 16: Create new areas of control on the head by splitting Polygons. So, we have looked at how to create new faces from the surface of old ones. However, what happens when you need extra control between two rows of vertices? Because the object is actually hollow, there are not any faces running cross-section through the bird.

The solution is to split extant Polygons to provide new vertices. Select Modeling | Edit Polygons>Split Polygon Tool. This tool will allow you to cut through polygons (or, in our case, faces) to create two new faces.

To use this tool, click from edge to edge. Figure 6.28 a-e shows the process as we work around the middle of the head. Remember to click right on the edge of the Polygon. When you have moved all the way around the head, the tool should snap back to the first place you clicked with the tool.

Hit **Enter** to finish using the tool. You will be left with a new collection of vertices to be manipulated.

FIGURE 6.28   (a-e) Use the Split Polygon tool to give yourself more vertices to work with.

Step 17: Adjust the vertices to match Figure 6.29. With your new vertices, new forms are possible. Make a few adjustments to create a more interesting head.

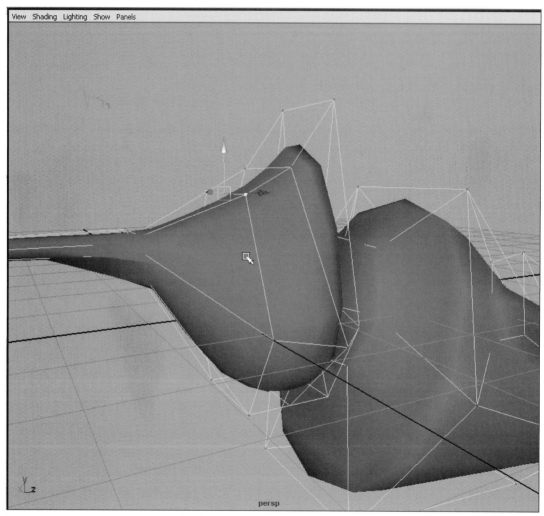

FIGURE 6.29 New shapes are available by altering new vertices created by splitting Polygons.

Step 18: Add the finishing touches with other objects. Figure 6.30 shows the finished shape. A couple of NURBS spheres were added for the eyes and a propeller was added for the tail. Customize yours as you wish.

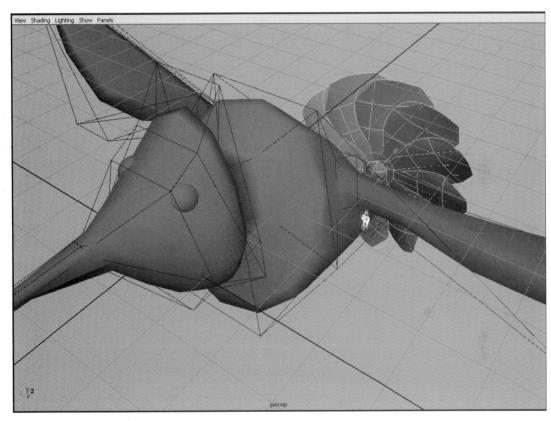

FIGURE 6.30   Finished bird.

CONCLUSION

Pretty powerful, eh? You can see how quickly we were able to create a single mesh shape that is complex in form and interesting in design. Along the way, we also looked at a variety of methods of altering faces that can be used to change Polygons with polygonal modeling.

This technique, though employed to make a simple shape here, is often used very successfully to create complex forms such as faces and bodies. Once you get the hang of what you can do with extruded faces, the possibilities are endless.

MATERIALS AND
TEXTURING

E ven though more than half of this book is done and has been dedicated to modeling, that does not mean that modeling should take half of your time for a 3D project. Although every project is different, most serious 3D artists spend *at least* as much time on materials and lighting as they do on the modeling process. This chapter will give an overview of lots of different techniques for utilizing Maya's texturing tools. Amazingly, these selected techniques will all fit into two chapters—a real departure from the six chapters used to cover modeling. However, mastery of these texturing tools takes time, require skill and creativity to master, but produce astounding work when all is said and done.

THE TEXTURING PARADIGM

So, what exactly does it mean to "texture" something? *Texture* (the verb) in 3D usually refers to the process of giving your models surface characteristics. These characteristics can be color, highlights, bump, and so on. Texturing objects is what makes a marble look different than a basketball; a bowling ball different than a baseball; and a marble floor different than a hardwood one.

In reality, everything within your Maya model is made of, well, nothing—it's all virtual. By default, things are shown in the Workspace as a sort of shiny gray plastic. This is just a default method of helping you visually understand the nature and shapes of the 3D forms you are building. Luckily, objects needn't remain in that gray, fake state. Indeed, making a computer-generated image look not quite so computer generated is largely a combination of effective lighting and cleverly constructed materials on the surface of models.

A simple way to think of texturing is to think of decals. If you have ever built a model airplane, you can remember that after constructing the body, the kit usually came with a collection of stickers that could be put on the plane to add color and pizzazz. In 3D, it is much the same, except instead of decals appearing like simple stickers of color, these 3D stickers can make a surface appear to be shiny, dirty, rough, smooth, metallic, cloth-like, furry, old, or new. Like decals, careful placement makes a big difference. Controlling how the material is placed on the surface of the model can help make a surface appear believable.

TERMS

Before we move on too much further, we should refine the terms we will be using. Although the general 3D market refers to this process of adding surface characteristics as texturing, *textures* can mean an entirely different thing in Maya.

Objects are either NURBS or polygonal objects. Often, these surfaces will include *UV Coordinates*. UV Coordinates constitute a collection of information about the nature of the 3D object. Think of these coordinates as a sort of map so that Maya will know how to attach the color, bump, and other information to the surface.

Maya creates visually different surfaces through the assignment of a *Shader*. Shaders usually include a *material*. Materials contain various channels that allow you to control different characteristics of the surface. Materials are actually nodes that can be adjusted dynamically and thus dynamically alter the surfaces to which they are assigned. Sometimes, materials may contain *textures* (sometimes called *Texture Maps*). Textures are actual images (photographs or otherwise) that help refine or explain the color or bump of a material. They are referred to as maps because they help map out what parts of a surface will be what color or what parts of a surface will appear higher than others. For instance, if you want a floor to look like maple hardwood, you can actually import a photograph of that hardwood to define the color of the material placed on the floor. On that hardwood floor, if you want to be able to define exactly how the planks are laid out, you can create an image in Illustrator to define what parts of the floor should be receded and what parts should rise.

Textures can also be *procedural*—that is, created mathematically. There are several procedural textures that Maya creates straight out of the box. Often, these procedural textures end up creating materials that look awfully canned so they usually are not advised. But, on occasion, they can be very helpful in making subtle tweaks to a material created from traditional texture maps.

TYPES OF MATERIALS

If you are coming from most other 3D applications, this delineation of material types may seem a bit foreign. In most 3D applications, you create a new material and define the characteristics of that material to suit your need. In Maya, there are actually different types of materials that you can choose from that contain certain editable characteristics that others may not.

The biggest difference between the material types is how the *specular highlight* behaves. The specular highlight is the glare or the sheen of a surface. A metal surface has a high, sharp specular highlight, while a piece of felt has a broad, very flat highlight. Depending on what you visualize your surface to be ultimately will determine which material type to pick. You can change a material's type at nearly any time during your work flow, so no need to fret too much over the decision.

The materials available in Maya are *Lambert, Blinn, Phong, PhongE,* and *Anisotropic.* Lambert essentially has no specular highlight—it is a matte texture. Chalky surfaces and many fuzzy materials are good candidates for a Lambert material. Blinn, Phong, and PhongE are all quite shiny materials. Most plastics and metals and even some woods are logical choices for these materials. Finally, Anisotropic is also shiny but bends the specular highlights in much more dynamic ways. Often, glass surfaces and brushed metals are best defined with an Anisotropic material.

Because you can switch between material types, and because the names of the material types are far from intuitive, there is no need to worry about memorizing what is what quite yet. As time goes on and you begin to build more and more materials, you will quickly develop a sense of what to use where. Figure 7.1 shows a quick breakdown of the different materials with the variation of the specular highlight as the primary difference.

FIGURE 7.1 From left to right the type of materials are: Anisotropic, Blinn, Lambert, Phong, and PhongE. Notice the biggest difference is size, shape, and crispness of highlights.

ANATOMY OF A MATERIAL

Although each of the material types discussed in the previous section have differences in the highlight department, they also have some identical attributes. Whenever a material is being edited through the Attribute Editor (more on this in a bit), you will be presented with a collection of editable attributes (Figure 7.2).

Following is a list of the common attributes seen in all materials and a brief description of what each attribute does:

- **Color**: Well, this determines the color of the surface. You can choose a color using traditional color pickers or you can import a texture. The texture for this attribute can be a procedural texture or a 2D texture image map.
- **Transparency**: Working on a glass surface? Plastic? This is the attribute that allows objects to be transparent or semi-transparent. Interestingly enough, you can use various texture maps here to make certain parts of a surface transparent, while other parts remain opaque. You can even use texture maps to make certain parts of a surface semi-transparent (Figure 7.3).
- **Ambient Color:** This is a fairly tricky attribute. Basically, it lets you change the color across all attributes of the material. This allows for quick lightening of the entire surface or tinting everything.
- **Incandescence**: This is a sort of "inner light." It makes an object look illuminated. The problem with this is that it tends to flatten out any interesting variations of the surface, giving you just the silhouette of the object. Also, this inner light only appears on the surface of the object the material is applied to—it does not actually cast any light into the scene. It is usually best to stay away from this, unless you are texturing something like a light bulb.
- **Bump Mapping:** This is the idea of painting a faux bump on a surface. What this means is that when Maya renders the surface, it "paints" the surface to look as though there are bumps in the geometry even though there are none. This is an important distinction. Figure 7.4 shows a sphere that appears to have a mighty bump. However, when the sphere is seen closer, notice that the edge (outline of the shape) is still smooth with no actual change in the geometry.
- **Diffuse**: Think of this as a dirt layer. Yes, this is over simplified but the idea is sound—you can set up any of the color, incandescence, and other attributes you wish to use and then with an active diffuse attribute with a texture map, you can layer a bit of dirt over everything making computer renderings less "computery." We will cover much more of this later in the chapter.

FIGURE 7.2 Attribute Editor. This illustration shows the attributes of a Phong material.

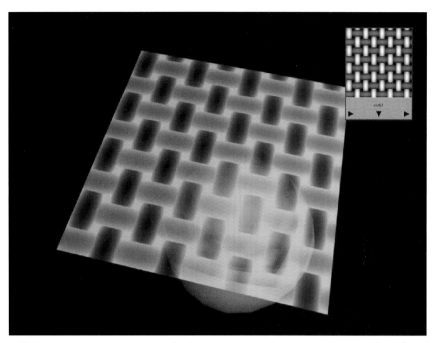

FIGURE 7.3   Using a texture map in the Transparency attribute can make parts of a surface render opaque, transparent, or semi-transparent.

FIGURE 7.4   (a-b) Bump maps only paint the surface to look bumpy. There is actually no change to the geometry.

- **Translucence:** This is fairly new to Maya (version 4 or so). It is a very nice attribute to have. Think of rice paper in a traditional Japanese room. From the outside, you can see the shadows of the people inside through the paper walls. You cannot see the people—the walls are not transparent but you can see the shadows. Figure 7.5 shows two planes; the one on the left is transparent and the one on the right is translucent. Notice how the light continues to pass through the translucent plane.
- **Glow:** It is interesting that this is a common attribute among the different material types, especially for Lambert. But it is. It will make any surface glow. Remember that this glow is a *post rendering* effect. That means Maya paints it on after it has finished rendering or calculating how the light rays work. That means a glowing object will not appear to glow in reflections (Figure 7.6).

Now, of course there are other attributes for each specific type of material. Some are related to the general common attributes listed earlier in this section and some are very specific to the nature of that material. As we work through the tutorials to follow, we will be looking at how to manipulate and utilize many of the attributes of all of the materials.

FIGURE 7.5   The plane on the right is using translucency that allows light to pass through the object without allowing you to see through it.

FIGURE 7.6   Because glow is a post rendering effect, it will not show up in reflected surfaces.

TEXTURE CREATION AND EDITING

Like most of Maya, there are multiple ways to work with materials and Shaders. However, most of the core work with materials takes place inside something called the *Hypershade*, which is kind of like a texture workshop. Within this editor, you can create new materials, decide how materials are organized or interconnected, and change how materials are applied to surfaces.

To pull up the Hypershade editor, select Window>Rendering Editors> Hypershade. This brings up the Hypershade as a floating window. You can also access the Hypershade by selecting the Hypershade/Persp layout (Figure 7.7).

Figure 7.8 shows the Hypershade as a free window, which is how most animators like to work with it.

Besides the pull-down menus along the top, the Hypershade essentially has four areas of interest. The first is the row of buttons immediately under the pull-down menus. These buttons primarily are involved with how the Hypershade is shown or organized. We will not go over all of these tools here although we will use them intermittently through the course of the tutorials.

FIGURE 7.7 Bringing up the Hypershade using preset layouts.

The second area is the Create Bar (the area to the left) that allows you to create, or (more accurately) activate, textures or materials. To the right of the Create Bar are two areas with tabs along the top. The organization here has always seemed a bit strange but the easiest way to think of it is that the top area is sort of like a shelf. Notice that there are several tabs for different types of things (Materials, Textures, Utilities, Lights, Cameras, Projects). These are different shelves of things that you may be using at different times but that stay out of the way until you bring them down onto your workbench. The bottom area also has a library (the Shader Library) but more important, it has the Work Area.

The Work Area is the workbench of this texture workshop. You can bring things from the shelf above down to the workbench when you want to use them. Most of what you do in the Hypershade will actually

Show/Hide Create Bar
Previous/Next Graph
Clear Graph
Rearrange Graph
Show Material of Selected Object
Show Upstream/Downstream Connections

Create Bar

Tabs

FIGURE 7.8   The Hypershade.

be done here in the Work Area. Keeping control of how this area is organized and its accessibility will greatly enhance your material building experience.

A final note on the Hypershade. One very interesting and effective part of Maya's work flow is the consistency of functions such as moving, rotating, and scaling your view. When you are working within the Workspace, you can use combinations of **Alt-**Mouse button to move, rotate, or dolly in on your scene. **Alt-**LMMB-drag (that is left and middle mouse buttons) will make the swatches in both the top and bottom tab areas smaller or larger. Think of it as moving a camera that is looking at the swatches closer or farther away rather than resizing anything within the Hypershade area.

So, enough talk. Now that we have the metaphor of a workshop worked out, we can actually get to work.

TUTORIAL

7.1 TEXTURING THE ROOM

After the brief modeling respite we had in Chapter 6, we are back to working with our room. In the course of this tutorial, we will be laying down the materials on the surfaces we created in earlier tutorials to bring the room out of the drab gray plastic world it is in now. This should be a fun process and one that leaves a lot of room for interpretation. If you do not like the green walls, change the color. Indeed, as we deal with most colors, there will be no call-out for exact numerical values for colors. Green can be almost any green you like.

ON THE CD

Along this same vein, the images in the book are in black and white (as you have undoubtedly noticed). Unfortunately, effective texturing is largely dependent on color. Because of this, make sure that you take time to look at the color versions of all of the images of this chapter. The images, in full color splendor, are on the included CD-ROM in the folder, Images/Chapter07. Also remember that the finished file that makes up this tutorial is included on the CD-ROM and can be a valuable resource if you get stuck.

Step 1: Open the modeled room. Wherever you have set up the room project, go to the scenes folder and open your room thus far. You may or may not have added other props; for this tutorial, we will just texture some of the objects we built through the course of the earlier tutorials. Make sure that as you learn, you expand out to include your newfound skills on other things in the scene.

Step 2: Set up your working space. Make sure that the Hypershade editor is open (Window>Rendering Editors>Hypershade). Or, to mount everything together, which is the view we will use for these tutorials, select Window>Saved Layouts>Hypershade/Persp. The result should look something like Figure 7.9.

Finally, make sure that your Outliner is visible (Window>Outliner). It will be an important tool to have when we need to apply materials to surfaces.

Step 3: Shift the Hypershade's organization. Your Hypershade's Create Bar probably shows Create Textures at the top, while Figure 7.9 shows Create Materials. LMB-click on Create Textures and choose Create Materials from the pop-down menu. This gives you a quick visual representation of the possible materials that are available.

Next, put your mouse on the top tab area and **Alt**-LMMB-drag to the left so that those swatches are smaller. For now, we want to be able to see all of the extant materials.

FIGURE 7.9   The Hypershade/Persp gives you the Hypershade, a perspective view, and a space for your Channels box (or later, your Attribute Editor). All are important for the material creation process.

Step 4: Create a new Lambert material. There are actually several ways to do this. For this step, select Create>Materials>Lambert from the pull-down menus within the Hypershade Editor.

This will do a couple of things. First, a new swatch with the word `lambert2` will appear in the Work Area. Also notice that a new swatch (high-lighted in yellow) appears in the top Material tab as well. Essentially, creating the new material places it on your Shelf and puts it on your workbench so that you can work with it. At various times, we will clear the workbench but the materials created there will remain on the Materials tab (Shelf) above in case you need to take it down and work with it again.

Step 5: Rename the material. Double-click the `lambert2` swatch in the Work Area. This indicates to Maya that you want to work with this particular material, so you will be presented with the Attributes Editor on the right (where the Channels box was). This Attributes Editor is a fairly important window and one that we will be working with quite a bit over the course of this tutorial. For this step, there is an input field at the top called `lambert`. Change the name from `lambert2` to `Walls_Material` (Figure 7.10).

FIGURE 7.10 Opening the Attributes Editor and renaming the new texture to `Walls_Material`.

Although the name is largely arbitrary, it is always helpful to be as indicative as you can. Name objects and materials as you go along so that you can find them again quickly when the need arises.

Step 6: Change the color of `Walls_Material` **to green.** In the Attributes Editor are several areas that allow you to define the attributes of this material. By default, the Common Material Attributes area should be expanded revealing a collection of sliders, swatches, and buttons.

The first will be Color followed by a gray box. Click once on this gray box and a color picker window will open (a slightly different color picker for the Mac or PC). Use the picker to choose a green color (I chose kind of an olive) as shown in Figure 7.11. Hit **Accept** (or **OK**).

Now, your Attribute Editor should have a different color than gray next to the word, *Color*. In addition, the swatch in both the Materials area (top tab area) and the Work Area (bottom tab area) should reflect this new alteration in the Color attribute.

FIGURE 7.11   Choosing a new color for the Color attribute. This is for the interface on a PC.

Step 7: Hide the layer, `Ceiling_Floor`. Show the Channels Box/Layer Editor (using the button shown in Figure 7.12). This hides the Attribute Editor, but not to worry; we will get it back when we need it. Hit the visibility button for the layer, `Ceiling_Floor`, to hide those objects. This will make it much easier for us to see what we do.

FIGURE 7.12   The Show Channels Box/Layer Editor button.

Step 8: Apply the material, `Walls_Material`, to the south wall. In the Outliner should be a group called `WallSouth_Group`. Select `WallSouth_Group` in the Outliner, and then in the Work Area of the Hypershade Editor, RMB-click-hold on the `Walls_Material`, and select Assign Material to Selection.

Tumble your view in the Perspective view so that you can see the wall. This will place this material on the entire group, wall, trim, and everything (Figure 7.13). It is important to notice that when a material is placed on an object or

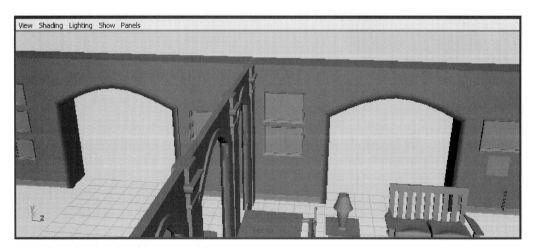

FIGURE 7.13   Results of applying a material to a group.

group, the children of that group also inherit the material. We will look at how to override this in a bit.

Your Perspective view should appear something like Figure 7.13. Hit **3** and **6** to make sure that you are seeing things shaded with the materials applied to them.

Step 9: Apply the material, `Walls_Material`, to the east wall. Besides the method described above, you can assign materials to objects or groups by MMB-dragging. Tumble your view around so that you can see the wall on the east side. This time, MMB-drag `Walls_Material` from the Work Area onto the wall. The mouse will change to include a small plus sign (+). As soon as you release the MMB, the entire group of the east wall will be green as well.

Step 10: Apply the material, `Walls_Material`, to the rest of the walls. Using whichever method you prefer, apply the material to all the other walls in the scene, including the wall in the middle of the room.

Step 11: Adjust Render Settings to allow for useful, targeted renderings. We are going to cover much, much more about rendering in the next chapters; however, as we work with materials, it will be important to be able to render on occasion. So, we are going to set up things briefly to give us a chance to perform some occasional renderings.

Figure 7.14 shows the three rendering buttons on the Status Line. The one on the far right, Display Render Globals window, allows you to change the settings for how Maya renders your scene. Click this button.

FIGURE 7.14   The Rendering buttons of the Status Line.

When the Render Globals window opens, we will change just one thing for now. Expand the Resolution section. By default, Maya renders out to a small, nearly unusable 320x240 image. For now, change these setting to Width = 800 and Height = 300. You may need to adjust this if you have a smaller monitor. Hit the **Close** button to save the new settings. This will render the scene out into long thin images that are big enough to actually see what is going on.

Step 12: Tumble and dolly into position and take a quick rendering. Figure 7.15 shows a close-up of the southwest corner of the room. Move your camera in the Perspective view to match roughly and hit the **Render the Current Frame** button (the left button shown in Figure 7.14).

A new window will pop up called the Render View. Within this window, Maya will render or draw the scene with the materials created so far. Notice that because we have not created any light sources, Maya is functioning with the assumption that there is a large floodlight immediately above the virtual camera through which you are looking.

At this point, the rendered view looks very similar to what is seen in the Workspace. However, as we begin to alter attributes further, the difference between the two will increase fairly dramatically.

Step 13: Add bump to the `Wall_Material`. Well, the walls are currently definitely green but that's about it. To give these walls a bit more interest, we will be working with a few more of the attributes to spice things up, dirty things down, and make things look a bit more "real."

Double-click `Walls_Material` again in the Work Area; this will open the Attribute Editor. The fifth attribute down is Bump Mapping. This is noticeably different than the other attributes as it has no slider. This is because a bump map will only work if it has a map to work with.

FIGURE 7.15 Close-up of the southwest corner of the room in the Render view.

Basically, the way that Bump Mapping works is Maya looks at an image and renders the parts closest to white as raised and those closest to black as flat (or they can be receded). Although color images can also be used as bump maps, grayscale images are usually the most effective.

To tell `Walls_Material` what to use for its bump map, hit the checkered button on the far right. This will open a new window called the Create Render Node. What we are doing here is adding a node to the material. This node will change the appearance of the material and will remain very flexible. As we edit the node (in this case, the bump map), the material will update as well.

Notice that the Textures tab is highlighted within this window. Maya understands that you will need to place a texture as the bump map. For these walls, we will use Brownian located under the 3D Textures area. Click on Brownian and the Create Render Node will automatically close.

The Work Area will all of a sudden be full of an awful lot of new swatches. These swatches represent nodes and texture maps that are attached to the material, `Walls_Material`. Notice that there are a variety of arrows drawn between all the swatches.

The problem is that often, when a new map/node has been created, the organization of the Work Area becomes hectic at best (Figure 7.16a). To fix up things a bit, hit the **Rearrange Graph** button at the top of the Hypershade window (Figure 7.16b).

Let's take a second to discuss what each of these nodes/textures mean.

Notice that at the far right is the final output (`Walls_Material`) of a collection of inputs. The first input (`place3dtexture1`) has to do with how the texture is going to be placed on the object. If you click the `place3Dtexture1` swatch, the Attributes Editor will change to match Figure 7.17a. This window allows you to adjust the position, size, or rotation of the texture.

Similarly, if you click the `brownian1` swatch, Figure 7.17c will appear in the Attributes Editor. This allows you to change things about the *procedural* (mathematically generated, not an image) texture. This will be slightly different for each procedural texture and different still when the texture is actually an image.

The next swatch, `bump3d1`, will produce an Attributes Editor window similar to Figure 7.17b and will allow you to do things such as control how high the bump will be.

Don't worry too much about the details of each of these nodes for now. We will cover many of them in steps to come. It is important to notice that they are all related and that they feed linearly into the final material, `Walls_Material`.

FIGURE 7.16 (a) Newly created nodes and textures can leave a messy Work Area. (b) Using the Rearrange Graph button puts things back into place.

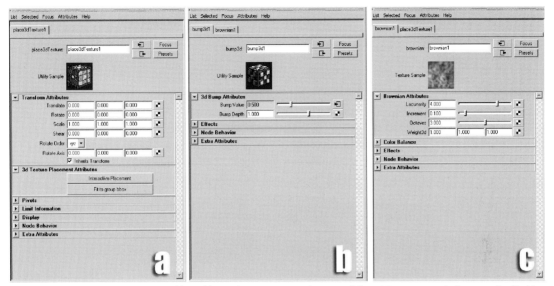

FIGURE 7.17   (a-c) The nodes created by adding a bump map to the material, `Walls_Materials`, are all editable and allow you to control various parts of how a material will ultimately look by affecting the textures that make up the material.

Step 14: Render to see the effects of the new bump. Hit the **Render the Current Frame** button to render out the corner (Figure 7.18). Bump seems a bit too intense, no?

FIGURE 7.18   Rendered corner with new bump map applied.

The important thing to notice here is that when we adjusted the material in the Hypershade, all the places where the material had been applied were updated automatically to reflect the changes.

Step 15: Adjust the height of the bump. The bump is a bit too intense. So, we need to reduce the depth of the bump map. To do this, click on the `bump3d1` swatch in the Work Area. In the attributes window, change the Bump Depth to 0.100. You can do this with the slider or by entering the value numerically. Figure 7.19 shows the results.

Getting closer. But still, the bump seems a bit too big on the surface.

FIGURE 7.19   Reduced Bump Depth provides a more gentle bump.

Step 16: Adjust the size of the placement. To make the size of the bump a bit smaller, we will edit the `place3dTexture1` node. Click its swatch in the Work Area. In the Attributes Manager, we now have control over how the texture is to be placed on the surface. As usual, there are three columns represented by the X, Y, and Z. Change the settings for Scale in the X, Y, and Z columns to `0.600`.

Take another render (Figure 7.20) to see how close you are getting. If you still feel like the bump needs adjusting, go ahead and do so to taste.

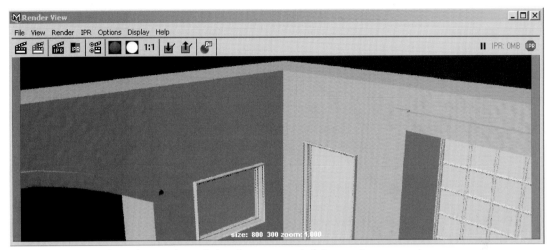

FIGURE 7.20   Bump adjusted in size through the placement node (`place3dTexture1`).

Step 17: Create a white painted wood material for trim. Last time, we created a new material through the Create pull-down menu in the Hypershade. This time, we will do it by MMB-dragging the Blinn icon from the Create Bar area into the Work Area. The benefit of doing this is you can choose where to place this new material. Select it in the Work Area and rename it `WoodTrim_Material`.

Change the color to a white shade by moving the slider to the right in the Attribute Editor on the Color attribute.

We will assume that this wood was a satin paint. This means that the specular highlight will be broad but not too shiny. We used a Blinn material because it allows us to work with the specular highlights.

Make sure that the Specular Shading area of the Attributes Editor is open. The Eccentricity setting has to do with how small the highlight is. Smaller values make for smaller highlights. The Specular Roll Off allows you to define how bright the highlight is. For now, change the Eccentricity setting to 0.500 and the Specular Roll Off to 0.300.

Notice that you can also define things such as the color of that highlight. We will change this setting later when we are working with metallic surfaces.

Step 18: Apply this material to floorboards, crown molding, trim, window trims, columns, ceiling, and crossbeams. This step will take a while. There are an awful lot of objects in the scene that need this white wood trim. Basically, everything but the walls, floor, furniture, and pictures on the wall should have this white material applied to it.

You can select many objects directly in the Workspace, then RMB-click-hold `WoodTrim_Material`, and select Assign Material to Selection. Remember that you can select an object in the Workspace and then hit the up arrow to move your selection up a hierarchical chain. So, for instance, you could make the `Ceiling_Floor` layer visible and select one crossbeam. Then, hit the up arrow key and your selection will expand to include the group that the crossbeam is in. You can then apply the material to the entire group.

You can also search out the needed objects in the Outliner, select them there, and then choose Assign Material to Selection in the Hypershade. Lastly, you can MMB-drag the material, `WoodTrim_Material`, to an object in the Workspace to apply it.

Notice that previously green trim changes to white when a new material is applied to it, thus overwriting the material that was applied to the group or parent that the trim is a child of.

Figure 7.21 illustrates the Workspace with the appropriate material applied in all the needed places. Notice that there are some problems—namely, the windows (including the glass) are painted white. Not to fear, though. We will fix that in a bit.

FIGURE 7.21 White applied to all the trim in the room.

Step 19: Create a new painted wood texture through duplicating the existing the `WoodTrim_Material`. That's right, duplicating works with materials, too. Select `WoodTrim_Material` in the Work Area and hit **Ctrl-D**. If you get an error, make sure to reset the settings for the duplicate.

Notice that this new material is called `WoodTrim_Material1` (make sure to double-click the material in the Work Area). Rename it `FrameTrim_Material`.

Step 20: Change the color and highlights of `FrameTrim_Material`. The frames in the room are a dark red. Click on the wide box next to the Color attribute and select a new dark red color.

For this wood, we want it to look like a high-gloss paint. So, in the Specular Shading section of the Attributes Editor, change the Eccentricity setting to `0.200` and the Specular Roll Off to `3.00`. This will make a small, bright highlight. Notice that by default the Specular Roll Off slider will only slide to 1. By entering `3.00` in the input field, we hyper-extend the value. This trick works often for textures to give you a bit of a boost.

Finally, you may wish to change the Specular Color to a light brown so that the gloss is not quite so intense (Figure 7.22).

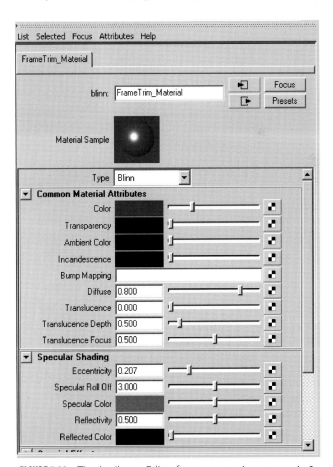

FIGURE 7.22 The Attributes Editor for `FrameTrim_Material`.

Step 21: Apply this new material to all the frames in the room. If you have all the frames grouped together, you can select the frames group in the Outliner and assign `FrameTrim_Material` to everything in one swoop. Do not worry that the pictures in the frames are also dark red; we will fix that later (Figure 7.23).

FIGURE 7.23   Frames with the newly duplicated `FrameTrim_Material`.

Step 22: Create a glass material for the windows. Create a new material by dragging Phong from the Create Bar area into the Work Area. You may want to hit the **Rearrange Graph** button at the top of the Hypershade to clean up things a bit in your Work Area.

Double-click the new Phong material in the Work Area to open it in the Attribute Editor. The key to this glass will be to create a material that has no color, high transparency, and some reflectivity.

To do this, use the sliders for Color and slide it completely to the right, making the color box black. Next, slide the Transparency slider completely to the right. This will change the preview box at the top of the Attribute Editor so that there is a checkered background behind the material. This is there to help you visualize the new characteristics of the material.

Now, to cheat a little bit, we are going to apply just a bit of a tint to things seen through the glass. I know, I know, true glass has no color, but for illustration purposes, we will view the world through blue-tinted glass. To do this, click on the Transparency color box and select a very, very light blue. This will help us see the glass a bit better.

Finally, in the Specular Shading area, Change the Reflectivity to `0.700`.

Step 23: Apply this `WindowGlass_Material` to all the glass panes. Remember that you do not want to apply this material to the entire window, just the pane. It is easiest to just tumble around your scene to see each window and MMB-drag `WindowGlass_Material` onto the pane.

Step 24: Render the scene. You will notice that when the scene is rendered, you can suddenly see through the windows to the black outside (Figure 7.24). However, there is no reflection even though we told the glass to reflect its surrounding. This has to do with how Maya is rendering the scene.

FIGURE 7.24   Rendered scene shows transparent glass but no reflections.

To get reflections, you must use *Raytracing* for the rendering engine. Raytracing is a more accurate rendering algorithm than the default Maya renderer, but also quite a bit slower. We will be talking much more about specifics of Raytracing later. For now, suffice it to say, we need to turn on Raytracing.

Step 25: Activate Raytracing. Open the Render Globals window (click the far right button of the bank of rendering buttons in the Status Line). There are a lot of different sections of this window, so look carefully for Raytracing Quality. Expand this, and for now, check the Raytracing option.

Do not worry about any of the sliders contained in this section; for now, having Raytracing on is enough. Hit **Close** to save the changes.

Step 26: Render the scene. Again, hit the **Render the Current Frame** button. Take a quick break and come back because Raytracing can be a slow process.

The results shown in Figure 7.25 show reflections alright. The problem is that although the window with the material, WindowGlass_Material, is reflecting, so are all the woods in the room.

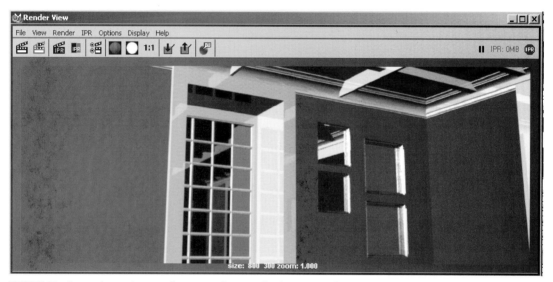

FIGURE 7.25   Raytracing activates reflection; unfortunately, things are reflecting that should not be.

The reason that this is happening is that Blinn, Phong, and PhongE all have Reflectivity active automatically. Select WoodTrim_Material in the Work Area and in the Attribute Editor, notice that within the Specular Shading section, Reflectivity is set at 0.500 even though we never activated it. Annoying, huh?

Step 27: Deactivate reflectivity for WoodTrim_Material and FrameTrim_Material. Simply select each material (one at a time) and in the Attribute Editor, pull the Reflectivity slider to 0.

Step 28: Render again. This time, when you render, the window will show the reflection of the trim around it in a more believable fashion. Additionally, the wood trim and frames no longer reflect (Figure 7.26).

FIGURE 7.26   After adjusting the Reflectivity settings, the glass panes reflect but the wood does not.

Step 29: Turn off Raytracing. For now, go ahead and open the Render Globals window again and deactivate Raytracing. For the kind of construction that we are going to be doing in the next chapter, we will want a speedier rendering than what Raytracing will provide. Remember, ultimately, we will want to raytrace the room, so keep a careful eye open that the Reflectivity setting is indeed at 0 as we create new materials.

CONCLUSION

We just barely got started on the powerful tools of textures in Maya, but in the next chapter we will be going over how to create custom texture maps. We will cover how to control more specifically how a material is applied to a surface, and we will get to move into the artistry of materials more specifically by making our stale models works of art.

CUSTOM TEXTURE MAPS IN MATERIALS

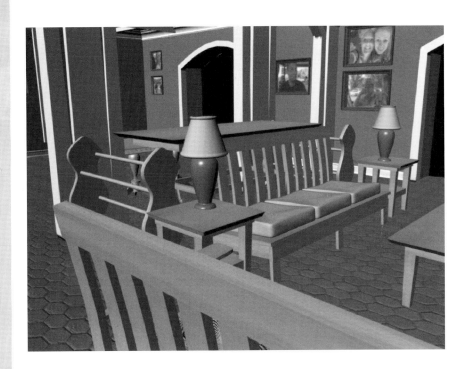

n the last chapter, we got a brief overview of how materials were created and a look at how they were edited. In that chapter, we looked at the workshop of material creation—the Hypershade and how the workshop was organized. We looked at how to use sliders and solid colors to affect a material's color, bump, and transparency. We even looked at how to use a procedural texture to determine how the bump map was supposed to look.

In this chapter, we get away from simply moving around sliders and choosing default options. In this chapter, we get to construct materials that are based on photographs. We get to create materials that are much closer to photorealism than any canned material would ever be.

Because so much of the work done here will be using photographs, there is quite a bit of Photoshop work. As outlined in the Preface, we assume that you are fairly familiar with this tool and covering many details is really beyond the scope of this book. However, there are a few places where we will actually be delving into the Adobe wonder and looking at how to prepare texture maps for use in Maya.

After we have the texture maps prepared, we will import them into our materials and apply these materials to create believable woods, metals, hanging pictures, and other items.

T U T O R I A L

8.1 TEXTURING THE ROOM, CONTINUED FROM CHAPTER 7

In this tutorial, we are going to continue to texture the room. We will put pictures in the frames and make the wood floor look like a floor. We will add texture to the furniture and make this room really look like it is part of the color age.

Step 1: Move the folders within Tutorials/Chapter08/Textures into your own Textures directory. On the CD-ROM, we have been placing files that are finished steps of the tutorials. The CD-ROM also includes some image files that you can use for textures in this tutorial. Within the folder, Tutorials/Chapter08/Textures, you will see several sub-folders. All of these sub-folders will contain some images.

ON THE CD

Although you could access them within Maya directly from the CD-ROM, this is unadvisable. When Maya imports a texture into a material, it links only to where that texture is located. It does not import the actual file. So, if you are working on your room, and you have been saving your scene files to your hard drive, and then you start pulling textures off a CD-ROM, that means that the

CD-ROM must always be in its drive when you are working on the room. If not, when Maya gets ready to render and tries to collect the textures it needs, it will not be able to find the images that are necesssary.

So, we want to make sure and get these textures copied to your hard drive where Maya will be able to consistently find them (at least as long as you are working with the room tutorials).

When you set up your project at the beginning of the whole room tutorial sequence, Maya created a large collection of folders for you. By default, when you tell Maya to save a new file, it tries to save it into the Scenes folder, within the Project directory, although you can tell Maya to save elsewhere.

ON THE CD

Figure 8.1 shows the Project directory we have been using while constructing this tutorial. All of the different versions of the room are housed within the scenes folder. However, the important part of that figure is the highlighted textures folder. When you can see all the folders of textures on the CD-ROM (in the directory Tutorials/Chapter08/Textures/), drag all of the folders into the folder textures on your hard drive.

You do not have to store textures in the textures folder. Doing so just keeps together all of the relevant files, if you take the time to organize and save things in the folders Maya created for you when you first defined your project.

FIGURE 8.1   Project directory with the important textures folder.

Step 2: Begin by opening the room you have built and textured so far.

Step 3: Organize your UI. Again, we will be doing a lot of work with the Hypershade, so make sure that you are using the UI layout Hypershade/Persp (Window>Saved Layouts>Hypershade/Persp).

Step 4: Clear out the Work Area. We will talk much more about the details of this a little later in the chapter and you might not need to do this step at all. If you did not exit Maya since the last time we worked, your Work Area is probably getting to be pretty messy. We could rearrange things or even clean them up, but for now, let us clean it off. RMB-click-hold on any black part of the Work Area and select Graph>Clear Graph from the pop-down menu. You will be left with a clear, black Work Area.

If you have closed your room and come back to it at the beginning of this tutorial, when you open the room scene again, the Work Area will be clean automatically; it's as if Maya cleans off your workbench when it knows you will not be in to work for a while.

Step 5: Tumble around your room until you are focused in on any one frame. The exact frame is unimportant; if your room is like the one shown in Figure 8.2, you probably have a lot of frames so you will have plenty of practice placing the needed textures.

For this first frame, do find a frame that is horizontal in format. We will do some vertically formatted frames, later.

FIGURE 8.2   Focused on one frame so we can see our work clearly.

Step 6: Import `ReunionPhotos` textures. Among the items you copied to your Textures directory is a folder called `ReunionPhotos`. These are actually photos from a recent family reunion of mine that we are going to put on the walls of the room. Before we can use these images, we need Maya to recognize that we are going to use the images as textures. There are several ways to do this. We will look at a few of them here.

In the top tab area, we have been working primarily with just the Materials tab. However, there are other tabs there, some of which we will discuss and some that are beyond the scope of this volume. The one that is important is the Textures tab. Click that tab to activate it. Within an area beneath the tab should be the `brownian1` texture that we used for the walls. All the tabs that you use for your various materials will be stored here. So, we can also import materials into this space.

Interestingly enough, if you use File>Import (pull-down menu within the Hypershade) or RMB-click-hold and select Import, the result will simply show you the image. For instance, Figure 8.3 shows the image, `Jake.jpg`, that was selected through File>Import (Hypershade pull-down menu). Rather than importing the file into the Textures tab area, it just opens it in the Fcheck (an image/movie viewer within Maya). So, the most intuitive choice does not work.

However, Maya will interact with the Explorer (or Finder if you're on a Mac). Simply open up the folder, ReunionPhotos, (from your own Textures

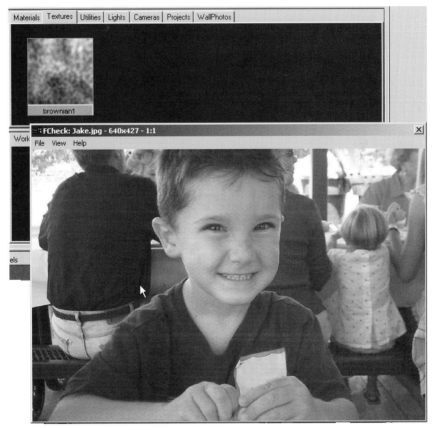

FIGURE 8.3 Using File>Import does not work. It simply opens an image into the Fcheck application.

folder) and LMB-drag the file, `Jake.jpg`, into the Textures tab area (Figure 8.4a). As soon as you do this, the image, `Jake.jpg`, will appear in a new swatch within the Textures tab area (Figure 8.4b).

FIGURE 8.4   (a-b) One way to import images for use as textures is to drag them from their locations on your disk into the Textures tab area.

The first method of dragging files to the Textures tab area can be an acceptable method. You can even drag multiple files at once and they will all be imported as textures. However, this can leave you with a huge amount of texture swatches all bunched up together in the Textures tab, thus making that "shelf" kind of junky.

Instead, wouldn't it be nicer to create new shelves where we could store textures? Turns out, we can.

1. Within the Hypershade, go to Tabs>Create New Tabs to open a dialog box similar to the one shown in Figure 8.5a. There are a lot of things that can be done in this window, but to keep us on task, we want to stay focused on just a few functions.
2. Change the New Tab Name to read `ReunionPhotos`. Although you can place a new tab in the Top or Bottom tab areas, it is often easiest to keep your "shelves" above the workbench (the Work Area), so leave the Initial Placement at Top.
3. The Tab Type we want is Disk. This tells Maya that we are going to create a new tab and that it will place the contents of a directory from a disk. You will notice that as soon as you do this, the bottom part of the dialog box changes to ask you where the Root Directory is (Figure 8.5b).

FIGURE 8.5   (a-c) Creating a new tab with all the images we need for textures.

4. Click on the folder icon to tell Maya what directory to import. Find the folder ReunionPhotos within the Textures folder of your Project directory and hit **OK** (Figure 8.5c). Finally, click on the Only Show Files (Hide Directory Tree) option. This will keep our new shelf (tab) clean. Hit **Create** and you will have a new tab (Figure 8.6) with all the contents of the Reunion-Photos already imported into swatches.

Pretty snazzy, eh? Everything is imported in one swoop and we can use this method to keep things organized.

Step 7: Create a new PhongE material. As a review, you can do this by selecting the Hypershades Create>Materials>PhongE or by MMB-dragging the materials from the Create Bar area into the Work Area. Rename this material to `JakePhoto_Material`.

Step 8: Place `Jake.jpg` into the Color attribute. In past tutorials, we have altered the color channel by changing the actual hue, and brightening and darkening the color. However, now it is time to bring in an actual photograph to define how the color of the material that we are going to place on the plane in the frame will look. Again, there are a couple of ways to do this. For this Step we will use one method and another in the next Step.

In the Attribute Editor, click the checkered button at the right of the Color attribute. In the Create Render Node window that pops up there, you can se-

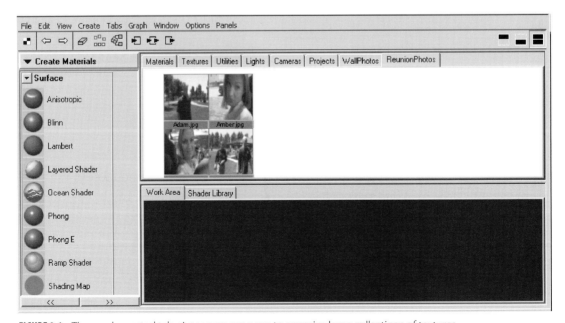

FIGURE 8.6   The newly created tab gives us an easy way to organize large collections of textures.

lect what file will be used to define the color. A number of procedural textures that Maya creates mathematically are listed in this window. However, in this case, we want to use an image. So, click the **File** button.

All sorts of things will happen. First, in the Work Area, there will be a couple of new swatches/nodes that pop up. You will see a swatch called `file1` and another yellow one called `place2dTexture8`. To see a little clearer what is going on here, RMB-click-hold within the Work Area on a black area (not on any swatch) and select Graph>Rearrange Graph from the pop-down menu that appears.

The yellow swatch (`place2dTexture8`) is, of course, the node that allows us to define how the Color attribute will be placed on the surface. The swatch called `file1`, of course, will be Jake—the photo or texture that `place2dTexture8` will be placing. Finally, `JakePhoto_Material` is the last swatch there (in green) that represents the material.

To get `Jake.jpg` into the `file1` swatch, make sure that it is selected in the Work Area, and the Attribute Editor will appear asking you to define (in the File Attributes) what image is to be used. In the Image Name input field, you can do the following:

a. Type in the path of the image you wish to use.
b. Hit the **folder** button and then guide Maya to where the image you wish to use resides.
c. MMB-drag the file, `Jake.jpg`, from the ReunionPhotos tab area (you may have to move down within the tab area to find `Jake.jpg`) into the Image Name input field. Choice c is the easiest for us here.

As soon as you do that, the path will appear immediately in the Image Name input field. More important, the `file1` swatch in the work area will show Jake grinning. The green swatch representing the material, `Jake Photo_Material`, will also show the results of the new texture that was imported into its Color attribute (Figure 8.7).

FIGURE 8.7   Rearranged Graph after importing `Jake.jpg` into the Color attribute.

Step 9: Place `JakePhoto_Material` **on the plane inside the frame.** As we discussed in the last chapter, do this by MMB-dragging the material (`JakePhoto_Material`) from the Work Area onto the plane at the center of the frame. Hit 6 on your keyboard to tell Maya to show you textures and you should have something like Figure 8.8.

Now, depending on how you built your frames, there could be some funny things that happen. For instance, your image might look something like Figure 8.9. If it does, not to worry—we can fix this.

The problem here is that the Color attribute is placed on the surface incorrectly. To adjust this, click on the `place2dTexture` yellow swatch. Your Attribute Editor will look like Figure 8.10. Because we need to rotate the placement, just enter `90.00` (or it may need to be `-90.00`) into the Rotate Frame option. Immediately, the Workspace will show the results and your photo will look right.

FIGURE 8.8 Placed `JakePhoto_Material`.

FIGURE 8.9 Material placed but by default, rotated incorrectly.

FIGURE 8.10   Attribute Editor for the `place2dTexture` swatch.

Step 10: Adjust other material attributes for the material, `JakePhoto_ Material`. To do this, click on `JakePhoto_Material` in the Work Area. This will bring up the material's attributes in the Attribute Editor. Scroll down to the Specular Shading area and change the Highlight Size to `1.00`. While you are there, change the Reflectivity to `0.00`.

Now, this is really cheating a bit. In reality, the photo would be one plane and a plane of glass would be another. However, because we are not going to be getting very close to any one image, we are going to give a bit of glass characteristics to the one plane that already contains the color information of Jake smiling.

One final note: we are using PhongE because it gives us the option of having Roughness in the Specular Shading area. This gives us a softer specular highlight as though the images were behind a high-quality, no-glare pane of glass.

Step 11: Clean up the Work Area before starting a new material. In the last chapter, we just created material after material in the Work Area; the problem is that this can become quite crowded. We can clear the workbench (Work Area) manually by RMB-click-holding and selecting Graph>Clear Graph from the pop-down menu.

Step 12: Move so that you are focusing on another frame. Again, for this one, find another horizontal frame.

Step 13: Create a new PhongE material and name it `GpaPhoto_Material`.

Step 14: Assign a Color texture directly from the ReunionPhotos tab to the new material. We are going to place the Color attribute a bit differently for this one. In the last steps, we used the Attribute Editor to find and place a texture. This time, we will place it by dragging the texture directly onto the material.

In the ReunionPhotos tab area, find the image called `Gpa.jpg`. MMB-drag this image onto the `GpaPhoto_Material` swatch in the Work Area. As soon as you release the MMB, a pop-down menu will appear asking you what attribute you wish to assign this texture (Figure 8.11). Choose color.

You might need to rearrange the graph to see a little more clearly what is happening. The thing that may appear odd to you here is that you are missing the `place2Dtexture` swatch that you had for the last material. It is actually there, just not visible.

The Work Area will display various graphs that show nodes and relationships between textures and materials. Sometimes, when editing attributes, relevant nodes will be shown in the Work Area. At other times—as in the method that we just used—some nodes are not shown by default.

In this case, `place2dTexture` is a node that helps the material, `GpaPhoto_Material`, know how to place the color information we introduced through the texture, `Gpa.jpg`. So, to see that node, we need to make sure that `GpaPhoto_Material` is showing all of its Input nodes. There are a couple ways to do this but the simplest is to select `GpaPhoto_Material` in the Work Area using the Input Connections tool at the top of the Hypershade (Figure 8.12). Click that button and your `place2dTexture` node will appear.

FIGURE 8.11   After releasing the MMB, you can choose directly what attribute to place the texture into.

FIGURE 8.12   The Input Connections button will show the inputs to a particular node or material.

Step 15: Adjust the Specular Shading attributes to match those outlined in Step 10.

Step 16: Assign the material, `GpaPhoto_Material`, to the plane of the picture frame. The Workspace should look something like Figure 8.13.

FIGURE 8.13   New photo and frame.

Step 17: Prepare to start work on another frame—a vertical one this time. Clear the graph in the Work Area and move around to find a vertically formatted frame in your room. Again, create a new PhongE material named `Seth-Photo_Material`. Change this material's Highlight Size to `1` (in the Specular Shading section of the Attribute Editor) and the Reflectivity to `0` to match earlier materials.

Step 18: Bring in `Seth.jpg` as the texture for the Color attribute. You can do this via the Attribute Editor or by dragging directly to the `SethPhoto_Material` swatch in the Work Area. Either way, make sure that you can see the `place2dTexture` node within the Work Area (you might need to use the Input Connections button). Your work area should look something like Figure 8.14.

FIGURE 8.14   New `SethPhoto_Material` with `Seth.jpg` as the Color attribute.

Step 19: Assign `SethPhoto_Material` **to the plane in your vertically formatted picture frame.** Remember, a quick way to do this is MMB-drag the material from the Work Area to the surface, itself. Figure 8.15 shows the result on my file. Yours may differ slightly in its orientation but you will definitely have a "squished" image.

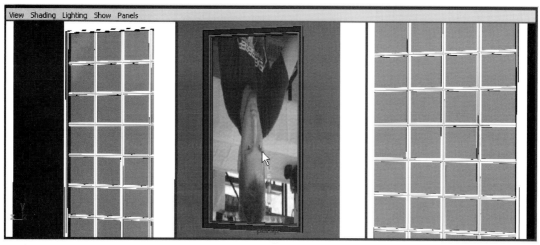

FIGURE 8.15   The squished and upside-down default placement Maya used.

Step 20: Adjust the Color attribute of `SethPhoto_Material` **using the** `place2dTexture` **node.** You may not need to rotate in your file, but if you do, select `place2dTexture` in the Work Area and change the Rotate Frame setting (in the Attribute Editor) to get the image looking the right way.

While we are here in the Attribute Editor and we are editing the placement, we can do something about the squished image. Notice that in the input fields such as Coverage, there are two columns. One is for the U coordinate and one is for the V. A simple way to think of UV is XY.

By default, the Coverage setting is at 1 and 1. This means it takes the texture (`Seth.jpg`) and covers from edge to edge the assigned surface, and does it exactly once. That is why the image appeared squished. To stretch it back out again, we need to change the Coverage settings. Depending on the exact proportions of your frame, this value may be slightly different, but for now, enter `2.50` in the first column. This should stretch out your material (Figure 8.16). The problem is, we cannot see Seth.

To get him centered again, we need to move or translate the texture that sits on the surface. In the Translate Frame input field, in the first column, enter `1.75`. You may need to adjust this value to accommodate your slightly different proportioned frame. The result should look like Figure 8.17.

FIGURE 8.16 By increasing the coverage, we stretch out the image to a more appropriate size but we move Seth out of the frame.

FIGURE 8.17 Translated placement moves the color across the face of the plane to where we can see Seth.

Finally, the texture is placed correctly. However, having to make blind guesses on values is a goofy way to place a texture/material. Read on to find out how to create Interactive Placement.

Step 21: Prepare for a new material and create a new PhongE named `AmberPhoto_Material`. Clear the graph. Create a new PhongE material and rename it `AmberPhoto_Material`. Change this material's Highlight Size to 1 (in the Specular Shading section of the Attribute Editor) and the Reflectivity to 0. Finally, move around in your scene so that you are looking at another vertically formatted frame.

Step 22: Bring `Amber.jpg` **into the** `AmberPhoto_Material`'s **Color attribute and assign the material to the picture plane (Figure 8.18).** Notice that in my image, again, the new material's placement is upside down and squished. Yours might not be upside down but it will be definitely squished.

Step 23: Use the Interactive Placement tool to adjust the texture's placement. Select `place2dTexture` in the Work Area. This will open this placement node in the Attribute Editor. Notice that above all of the input fields we adjusted in earlier steps there is a button called Interactive Placement. When you click that button, your mouse will change to one similar to the one shown in Figure 8.18. When you use this new tool to LMB-click on the plane that has `Amber-Photo_Material` assigned to it, a red line with several handles will appear.

These handles encompass the texture and its placement. When other handles are MMB-click-dragged, they affect different aspects of the placement. The corner handles allow you to rotate the placement of the texture while the ones at the top, bottom, and both sides allow you to resize a texture to make it smaller. Notice that you will not be able to stretch the texture larger using the Interactive Placement tool. However, do take a minute to play with rotating the texture by MMB-dragging the corner (Figure 8.18).

Notice that as you rotate or change the texture placement with the Interactive Placement tool, the corresponding numbers in the Attribute Editor change as well.

Change the U Coverage (first column in the Coverage of the Attribute Editor) to 2.5. If you are not in the Interactive Placement tool already, click the **Interactive Tool** button again. This time, MMB-drag the middle red handle to move the texture along the surface to a new placement (Figure 8.19). This is

FIGURE 8.18   Rotating a texture using the Interactive Placement tool and MMB-dragging a corner.

FIGURE 8.19   Using the Interactive Placement tool to place the texture on the surface visually.

more intuitive as you can eyeball the new placement. Also, you can use the Interactive Placement tool to MMB-drag the texture thinner if you need to.

Step 24: Use the techniques described earlier in this tutorial to place materials on all the remaining frame picture planes in the room (Figure 8.20).

FIGURE 8.20   Lots of placed textures in the room for all the frames.

Step 25: Create a new tab in the top called FloorTextures. Remember, to do this use Tabs>Create New Tab (Figure 8.21). Be sure to designate the folder FloorTextures as the directory to import. This folder was one of those that you copied from the CD-ROM to your hard drive at the beginning of this tutorial.

Now, there are a lot of images for use in textures in this folder. We will not use all of them in this tutorial. However, they are provided so you can do some experimentation and play with the settings available.

FIGURE 8.21   Creating new tab with floor textures.

Step 26: Create a new Blinn material and name it `Floor_Material`.

Step 27: Make `TileColor.tif` **the Color attribute for** `Floor_Material`.

Step 28: Assign the new `Floor_Material` **to the Floor object and render.** The result is obviously wrong (Figure 8.22). Taking one copy of our color texture and stretching it over the entire floor makes for huge tiles.

FIGURE 8.22   The default placement of the new color texture leaves much to be desired: it is too big.

However, we know how to resize a texture across a surface. In the Work Area, make sure that you can see the Inputs of `Floor_Material` and open the placement node in the Attribute Editor (double-click `place2dTexture`).

For our photos, we changed the coverage to make the texture bigger than the surface it was assigned to. In this case, we want to do the opposite. However, if we reduce the Coverage settings to below 1, parts of the surface will be without any color texture. Instead, we want the texture to have full coverage but repeat itself many times.

To do this, we want to enter new values in the Repeat UV Input Fields. Enter `10` in the U column and because the room is twice as long as it is wide, enter `20` in the V column. This will produce a floor with the tiles correct (Figure 8.23). Although you can see this in the Workspace, take a quick render.

FIGURE 8.23   Correctly shaped and sized tiles.

Step 29: Add a bump map to the material, `Floor_Material`. The color is a good start for this material but it looks very flat. To fix this, we will be adding a bump map to give some depth to this surface. Within the FloorTexture tab is another image called `TileBump`. (For details on how to create these custom maps, see Appendix C).

Assign `TileBump.tif` to `Floor_Material`'s bump attribute by MMB-dragging it from the FloorTextures tab onto swatch, `Floor_Material`, in the Work Area. Take a minute to clean up the graph and make sure that you are seeing all of `Floor_Material`'s inputs. Your Work Area should like Figure 8.24.

There are some interesting things to note here. There are essentially two branches of information feeding into the final output of `Floor_Material`: the color and bump. You can see that each of these input branches has a file that helps define what is happening. However, the biggest issue is that there are two placement nodes. Unlike most applications, you can actually map the color and bump differently. The problem with this is that we have carefully created the tiles' placement with the color. It will be important that our bump texture's placement matches our color texture's placement.

FIGURE 8.24   Work Area with newly placed bump map.

Step 30: Make the color's placement node an input for the bump map. Because we have defined the placement for the color, this is the keeper. Select the `place2dTexture` for the bump map (Figure 8.25a) and delete it (Figure 8.25b) using the **Backspace** or **Delete** keys.

Then hold down the **Ctrl** key down and MMB-drag the `place2dTexture` node (the one associated with the color texture) to the `TileBump1` swatch. When you release the mouse (Figure 8.25c), you will see a new connection between the placement node and the bump map.

What this has done is make the placement node the input for both the texture that defines the bump and the texture that defines the color. If you pull the placement node a little ways away, you can see the new arrows emerging from it to both branches of inputs (Figure 8.25d).

FIGURE 8.25   (a-d) Creating new connections (Inputs) within the Work Area.

Step 31: Tone down the bump height. If you take a render now, the bump will be a bit severe. To turn this down a bit, select the `bump2d1` node in the Work Area. In the Attribute Editor, change the bump depth to `0.10`. The result of all of this should look similar to Figure 8.26.

FIGURE 8.26   Final floor with bump and color.

Step 32: Create materials for the rest of the room. A tall order for sure. Remember that there are some extra textures for your use included in the Floor-Textures tab. Namely, there is a texture called FurnitureWood. In Figure 8.27, this texture was used to create all the materials that went on all the furniture.

FIGURE 8.27 Finished textures.

Other materials such as the lamp base and the lamp shade were simply done with procedural textures. Even the cushions of the room were done with procedural textures. Play with a variety of things and throw a bunch of colors on everything. There is really no right or wrong—just let it flow.

CONCLUSION

Many pages have gone in the pursuit of texturing excellence. The amazing thing is we have barely scratched the surface. Unfortunately, this book is not big enough to explore all the nooks and crannies of Maya's texturing monolith. However, we have covered most all of the general tools and concepts within Maya's paradigm. This probably does not mean that you are an expert at texturing at this point, but with the knowledge you have now, you should be able to continue to manipulate and learn new techniques in texturing as you work.

ON THE CD

Remember that the results of this chapter's tutorial are on the CD-ROM. If you would like to take apart any of the materials created to see the details, just open the file and begin a'ripping. A lot can be learned by looking at someone else's files—it is kind of a view to their thought process. Or, if you are comfortable with the things we have covered, then you are set to move on.

Texturing is truly an art form. However, as the final figure in this chapter shows, texturing is only half the battle. Even with all of our materials created and placed, the room is still stale, unbelievable, and uninteresting.

The other half of effective texture work is actually lighting. In the next chapter, we will go over Maya's lighting tools and look at ways to manipulate them to highlight our modeling strengths and even hide weaknesses. So, take a break and then read on. The best eye candy is yet to come.

LIGHTING AND RENDERING

We are getting closer and closer to the desired image shown way back in Chapter 2. In the last chapter, we finished up the methods of adding color to the objects in the scene. Although that was simply an introduction to the many facets of Maya's texturing capabilities, we still covered enough to create some solid materials for the room.

In this chapter, we get to help ground things with shadows, color things with lights, and give the stale room character and mood. All of this is done with the creation and manipulation of lights.

Also in this chapter, we will be taking time to cover how Maya renders. In most of the documentation that comes with Maya, lighting and rendering are listed together; this is because the two are very inextricably linked. Although the Workspace will show you a kind of preview of what your lighting is doing to the scene, it is just a preview. Without rendering, there are no shadows, no interplay between lights, and no real depth. So, we will be covering Maya's default rendering algorithm and some Ray-tracing. Lots of great things are yet to come.

Before we really get going, let us look a bit at the different types of lights and some general settings of how they work. If you are familiar with Maya's lighting instruments already, skip on down to the tutorials.

For now, we are going to look at how different types of lights affect an area. Figure 9.1 shows our mini lighting lab. It contains a box with a bunch of spheres and some strong vertical elements. The spheres have a Phong material on them and the box that contains it all has a Lambert.

The first thing that is important to know about Maya and its lighting-rendering relationship is that if there are no lights in the scene, Maya will render the scene as though lights were present. For instance, Figure 9.2a shows the uninteresting screens after hitting 7 on the keyboard. Hitting 7 shows the scene with an estimate of how the lighting in the scene will work. Without light sources in the lighting lab, it looks black. However, upon rendering (Figure 9.2b), you can see that Maya renders the scene as though there is a floodlight sitting right above the camera.

It is important to note that as soon as you place a light in the scene, Maya no longer assumes you want a floodlight.

FIGURE 9.1   The lighting lab.

FIGURE 9.2   (a-b) Even without lighting, Maya will render the scene as though there is a light.

LIGHT ATTRIBUTES

Before we get going on looking at all the different types of lighting instruments, we should talk a bit about which attributes Maya lets you control for lights. With any light, you can select the light and then open the Attribute Editor (**Ctrl-a**) to see and alter the available editable attributes.

Figure 9.3 shows the Attribute Editor of a spotlight. Notice that there are a couple of swatches at the top (Intensity Sample and Light Shape) that help give you some visual clues about the light selected.

FIGURE 9.3   Spotlight Attribute editor.

Immediately below that are several expandable sections that contain collections of attributes. There is some variation among the different light types once you get into these areas, but generally, here is how they break down:

- **X Light Attributes:** This area has the largest variation among the different light types. It contains details such as the ability to define or change the type of light that identifies the instrument. You can change the color, intensity, decay (light falloff), and shape here (Figure 9.4).

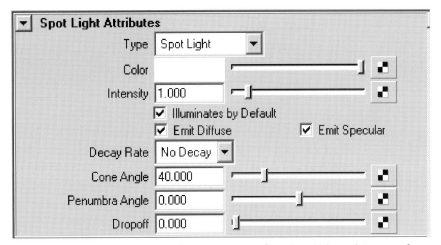

FIGURE 9.4   X Light attributes. Note these are not specific to Spot Lights; other types of lights also share many of these attributes.

- **Light Effects**: This generally details attributes such as Light Fog, which is similar to volumetric or visible light in other 3D apps. It also allows you to define things such as lens flares (Figure 9.5)
- **Shadows**: This is actually a very complex group of tools. Notice that when you expand the Shadows section, two new sections appear

FIGURE 9.5   Light Effects.

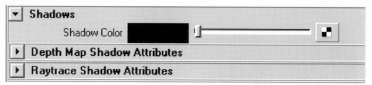

FIGURE 9.6   The Shadow Attributes and sub-attribute sections.

beneath it: Depth Map Shadow Attributes and Raytrace Shadow Attributes (Figure 9.6). The differences here are complex, but an over simplification of the two types of shadows can be summed up as Depth Map Shadows render faster, are mostly hard edged, have a constant color/transparency, and are typically less realistic (Figure 9.7a). Raytrace Shadows render considerably slower, can be soft, have varying color/transparency, and tend to produce much more realistic results (Figure 9.7b).

- We will talk much more about the difference between Depth Map Shadow and Raytrace Shadow differences. In general, you should try to make things work with just Depth Map Shadows, but if the need arises, use Raytracing Shadows. Part of the reason for this is that to see Raytraced Shadows, you must activate Raytracing in the Render Globals. Although Raytracing can indeed produce some beautiful renderings, you pay for it in render time.

- **Fur Shading/Shadowing**: Because we are not going to have the time or space in this book to get into fur or hair, we will not talk much about this. The core idea though is that when creating hair or fur, there are some specific shortcuts that Maya does to be able to render the fuzzy stuff without taking years to render. In this area, you can help define what those shortcuts are and how they work.

FIGURE 9.7   (a) Depth map shadows. (b) Raytraced soft shadows.

FIGURE 9.8   Remaining general light attributes. Typically, you do not use these much for lights.

- **Object Display, including the areas of Bounding Box Information, Drawing Overrides, Node Behavior, and Extra Attributes:** These remaining attributes are really something that affects your work flow when modeling. Here, you can determine if the light is visible, how detailed it displays (LOD—Level of Display visibility), whether it is templated, and so on. This group of attributes is available for most all objects created in Maya but it does not have a lot of relevance for a light. So, no need to be concerned with these (Figure 9.8).

Details of all these attributes will be explored as we work through the tutorials.

LIGHT TYPES

Maya creates several different types of lighting instruments. Each of them has slightly different characteristics, and the light that these virtual instruments give off in your scene all have slightly different attributes and editable characteristics. All are available via the Create>Lights> pull-down menu. The different light instrument types and some general descriptions are listed in the following sections.

Ambient Light

An *ambient light* is essentially a light that is everywhere. It never falls off and its light radiation goes forever in all directions. Although an Ambient Light has a source, you have very little control over where the light goes or how it reacts in the scene.

Figure 9.9 shows an Ambient Light placed in our lighting lab. On the left is what the Workspace shows; the middle is the Attribute Editor with the Ambient Light selected; and on the right is the default rendering result.

FIGURE 9.9   Ambient light placed in the lighting lab.

There are several things to notice here. First, despite having a Phong material, the rendering shows no specular highlights. The colors are still extant but there are no highlights. Second, notice that there are no shadows in the scene. In the Attribute Editor, there is an area set aside for Shadow Color but there are no Depth Map Shadows available to activate.

One caveat to this is the ability to create Raytrace Shadows. Figure 9.10 shows the same scene shown in Figure 9.9, except this has the Ambient Light's Use Ray Trace Shadows attribute checked. The scene is also rendered using Raytracing. Notice that all of a sudden, we have a plethora of shadows, but all of the colors are blown out.

In general, you will probably want to avoid Ambient Lights. They are seductive as a way to all of a sudden flood the scene with light, but you lose all control when you do so.

FIGURE 9.10   Raytraced scene with an Ambient Light and Ray Trace shadows.

Directional Light

The best way to think of this is sunlight. Most of the lights we will be creating in Maya create light rays that emanate from a single point. This gives us angled shadows that can splay or taper. *Directional Light* is a whole lot of light rays that all run parallel to each other. They come from infinitely far away and throw light to an infinite distance. In fact, in the Directional Light Attributes, there is no option for decay at all; the light keeps going forever and ever.

To better understand this light a little bit, take a look at Figure 9.11 and that image's inset. This is a Directional Light that has been turned a bit so that it faces downward. The light had its Depth Map shadows activated. Notice that the symbol that represents the Directional Light is sitting in the middle of the room, but the rendering on the far right is completely black! This is because the box of our lighting lab is stopping all the light from entering—in essence, the box is casting a shadow on its own inside. This suggests that even though the symbol is inside the box, the light is actually emanating from a point outside of the box.

FIGURE 9.11   Directional light inside the box, although obviously, the light radiation comes from some point outside of the box.

So, think of Directional Light as sunlight. You can place the actual instrument wherever you wish in your scene. The results will be a faraway light source that blasts through the entire scene. For illustration's sake, Figure 9.12 shows our lighting lab but the box has temporarily been set not to cast shadows. Notice the nature of the light and the shape of the shadows.

FIGURE 9.12 Directional light and its shadows.

Point Light

This is a tremendously useful instrument. Think of Point Lights as light bulbs. That is, there is one point from which the light emits and this light emits in all directions. This may seem to be similar to the ambient light we discussed, earlier. However, there are some important differences—namely, the ability to set a decay for the light, and the ability to produce Depth Map shadows.

Figure 9.13 shows our lighting lab with a Point Light set in the middle of the room. Depth Map shadows are turned on so, of course, quickly rendered shadows are present for all of our objects. Also notice that the specular highlights of the spheres with a Phong material on them show up great.

One more note on Point Lights. Figure 9.14 shows the room using Raytracing as the rendering engine and with Ray Trace Shadows activated. Notice the nice shadows and the reflective surface.

FIGURE 9.13 Point light with Depth Map Shadows activated.

FIGURE 9.14 Raytraced lighting lab with one Point Light.

Decay

Figure 9.15 makes use of one of the most important parts of creating realistic interior images—*decay*. Decay refers to how the light loses power as it travels further from the source. A light in a room that is not very bright does not light every corner of the room. Point lights allow you to set a Decay Rate (Linear, Quadratic, Cubic) that defines how the light will fall off. The easiest to control, although the least realistic, is linear decay.

Maya's implementation of controlling the decay of a light is really goofy. The only way to control how far a Point Light with decay throws light is to take the Intensity attribute up and down. Often, the best effects are combinations of changing the color and intensity to get the intensity and throw you want. We will look a bit more at this in Tutorial 9.1.

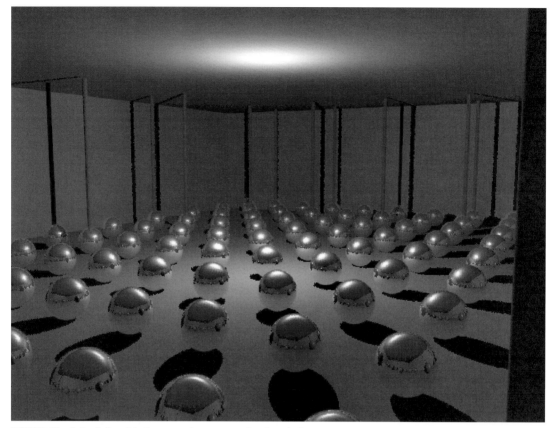

FIGURE 9.15 Point light with decay renders a room that has dark corners.

Spot Light

Another of the real staples of effective lighting, the *Spot Light* provides one of the ultimate instruments in control. Spot lights are lighting instruments whose light rays emit from one point. The path that these rays take is like a cone; they emit outward in the directions you define. Spot lights allow for decay and all types of shadows.

Figure 9.16 shows a Spot Light pointed (which is an important power of Spot Lights) downward into the light lab. Notice that the light is thrown only in the direction of the Spot Light. Specular highlights work well as do Depth Map shadows.

The Attribute Editor for a Spot Light includes sliders for changing the angle of the Spot Light, allowing you to have a broad or tight ring of light. Also in the Attribute Editor, you can change the Penumbra Angle and the Dropoff. These two features help define the sharpness or softness of the

FIGURE 9.16   Spot light using Depth Map shadows.

light's radiation. In Figure 9.16, the Penumbra Angle is set at 0. Figure 9.17 (a & b) shows the Penumbra Angle at 10 and –10. You can see how this allows the light to spread out gently, or contract, in creating a soft effect.

One final note about spotlights is that they work well with Raytracing.

FIGURE 9.17   (a-b) Altering the Penumbra Angle creates a light with a softer edge.

Area Lights

These are like giant walls of light. Although when they are first created, they are represented by a small square, they can be expanded to be the size of a wall or ceiling. They can have a Decay Rate assigned and use Depth Map Shadows and Ray Trace Shadows well (Figure 9.18).

Out of the box, Maya does not include any sort of *radiosity* renderer. Radiosity is a powerful but slow rendering engine that calculates bounced

FIGURE 9.18   Area Light. Notice, it is easy to overexpose a scene with this light instrument.

light in a room. Raytracing does not. However, with strategic placing of Area Lights, you can fake bounced light from any source. Effective use of Area Lights can add a subtle depth that is important for believable scenes. In the tutorials later in this chapter, we will be looking at ways to utilize these powerful but underused tools.

Volume Light

This light is finally what you would expect from a light source if you were coming from another 3D application. *Volume lights* give you a geometric 3D shape that is the absolute falloff of the light radiation. This is essentially the outer limit falloff of other applications. The powerful thing about this tool is that instead of creating just a spherical shape, you can also choose to have the light radiation fill boxes, cylinders, and cone shapes. Additionally, you can alter many of these shapes further into half spheres, and so on. Volume lights work great with both types of shadows.

Figure 9.19 shows a Volume Light using the Sphere shape. Notice on the left that the Sphere fills the middle of the room but does not reach the corners. The resulting render shows that absolutely no light reaches any of those corners. There is a lot of power and control in this instrument. We will be playing with it in later tutorials in this chapter.

So, that was a brief rundown of the different light types. We will be using many of them in the tutorials coming up. However, before we do, we have a bit more background information to catch up on. It will be important to know how to manipulate lights and what are the various parts of the light's anatomy.

FIGURE 9.19 A Volume Light has definite falloffs. Basically, if an object is within its sphere of influence, it is illuminated; if an object is not, it is in the dark.

LIGHT ANATOMY

To discuss the different parts of the light, we will use a Spot Light. Each type of light has slightly different characteristics that can be altered in the Workspace or Attribute Editor. However, the Spot Light has quite a few that can be seen in the Workspace, so we will use it for illustration.

Figure 9.20 shows a Spot Light as it appears when it is first created. Important things to notice are the large arrow in the middle that indicates the direction of the light's radiation. Directional lights have a series of similar arrows that become invaluable. Some light sources, such as an Area Light, simply have a line to indicate which way it is shooting.

The second thing to notice about Figure 9.20 is that the light's manipulator is at the source of the light's radiation. Using the manipulator, you can move, rotate, or scale a light however you need to.

Finally, for a Spot Light, you can see the cone that indicates the width or narrowness of the Spot Light's beam. Not all lights have a cone of light but light types such as Volume Lights have other shapes that indicate the "shape" of a light's influence.

Rotating a light into position is certainly one way to get a light to illuminate the desired objects. However, there are more eloquent ways to do this. In the Toolbox on the left of the UI is the Show Manipulator Tool (Figure 9.21). When you click this tool, a whole new set of iconography appears on and around the light (Figure 9.22).

There are two main manipulators that appear. The first is the Center of Interest (COI) manipulator. Think of this manipulator as a light target. When this is visible, the light will always be pointing at it. Area lights and Directional Lights also have such a manipulator. They make it easy to

FIGURE 9.20 A Spot Light with manipulator and directional arrow.

FIGURE 9.21 The Show Manipulator Tool.

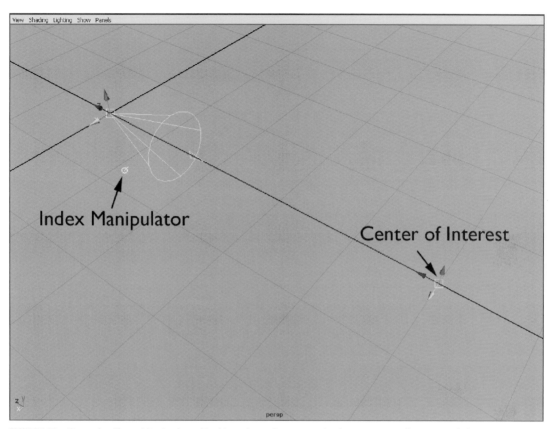

FIGURE 9.22   Once the Show Manipulator Tool is activated, new manipulators emerge for a given light.

point the light at exactly the place or direction you want it. Use the Move tool to reposition the COI and the light source will rotate to match.

The second manipulator—the Index Manipulator—is actually just a button to pull up other manipulators. When you click the Index Manipulator, new collections of manipulators that allow you to adjust various aspects of the light visually will appear.

Figure 9.23 shows the manipulators that show up for various positions of the Index Manipulator. The first position simply shows the COI and the manipulator for the light origin (Figure 9.23a). Click the Index Manipulator again (Figure 9.24b) and a new handle emerges that allows you to adjust the center of rotation for the light, just in case you want to be able to rotate a light from another place besides the source.

Figure 9.24 shows the next two collections of manipulators that appear if you continue to click the Index Manipulator. Figure 9.24a shows a new handle that appears to let you adjust the width of the angle of the Spot Light interactively. Figure 9.24b gives you a new manipulator that

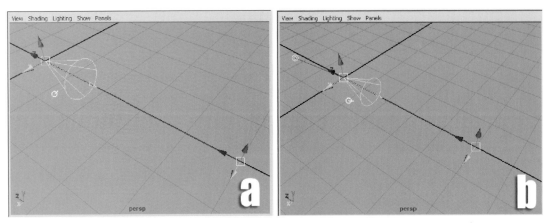

FIGURE 9.23 (a) The COI and source manipulators. (b) This blue handle manipulator allows you to define a new axis of rotation.

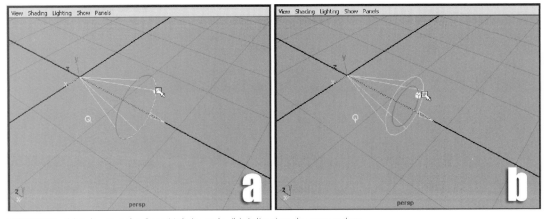

FIGURE 9.24 (a) Adjusting the Spot Light's angle. (b) Adjusting the penumbra.

allows you to adjust the *penumbra*, which changes how hard or soft the edge of the light appears. These are obviously some fairly specific manipulators available only to the Spot Light.

Finally, the last two sets of manipulators are shown in Figure 9.25. Figure 9.25a shows the various levels of decay that the Spot Light calculates. You can actually maneuver these manipulators to adjust the rate of decay, although this is very technical, and usually requires much more work than it is worth. Figure 9.25b shows the last option, which essentially is a rehash of manipulators seen in the past—the COI, light manipulator, and decay.

Once manipulators are shown, they can be altered independently of each other. With a light selected, the first time you hit the Show Manip-

FIGURE 9.25   (a) These manipulators can be used to define rates of decay. (b) The final collection shows the COI again, the light's manipulator, and the rates of decay.

ulator Tool, you will have the light's manipulator and the COI. This allows you to move the light quickly and use the COI to point it.

Enough of the theory of what the lights are and the basics of how they work. Let us get on to lighting our room. We will do two tutorials here. The first will light the room for nighttime and then we will light it for day.

TUTORIAL

9.1 NIGHTTIME

Interestingly enough, creating the lighting for night scenes is easier than daylight. The reason is that there is simply less light in the scene. Further, the man-made light that is produced by lamps, sconces, and other electric driven light sources is much easier to emulate virtually. Natural light, and its play inside a space, requires a bit more thinking.

Step 1: Open your room. Wherever you have been saving your room (which by now is modeled and textured), open it up; the fun is about to begin. Now, because we are going to be lighting this in two different ways, immediately use File>Save Scene As and save the room as `RoomDaylight`; this file will be used later. Then, again, immediately use File>Save Scene As and save the scene as `RoomNightLight`; this is the scene we will be lighting right now.

Step 2: Organize your Workspace. For light placement, it will be important at first to be able to see multiple angles of the room. Set up your layout to allow for a four panel layout (Figure 9.26). Also, move your mouse over the Perspective

FIGURE 9.26 Setting up your Workspace to light.

view and hit **7** on your keyboard to be able to see what your room looks like with the placed lights. Right now, it should look awfully dark.

Step 3: Set up your Render Globals. We will want to do frequent renders as we build and adjust our lighting setup. However, as our lights increase, so will the render time. Click the Display Render Globals Window button and change your resolution to either 320×240 or 640×480. Of course, the 320×240 will render quicker but will be a bit harder to see. You might want to start with 640×480 and then downsize to 320×240 if the render times get too long.

Step 3: Create and place a Point Light in a lamp. Create the light with the Create>Lights>Point Light pull-down menu. This will place the light source right at 0,0,0, which of course is in the middle of the floor where it is of no use to anyone. The light is just like any other object, so it can be moved by hitting **w** and then LMB-dragging it into place. Put it in the lamp on the south side of the couch. Render and take a look (Figure 9.27).

FIGURE 9.27   Placed Spot Light with unchanged attributes.

Right away, you can see that things are changing. All of a sudden, there are dark sides to objects, and there are lighter areas on the scene. However, there are also things that are not quite right. For instance, if a surface is facing this light, that surface is bright—artificially well lit. Also, everything seems to be floating; the couch does not quite sit on the ground and the lamps do not quite sit on the tables. We need to adjust the light's attributes.

Step 4: Rename the light. Open the Outliner and double-click on the light. Rename it `LampLet_pointlight`. Tumble and dolly around a little closer to the light/lamp.

Step 5: Add the ability to cast shadows to this Point Light. Hit `Ctrl-a` to open the Attribute Editor. As we discussed before, this allows you to define how the light is to act. Open the Shadows section and in the Depth Map Shadow Attributes area, check the Use Depth Map Shadows button. Render (Figure 9.28).

FIGURE 9.28   To make a light cast quick shadows, open the Attribute Editor and activate the Use Depth Map Shadows option.

Some interesting things happen here. In the render, you can see that indeed, shadows are being cast. A shadow is caused when a surface stops the light from passing through it. In this case, the lamp shade and the lamp below it are stopping most all of the light from passing through to anything. As a result, everything is dark but the top of the table.

Step 6: Stop the lamp shade from casting shadows. We need just the lamp shade to quit stopping light, to stop casting shadows. To do this, LMB-click on the lamp shade in your Workspace. Because your Attribute Editor is already open, the attributes for the lamp shade surface will be displayed. Look for the Render Stats section and expand it.

Here are many attributes that define how this particular surface is going to be rendered. The important one for us is the Casts Shadows option, which by default is checked. Deselect it and render (Figure 9.29).

Getting closer but there are still some things that do not quite jive.

FIGURE 9.29   Deselected Casts Shadows option for the lamp shade allow the Point Light's radiation to pass through it into the room.

Step 7: Adjust the lamp shade's material to "sell" the light source. Part of what makes believable lighting convincing is not only the light that hits the walls, but also the object that the light is supposed to come from. There is no need to model a lightbulb in this instance because we will never see inside the shade. However, it is important that the shade looks as though there were a lightbulb within it.

To do this, we need to adjust a few of the shade's material's attributes. The lamp shade's material was one that you created on your own at the end of the last chapter. Open the Hypershade, track down in the top Materials tab the material, and LMB-click it. The attributes for that material will appear in the Attribute Editor. In the Common Material Attributes section, change the Translu-

FIGURE 9.30   New lamp shade with Translucence and Glow activated.

cence setting to `1.00`. This will allow the surface to show that there is a light source beneath it.

Open the Special Effects section (still within the Attribute Editor) and enter `0.075` into the Glow Intensity input field. Render (Figure 9.30).

Step 8: Activate the `LampLeft_pointlight`'s decay. The problem with the scene right now is that the light from this Point Light is as intense right next to the lamp as it is across the room—clearly not what it would do in reality. We need to tell this light to calm down and not throw its light quite so far.

In the Outliner, find `LampLeft_pointlight` (probably near the bottom) and select it. Its attributes will appear in the Attribute Editor. In the Point Light Attributes section, change the Decay Rate to Linear. Render and take a look at the results. The decay at default for the size room we have is too drastic. The light decays too quickly. To fix this, turn up the Intensity to `2.0`. Bringing up the intensity will throw the light a bit farther (Figure 9.31). Render.

FIGURE 9.31   Decay turned on and Intensity turned up.

You might find that with the higher intensity, the translucency and glow on the lamp appear a bit intense. If need be, go back and alter the translucency and glow to lower values until the render makes sense.

Step 9: Duplicate the lamp. Instead of repeating this whole process again, select the lamp on the other side of the couch and delete it. Now, select the lamp (base and shade) and choose the `LampLeft_pointlight` and group these together. Rename the group `Lamp_and_Light`.

Select Edit>Duplicate (Options) and reset the settings. Although you may not have needed to reset the settings, because it has been awhile since we used the Duplicate tool, its always a good idea to do so. Hit the **Duplicate** button.

Place the new `Lamp_and_Light1` group on the other table and render (Figure 9.32).

Starting to look a better better, no? To spice up the room a bit more, we will continue to add a few more light sources.

FIGURE 9.32   Duplicated lamp and light.

Step 10: Create a sconce from a Revolve surface. Create a CV curve and make a Revolve surface from it. Make sure that when you create the Revolve surface you set the End Sweep Angle to only 180. Place the new surface on the pillar so that it approximately matches Figure 9.33. The details are up to you.

For this exercise, let's pretend that this sconce is metal; it does not really go with the room, but let's just do it for fun. So, create an Anisotropic (or Blinn or Phong) material and make sure to adjust the Specular Shading attributes so that you have a high, tight specular highlight.

FIGURE 9.33   Sconce created with a Revolve surface and textured with an Anisotropic material.

Step 11: Create a new Point Light to place in the sconce. Again, select Create>Lights>Point Light. Move the new light so that it sits in the sconce. Again, activate the Depth Map Shadows, change the Decay Rate to linear, and render. We need to make sure that this sconce overcomes the shadows cast by the other lights in the room, so turn up the Intensity to 2.5, and turn down the color to a gray. This will give us a nice bright light close to the light source but not blast away everything else. Render (Figure 9.34).

FIGURE 9.34   A sconce created with a new Point Light.

This does some interesting things. First of all, because the sconce is solid and it casts shadows, it helps to define the shape of the light. Although that shape would have been made with a Spot Light, it was more accurate by letting the shape of the sconce shade do the work.

Step 12: Create a bit of bounced light. With a high-intensity sconce shooting straight up to a white painted ceiling, we would have some light bounce off of that ceiling, washing objects below with a soft light. To fake this, we will use an Area Light.

Create the Area Light with Create>Lights>Area Light. Use the Move tool to move it up and above the sconce (Figure 9.35a). Now, hit the Show Manipulator tool and move the COI manipulator so that it sits directly below the Area Light, in effect, telling the Area Light to aim its light radiation down (Figure 9.35b).

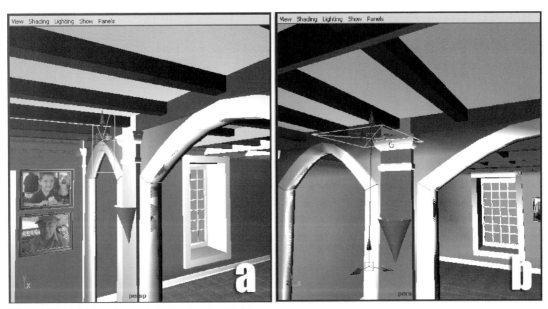

FIGURE 9.35 (a-b) Creating and aiming the Area Light.

Increase the size of the Area Light so that it roughly matches that of Figure 9.36. In the Attribute Editor, make sure to turn down the Intensity to 0.500 as it is bounced light. Change the Decay Rate to Linear and turn on Depth Map Shadows. Render (Figure 9.36).

Notice the top of the table behind the couch; this fake bounced light bathes the corner of the table in a soft light.

FIGURE 9.36   Sconce with bounced light.

Step 13: Group together the sconce, `pointLight`, and `areaLight`, and place duplicates around the room. Where exactly you place these is up to you. Figure 9.37 shows a suggested output. Because you are copying the bounced light along with the sconce, you create the fake radiosity automatically as you go along.

FIGURE 9.37   Duplicated and placed sconces (including the bounced light).

Step 14: Create a small light to light the artwork on the walls. Figure 9.38 shows a close-up of a small lamp that will hang over some of our pictures to illuminate them. Again, this is just the geometry—there is no light source presently in them.

FIGURE 9.38 Geometry of the art lamps.

Step 15: Create a Spot Light to go in the art lamp and position it. Create the Spot Light with Create>Lights>Spot Light. Move the light so that it approximates Figure 9.39a. Show the manipulators and move the COI so that it is towards the bottom of the picture (Figure 9.39b).

FIGURE 9.39 (a-b) Positioning and pointing a Spot Light.

Step 16: Adjust Spot Light settings to light the photos appropriately. Right now, the Spot Light is narrow, the light will shoot forever, and it will not cast any shadows. So, we need to adjust a slew of attributes.

Activate Linear Decay: we do not want the light from this small lamp running rampant through the scene. Change the Cone Angle to 85. You can do this with the manipulators if you wish, but it is just as easy and interactive in the Attribute Editor.

To give the light a bit of a soft edge, change the Penumbra Angle to 10. Make sure to activate the Depth Map Shadows. Lastly come the Color and Intensity settings. These can be rather tough. Because we have decay on, we are definitely trying to control how far the light throws—we do not want too much light emerging. Often, finding the right balance is a matter of reducing the color (closer to a gray) and increasing the Intensity. For Figure 9.40, the Color is about halfway gray (on the slider) and the Intensity is set at 5.00.

FIGURE 9.40   Adjusted Spot Light to highlight art work.

Step 17: Finally, add a small lightbulb in the lamp and give it some of its own inner light. Of course, this lightbulb will not actually be giving off any light—the Spot Light is taking care of that. What the lightbulb will do is make it appear as though there is indeed a hot tungsten source inside the lamp. This can be quickly modeled with a cylinder (NURBS or Polygon) with a material (we used Lambert) with a high Incandescence setting. For a little extra pizzaz, open the Special Effects section for the material you are placing on the lightbulb and activate the Glow Intensity by increasing the value to 0.25 (Figure 9.41).

FIGURE 9.41 Lightbulb with an incandescent material with glow activated.

Step 18: Group all of the objects related to this artwork lamp, and dupli-cate the lamp to pieces of artwork you wish to highlight (Figure 9.42).

FIGURE 9.42 Placed art lamps.

Step 19: Add any other lights inside of any other lamps that you see fit. Remember that believable light comes from a believable source. This means you might need to model some additional objects to get things working like you want them. Remember that the room does not need to be completely bathed in light; oftentimes, what you cannot see is almost as interesting as what you can see.

Step 20: Group together your lights and place them on a new layer called `NightLights`.

Step 21: Create a new layer for just the lights, not the surfaces. In the Top view, choose Show>None (from the Top View panel's pull-down menu). This makes the Top view completely empty. Now again, in the Top View panel, select Show>Lights. The result will look something like Figure 9.43.

Create a new layer in the Layer Editor and name it `NightLight_ Instruments`. Select all the lights in the Top view by marqueeing around them, and add them to the `NightLight-Instruments` layer (RMB-click-hold on the layer in the Layer Editor and select Add Selected Objects). Finally,

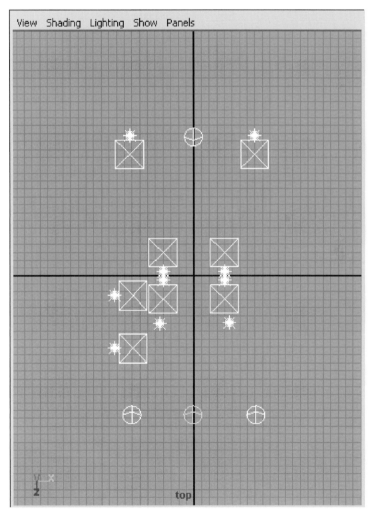

FIGURE 9.43   Showing just the lights in a scene.

hide this layer, but make the layer, `NightLights`, visible. You now have the geometry of the light objects in the scene but the actual lights have been made invisible.

Step 22: Save and close the file.

Well, that's it for this tutorial. We have covered Point Lights, Area Lights, and Spot Lights. We certainly did not explore every nook and cranny of these light tools but we did use many of them. Remember that if you want to see the exact setting of any of the lights used in this tutorial, the completed Maya file is on the CD-ROM; take a look. Also, many of the figures will simply not make a whole lot of sense unless you look at the color versions; these also are on the CD-ROM.

Keep reading. In Tutorial 9.2, we will be lighting the scene for daytime. This will actually require fewer lights but it will take a bit more finesse to get just right.

T U T O R I A L

9.2 DAYTIME LIGHTING

For the daytime lighting setup, we want a clean lighting slate. Remember that at the beginning of the last tutorial we saved a copy of the scene as `Room-Daylight`. Find this scene now and open it up.

Step 1: Create the sun. As discussed earlier, the best light type for this is a Directional Light. Create this with Create>Lights>Directional Light. Also, part of the plan was to have the light coming in from the east.

Although we have seen how a Directional Light does not actually need to be outside of a room, it is just more intuitive to set it up that way. Show the manipulators and move the COI so that it is on the floor of the room allowing the Directional Light to come streaming through the windows (Figure 9.44).

Finally, rename the Directional Light to `Sun_Light` in the Outliner.

Step 2: Adjust the attributes of the Directional Light. Your Attribute Editor may not be open if you were working with the Layer Editor from earlier. So, make sure of this and hit **Ctrl-a** to access the attributes. Turn up the Intensity to `3.00`. Turn on the Depth Map Shadows. Render.

This should be a fairly fast render; indeed, the scene will render quickly because it will be completely dark inside of the room. But why? We do have transparent glass after all. The reason is that the default renderer in Maya does not understand how transparent glass works. So, what is happening is that the glass windows that should be allowing light through are stopping everything up and not letting any light enter the room.

FIGURE 9.44   Setting up the sunlight with a Directional Light and a COI on the floor.

Now, we could get around this in several ways. One way would be to turn on Ray Trace Shadows for the Directional Light and then use the Raytracing engine to render but this adds a lot of rendering time—more than we want to deal with now.

Step 3: Make the glass not cast shadows. A more effective way will be to make the glass of the windows so that they do not implement the Cast Shadows feature. This means that they do not stop light so the light will be able to come streaming in unhindered.

Select the glass pane (just the pane—not the whole window) and in the Attribute Editor, expand the Render Stats section, and turn off Casts Shadows. Repeat this for all the glass in the room. Render (Figure 9.45).

Sure enough, the light is streaming in. However, it's not quite right yet. In a real room, if there were sunlight streaming through the windows like that, the entire room would be bathed in a gentle light from all the bounced surfaces. The light would bounce off the floor, the ceiling, all the walls, and so on.

FIGURE 9.45   With the glass not stopping light, the light from the Directional Light comes in to illuminate the room.

Step 4: Add bounced light. As we did in the previous tutorial, we will utilize the ever-useful Area Light. Create a new Area Light (Create>Lights>Area Light) and position it near the ceiling (just below the beams). Use the manipulator (show the manipulators first) to point the Area Light straight down on the ground. Finally, resize the Area Light so that is about the size of the side of the room closest to the east wall (Figure 9.46).

Rename this light in the Outliner to `BouncedEastCeilingLight`.

FIGURE 9.46 Placement of the Area Light for the bounced light from the ceiling.

Step 5: Adjust the attributes for `BouncedEastCeilingLight`. You might try and adjust these before reading this step. Much of this sort of adjustment starts out as good guesses and then is refined to the correct setting (which is then written here). If you would like to compare your results, change the Intensity to `0.300`. Make sure that the Decay Rate is set to Linear. Turn on Use Depth Map Shadows.

You were probably able to get all of these kinds of things right to begin with. There is one more cheat that we will want to use here. The bounced light that this ceiling will be giving off would be a soft, diffuse light that would also be bouncing off of a multitude of other surfaces. So, the shadows that this bounced light would cause would be quickly washed down to a much lighter color. To simulate this, move the Shadow Color slider to about midway—a light gray. This actually creates semi-transparent shadows that do not appear as harsh. Finally, render (Figure 9.47).

Starting to look a bit better now. We now need to add the light that would be bounced off of the floor.

FIGURE 9.47   Bounced ceiling light.

Step 6: Duplicate the light, `BouncedCeilingEastLight`, and position it on the floor pointing up. Remember to use the manipulators. Rename the light `BouncedFloorEastLight`. Also remember that this bounced light needs to be just above the floor of the room.

Because this bounced light would be the first as the sunlight strikes this surface in the room first, turn up the Intensity to `0.400`. Render (Figure 9.48).

Getting awfully close here now. While we are working on these two surfaces, let's create the bounced light for the west end of the room.

FIGURE 9.48 Bounced light added from the floor.

Step 7: Duplicate `BouncedCeilingEastLight` and `BouncedFloorE-astLight` and move them to the west end. Rename them to `Bounced-CeilingWestLight` and `BouncedFloorWestLight`. Finally, because the light will have traveled the farthest here, reduce the Intensity of `BouncedCeilingWestLight` to `0.200` and `BouncedFloorWest-Light` to `0.300`. Also, we want the shadows from these bounced lights to be extra light, so turn the Shadow Color to a lighter gray still. Render (Figure 9.49).

FIGURE 9.49 Bounced light on the other side of the room.

Step 8: Add a sunlight wash from windows. There are some really nice things happening here now. Figure 9.50 shows some great renderings of what we have thus far. The only problem is that there are still some really dark surfaces on objects that are facing other windows.

On a sunny day, there would be light coming in from all the windows, even though there would be one primary light source. All the other windows in the room would be letting light radiate from the outside in. So, we need to fake this with some extra light sources.

FIGURE 9.50   Room thus far.

Step 9: Add Area Lights the shape and size of the windows. Create new Area Lights and resize them so that they are the size of a window. Make sure that they are pointing into the room. Finally, make sure that the intensity is set low (0.100). For these objects, you can choose to turn shadows on or not. Leaving off the shadows can help give you a nice gentle wash but it can also create hotspots below the window. Figure 9.51 has the shadows turned off. However, from Figure 9.52 on, the shadows are on. Place one in each window and render (Figure 9.51).

FIGURE 9.51   Added Area Lights for the window radiation.

Step 10: Add a cyc. All of this lighting seems to work great. The only problem is regardless of how the lighting looks on the wall and furniture, when you look out the window and it looks black, we do not believe the lighting. To fix this, we will use an old theatre trick.

A *cyclorama*—cyc for short—is a backdrop that sits at the back end of a stage. It is usually just a drop painted to look like a skyline, fields, or whatever is appropriate for the play. What we want to do is create just such a cyc for the outside of this room.

Good cycs are actually curved. So, first—for the West end of the house— build your cyc by creating a CV curve in the Top view (Figure 9.52). Duplicate it, move it up, and create a loft surface between the two curves. Rename the `loftedSurface` to `WestCyc`. Once the surface is created, a material needs to be placed on it (Figure 9.53).

FIGURE 9.52   Create a cyc by starting out with a CV Curve.

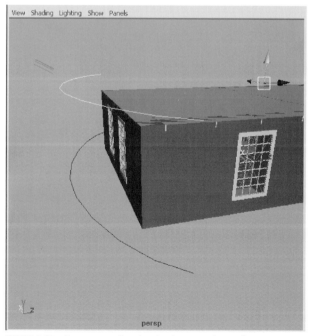

FIGURE 9.53   Create a surface by duplicating the surface.

Copy from the CD-ROM Tutorials/Chapter09/Textures the folder called Cycs to your hard drive into whatever directory you are storing your textures. In this folder are a couple of long photographs. In the Hypershade, create a top tab and define it as a Tab Type: Disk. Point Maya to the Cycs folder to use as the directory and hit Create.

Create a new Lambert Material and place the texture, `WestSideCyc .tif`, in the Color and Ambient Color attributes. We want to make sure that the cyc is not reliant on any light sources to illuminate it. Rename the material to `WestSideCyc_Material` and place it on the lofted surface.

Before rendering, there are a few other things we need to do. This cyc should not block any light coming into the room, so select the cyc, and in the Attribute Editor, open the Render Stats section. Turn off the Casts Shadows option.

In addition, we want to make sure that the lights in the room do not cast a shadow onto the cyc—it destroys the illusion. So, also uncheck the Receive Shadows button (Figure 9.54).

Tumble and dolly around until you can see out of the windows to the cyc. Figure 9.55 shows the result (be sure to look at this image in color). The problem is that the surface's colors are completely blown out. The reason for this is that the light from inside the room is bleeding out through the windows, and the Directional Light is lighting it as well. Too much light is not a good thing, so we need to tell all these overzealous lights to ease off.

FIGURE 9.54   The cyc setup.

FIGURE 9.55 Overexposed cyc.

Step 11: Refine the relationships of lights and objects. Select any light in your scene and make sure the Attribute Editor is open. Look carefully in the Area Light Attributes section and notice the Illuminates by Default option (Figure 9.56).

FIGURE 9.56 Illuminates by Default for a light.

What this means is that by default, this light's radiation will be "felt" by all objects in the scene (unless covered by a shadow). This is how real light works, of course. However, because since we are in a virtual environment, we can bend certain rules and have lights simply not shine on certain objects.

Managing this sort of trickery is done in the Relationship Editor. There are several types of Relationships Editors that can control everything from display layers, to render layers, to defining all the objects a light effects, or in this case, defining all the lights that affect an object. Choose Window>Relationship Editors>Light Linking>Object Centric. We want to use Object Centric as it will allow us to select our `WestCyc` and tell all the lights not to bother it at once rather than selecting each light, finding `WestCyc`, deselecting it, and moving on to the next light.

Once the Object Centric Light Linking window is open, click on `WestCyc` in the left column (Illuminated Objects). In the right column (Light Sources) all the lights in the scene will of course (by default) be highlighted. Simply start at the top and click-drag to the bottom. This will deselect all the lights, meaning that none of them will illuminate the `WestCyc` object (Figure 9.57).

Take another render (Figure 9.58).

FIGURE 9.57 Removing the light link for all lights on the `WestCyc` object.

FIGURE 9.58 Rendered cyc with no lights on it. The "illumination" comes from the material, only.

Step 12: Repeat steps 10 and 11 for another cyc for the east side called EastCyc. You can actually just duplicate WestCyc and rotate it around so that it is curved in the right direction. Rename it EastCyc. Create a new Lambert material and place the image texture, EastCyc.tiff, in the Color and Incandescence (or Ambient Color) attributes. Place the new material (renamed EastSideCyc_Material) on the object, EastCyc. Lastly, make sure that in the Relationship Editor, the lights in the scene do not affect EastCyc. Finally, render (Figure 9.59).

Step 13: Save your file and take a break. This is just a start for this room. There could be a lot more fine-tuning to do and you might find some areas that could be adjusted to match more closely your vision for what the room should look like. Now that you have the tools, you can do anything with the lighting in the room (Figure 9.60).

FIGURE 9.59   `EastCyc` in place and rendered.

FIGURE 9.60   Final lit room.

RENDERING

To look at rendering, we will just go over the Render Globals windows. We will also talk briefly about the IPR (Interactive Photorealistic Rendering) function.

Figure 9.61 shows an overview of the Render Globals window. We will not be covering all of each option available here. Those details are available in the Maya documentation and would make for some very dry reading. What we will look at are some core ideas and tips.

FIGURE 9.61   The Render Globals window.

IMAGE FILE OUTPUT

This area (Figure 9.62) allows you to set up the general rules about how Maya is going to save the objects it renders. You can define how it is going to save the strings of stills that make up animations (as in, which image format it will use), and you can even determine how it is going to

FIGURE 9.62   The Image File Output section.

number these frames (by the "File Name Prefix," plus the frame number, or by "Frame/Animation Ext" plus the frame number). Within this area, you can also define which camera Maya will use to render when it is rendering things such as animations or batch rendering things.

The last important part of this section consists of the Channels options. In general, you need not mess with these, although if you plan to do any sort of compositing, you want to be sure that the Alpha Channel option is active.

RESOLUTION

If you have worked much with digital imagery, this area is fairly straightforward. Remember that Maya is rendering in absolute pixels. So, if you are working in video, you want to render 640×480; DV 720×480. There is a collection of presets here that can set up things for you.

If you are working in print, make sure to do the necessary calculations. If you have an image that an editor wants at 4"×3" and she wants it in 600dpi, make sure that you enter 2400 for the Width and 1800 for the Height. Remember that rendering this large an image will take a long while, so plan ahead.

FIELD OPTIONS

This has to do with how a television displays an image. This is well beyond the scope of this volume, but when you get to the point that your work is ready for broadcast, there is much written about the theory and implementation of field options.

ANTI-ALIASING QUALITY

Anti-aliasing is the process in image creation of evening out the jaggies that often appear when a program is creating a large collection of pixels. The Anti-aliasing Quality section allows you to choose how Maya builds the images and how much time it takes to smooth the visual lines of pixels (Figure 9.63).

FIGURE 9.63   Anti-aliasing Quality.

If Maya takes a lot of time to work out the anti-aliasing, the rendering slows considerably. However, if Maya does not anti-alias, your image quality can suffer. Like most of Maya, the depth of tools here is fairly intense. In general, the Presets and Edge Anti-aliasing settings are all you need to worry about. The other sections are powerful but technical and more than we want to cover here.

In general, keep the presets set at Preview Quality as you work. When you are happy with your image and you are ready to make that "final" render, come back in and turn up the presets to Production Quality. This preset will kick up all the settings to where they need to be for a great quality image.

RAYTRACING QUALITY

As we have looked at earlier, this section allows you to decide whether to activate Raytracing at all. In the tutorials we have been taking on thus far, we have been making sure to use Maya's plain-Jane, out of the box, fast-as-it-can-go render. There are some definite drawbacks to this rendering engine. It does not handle shadows all that well and it does not do reflections at all. Raytracing can help solve some of those problems. As we discussed earlier, Raytraced shadows look better and Raytracing can handle reflective surfaces of any type. The drawback is this is all tremendously expensive in render time.

The Settings, Reflections, Refractions, and Shadows have to do with how many times the Raytracing engine is going to calculate the surfaces or reflected surfaces. Higher values make for more accurate images but also slow down the rendering. Keep these as low as you can. For example, if you have an error such as you begin seeing black planes where two reflective objects face each other, then come in and adjust these. In most cases, the default settings are fine. Fooling with them too much without a solid need and understanding can make the usually long rendering process even more excruciating.

If you are serious about rendering a large amount of animation or stills that need heavy reflections or other Raytracing-specific functions, you probably should be considering third-party options such as Mental-Ray. Other functions that programs such as MentalRay allow you to do include caustics, more accurate refracted light, bounced light, and other radiosity and radiosity-like functions. Although Maya's renderer has been making strides over the past versions, it is still dog slow and there are just better alternatives available.

MODIFY EXTENSIONS AND RENUMBER FRAMES

This area also deals with what to do with frames once they have been rendered.

MOTION BLUR

When you are playing back a VHS tape or even a DVD and hit the Pause button, often, the moving parts of the image are blurred beyond all visible recognition. This is a result of the shutter of the camera only being able to open and close so fast. In 3D, you can fake this effect and often give a bit of realism to animation by activating Motion Blur.

Motion Blur always takes longer to render and depending on the type of Motion Blur you use, it can dramatically increase the time needed. If you are doing heavy Motion Blur scenes, you are probably not using Maya's renderer—it's just too slow. If you wish to dabble with it, Maya's documentation has a fairly good overview of what it does and how to use it.

RENDER OPTIONS

Again, another area that is for high-end users. This allows you to define plugins or how MEL scripts will be used in the rendering pipeline. The notable exception is the Environment Fog. This is a fairly goofy implementation of the idea of adding fog to your scene. However, for quick and dirty fog effects, you can choose the colors, opacity, and density of the fog via the Channels box once the fog is activated. Figure 9.64 shows the room with fog added.

FIGURE 9.64   Fog added through the Render Options area of the Render Globals section.

MEMORY AND PERFORMANCE OPTIONS

By default, the settings within this area are set to try and optimize the power of your machine. There is usually not a large need to change them.

IPR OPTIONS

IPR stands for Interactive Photorealistic Rendering. It is an interesting idea to allow Maya to take a little longer to render certain parts of a scene so that as you change elements in your Workspace, they are "instantly" updated to reflect the changes. For some things, it really does work remarkably well—for example, light intensity, some texture work, and so on. However, for many things, IPR just does not do the trick.

The way to use IPR is simple. Along the top Status Line next to the Render Globals Window button is a clapboard with the symbol IPR on it. With the view you wish to render active, hit this button. Render time takes a bit longer.

When this is done, the Render View window will show the scene with a prompt on the bottom of the screen to "Select Region to begin Tuning." Right then, you can marquee around a section of the image that you wish to update quickly as you tweak your scene. It is probably not a good idea to marquee around the entire object, but small sections can work out.

You will then get a red box that is the updating region. As you make changes to your scene in the Workspace, Maya will update the area highlighted in red as quickly as it can. For details such as how high a bump map is, or how bright a light is, this works great.

In general, it is usually best to see how things are functioning on a macro level, so render the entire scene as you want to see the interplay of the light, the composition of the scene, and so on. For these sorts of things, sacrificing the time to render with IPR is usually not worth it. However, you might find IPR tremendously helpful for your work flow.

RENDER LAYER/PASS CONTROL

Full exploration of this area is the subject of another volume. Maya has the incredibly powerful option of rendering an image in layers—that is, rendering only parts of the scene in each pass that can be assembled together later. This means that Maya needn't deal with the entire scene all at once. It also means that you can separate the walls from the floor, and if you need to adjust the color of the walls, you can do so with just the Wall pass without having to re-render the entire scene.

CONCLUSION

Whew! That is really a whirlwind overview of the rendering options. There are lots of options to tweak here—so many that there are entire books written simply on optimizing and working with Maya's rendering engine. Hopefully, the view given here lets you know where things are, so if you run into problems you know where to go to begin tweaking.

Earlier in the chapter, we got to explore lots of the lighting tools. In reality, Maya's lighting is not as refined as many of its competitors. However, with a bit of understanding of the tools and a lot of creative thinking, you can create some great looking images. Remember to refine, re-fine, refine.

With this, we leave the room behind. In the next chapter, we will be looking at how to animate within Maya—how to make things come to life through movement. Come back and experiment with this room. There are lots of props to be added, new materials to be created, and new lighting setups to explore. Better yet, take the ideas covered in these chapters and create your own room. Be a set designer and interior de-signer. Interiors make for great laboratories to explore man-made objects, dynamic lighting, and rendering solutions. They are a great place to learn.

ANIMATION

We have been busy creating images. These still images we have created have been done with an interesting collection of a number of modeling techniques, texturing tricks, and rendering manipulations. However, in the big scheme of things, they are only the means toward an end.

Although there is certainly some incredible 3D still work out there, the biggest market is undoubtedly in the animation field. Actually making things move is what brings in the bucks and is what delights the audiences. In fact, many argue that the movement itself is more important than what is moving.

Because of its importance, and vast breadth and depth of concepts, we are unable to get into aspects of the technique or even the art of effective animation. However, we will look at the core tools that make Maya one of the greatest animation packages in the world. As you master the technique of animation, you can put the tools that we cover here in your back pocket and pull them out to create your masterpieces.

WHAT IS IT?

Before we get started on how to animate in Maya, let's look at a few core ideas behind animation.

First, *animation* (or any moving picture) is actually a string of still images that when played quickly enough in succession create the illusion of movement. Each of these still images is referred to as a *frame*. The number of frames played in each second help to determine how smoothly a motion plays. To complicate matters, different formats of media use different frames-per-second (fps).

Movies use 24 fps and this is the default setting for Maya. It will be important to know how to change this as most of the time, beginning animators are not animating for film but for other media such as video or broadcast. In the US, NTSC fps rate is 30 (actually 29.97), while in most of Europe, PAL standards dictate 25 fps. The variation never ends.

For the purpose of our discussion here, we will assume that we are dealing with 30 fps. What this means is that the arithmetic is always done with 30 as the core number. If you want to create a three-second animation clip, you will need 90 frames (30fsp × 3 = 90). If you want to know how long 300 frames will actually play out as, just divide the number of frames by the fps (30) and you know that it will play for 10 seconds.

It is rather awkward at first to take a linear idea such as time and look at it on a Timeline that is shown in terms of frames, but mastering the idea of timing via frames is important. It will come easier as time goes on and you do more timing/animation work.

So, we now know that we need 30 frames for every second of finished animation. How do we get those frames? There are several ways to do this but the most common is called keyframe animation.

KEYFRAME ANIMATION

Because so many frames are needed to create animation, it is not feasible for the master animator of a studio to draw every single frame. Studios have developed an interesting method of creating effective animation while keeping its most talented staff moving the key motion forward.

The master animator will come in and draw the character's first step, last step before leaping over the log, positioning for the jump, the character at the height of her jump, and then the frames where she lands. This leaves lots of empty frames but the most important ones—the frames that define the movement—have been dictated by the master animator. These frames created by the master animator to define the motion are called *keyframes*.

Then, the more junior animators will come in and use the keyframes created already to draw the frames in between. In fact, often when watching a movie, you can see the credits for an *in-betweener*—one who draws the in-between frames. So, interestingly enough, the junior animators often end up creating most of the frames for a production. However, the important thing to note is that the ultimate movement is still determined by the senior master animators.

Computer-generated keyframe animation functions much on the same premise. *You* are the master animator. *You* define the keyframes that determine how and when motion is to happen. Then, the computer becomes the in-betweener; it does all the grunt work of creating the frames that go in between the frames you define. On occasion, it creates bad in-between frames, and you have to go in and create more keyframes to help it along. However, most of the time, remember to let the computer do the majority of the grunt work for you. Work smarter not harder; keep the actual number of keyframes you must create to a minimum.

SETTING UP MAYA FOR ANIMATION

Before we get into the tools that allow us to create and modify keyframes, we need to make sure that Maya understands the rules of the animation game. To do this, select Window>Settings/Preferences>Preferences.

On the left are the categories of preferences that can be set. The organization of what is where is really odd, so take careful note. First, go to the Settings category. Here, you can define the Working Units of everything, including time. Change the Time setting to NTSC (30 fps) as shown in Figure 10.1.

Next, jump down to the Timeline category. Make sure that the Timeline lists 1.00 as the Playback and Animation Start/End value. The End value is irrelevant for now; it can be changed easily later. Also, move down to the Playback area of the same window and change the Playback Speed to Real-time (30 fps) as shown in Figure 10.2.

This is actually quite important. Without telling Maya to play in real-time, it instead attempts to show you every single frame, as fast as it can,

FIGURE 10.1 Changing the animation to work at 30 fps.

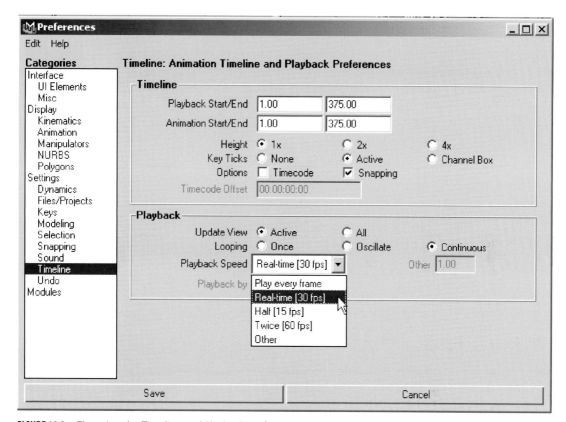

FIGURE 10.2 Changing the Timeline and Playback preferences.

when you are previewing the motion. This means that if nothing is happening, it flies through those frames, while if lots of complex things are going on, it crawls through those frames. With real-time selected, Maya will drop frames if necessary, in order to keep up. This actually gives you a much better idea of how the timing of your motion really works.

Hit the **Save** button to save your changes and exit this window.

THE ANIMATION TOOLS

Maya provides a surprisingly powerful collection of tools in a very small space in the default UI. Right toward the bottom is the Timeline (Figure 10.3). Within these two rows of tools are most of the tools to create most any type of keyframe. Although there is much refining to do within other editors, most of the "blocking-out" of animations can be done solely through this collection of tools.

FIGURE 10.3 The Timeline.

Time Slider and Current Time Marker

The actual Time Slider is the collection of numbers and hash marks at the top of this collection of tools. The numbers there represent frames. Notice that Figure 10.3 illustrates one specific black line that goes from the top to the bottom of the Time Slider; this is the current time marker. It lets you know where you are in time. The Workspace will show the state of your 3D universe at the time indicated by the current time marker in the Timeline. If you LMB-click anywhere in the Time Slider, the current time marker will jump to that new time.

Just to the right of the Time Slider is a small input field that shows numerically which frame you are on. You can also enter values there to move the current time marker to a new time manually.

Playback Controls

At the top-right corner of the Timeline are the Playback controls that allow you to navigate or play the animation you have created. Notice that from the far left, the buttons are: Jump to the Beginning of the Animation, Move Back 1 Keyframe, Move Back 1 Frame, Play Backward, Play Forward, Move Forward 1 Keyframe, Move Forward 1 Frame, and Jump to the End of the Animation. These are fairly intuitive and anyone who has worked a VCR will be familiar with the interface paradigm here.

Range Bar

The tool that takes the most space below the Time Slider is the Range Bar. Notice that this bar has two square handles at either end. Next to those handles are numbers that indicate which frames are visible in the Time Slider immediately above it.

If you drag one of the Range Bar handles in or out, you will be able to see less or more of the total frames of the animation. This can help you zoom in on certain keyframes and be more exact in your placement when you need to.

Similarly, on both sides of the Range Bar are pairs of input fields. They indicate both the length of the entire animation (on the outside of both sides) and what frames are visible in the Time Slider (on the inside of both ends of the Range Bar).

Auto Keyframe Button

As we work, we will begin to create keyframes. You can maintain complete control over which keyframes are placed where by defining manually what type of keyframe is to be placed at the current time marker (more on this later). However, you can also set a starting keyframe, and then with the Auto Keyframe button depressed, whenever you change the parameters at a different time of that original keyframe, a new keyframe is placed for you automatically. Be warned though: this is a seductive tool and one that often ends up creating more trouble than it is worth. Maya will be happily placing keyframes while you are working through details of placement or movement even if you do not mean to record any animation. In general, for now, leave this off.

Animation Preferences Button

Click this button to pull up the animation preferences that we changed earlier in this chapter. It is the same as selecting Window>Settings/Preferences>Preferences and then selecting the Timeline category.

ANIMATABLE ELEMENTS

Turns out, in Maya, most everything can be animated. If it has a numerical value, you can record a keyframe for it. Then, change the value later, record another keyframe, and Maya will animate the difference.

For our introduction here, the important ideas will be the ability to animate movement, scaling, and rotation. This is reasonably intuitive if you have gotten used to using the keyboard shortcuts for the Move tool (**w**), Rotate tool (**e**), and Scale tool (**r**). To record a motion keyframe hit **W** (or **Shift-w**). Similarly, rotation keyframes are **E** (**Shift-e**), and to record a scale keyframe, hit **R** (**Shift-r**).

The core idea of keyframe animation is that any motion is generated by two keyframes. The first dictates where the object is to start and the second indicates where the object is to end. So, to create an object sliding across a room over 30 frames, you would begin by moving the current time marker to frame 1. Then, select the object, move it to where you want it to start, and hit **Shift-W** to tell it, "Start Here." Next, move the current time marker to frame 30, move the object to the new location, and again hit **Shift-W**. This tells the object, "At frame 30, I need to you be here." Maya then figures how to get it there in the interim frames.

Enough talking about animation. Let's make some motion. To do this, we are going to animate a little character—a kind of mechanical hummingbird—flying through the room you have been creating in previous chapters. (Use the hummingbird we created with subdivision surfaces in Chapter 6.) Through the process, we will be creating several kinds of keyframes and altering how Maya decides to move between them.

T U T O R I A L

10.1 MECHANICAL HUMMINGBIRD

Step 1: Open your room. The daytime or nighttime lighting will work; either one you prefer. For the figures in this tutorial, we will be using the daytime lighting just so things will be seen easier.

Step 2: Set your animation preferences. As we discussed earlier, it's important that Maya knows the parameters that we are going to be using for the animation. Hit the **Animation Preferences** button at the bottom right of the Timeline. When the Preferences window appears, jump up to Settings and change the Time to NTSC (30 fps). Then, jump back down to the Timeline category and make sure that the Playback Speed is set to Real-time (30 fps). Click **Save** to save the changes and close the Preferences window.

ON THE CD

Step 3: Use the hummingbird model you created earlier, or import the one provided on the CD-ROM. If you want to use some of the techniques to design and build a new hummingbird or some other small flying critter, go right ahead. However, if you'd like to move quickly into animation, you can use the one we created earlier.

ON THE CD

To bring one model contained in one Maya binary file into another scene, use the Import command. Choose File>Import and then, in the resulting dialog box, go to the CD-ROM. In the Tutorials/Chapter10/ folder is a file called `Tutorial 10.1 Birdie Import.mb` Choose this file and hit the **Import** button.

This will import the small hummingbird right at 0,0,0 in your scene. It will be so small that it will be hard to grab in the Workspace. Make sure that your Outliner is visible and find the group toward the bottom called Birdie. Select it there and move it up to the middle of the room (Figure 10.4).

There are several things to notice about the model. First, in the Outliner, if you expand the group, Birdie, you will see that it contains the two Spheres that are the eyeballs, the `subdivCyliner1` that is the body, and a group called Propeller. Take a moment and rename the `sudivCyliner1` to `Body`. Name the two `nurbsSpheres` to `EyeballL` and `EyeballR` (Figure 10.5).

The organization here is fairly important. The Propeller is going to spin and will have its own collection of keyframes, but we also want it to move along with Birdie whenever it goes anywhere. Because Propeller is a child of Birdie, it will always travel with Birdie, regardless of the keyframes it has, itself.

FIGURE 10.4   Imported Birdie.

FIGURE 10.5   Organized Birdie.

Step 4: Prepare the Timeline. We are going to create a 10-second animation. So, we will need 300 frames. For now, in both the Animation Start Frame and Range Start Frames input fields, enter 1. In both the Animation End Frame and the Range End Frame, enter 300. This tells Maya that our animation will be 300 frames long and we want to see them all in the Time Slider, above.

Step 5: Record a rotation keyframe for Propeller at frame 1. When recording keyframes the order is important.

First, move the current time marker to the frame where you wish to record the keyframe (in this case, frame 1). You can move the current time marker to frame 1 by clicking on frame 1 in the Time Slider or by entering 1 in the Current Frame input field.

Second, select the object to be animated; in this case, Propeller. It is probably selected most easily by clicking the group in the Outliner.

Third, set the rotation to the value you want. In this case, we want Propeller to just start off at its current setting of 0 degrees.

Fourth, record a rotation keyframe. Hit **Shift-e**.

To see what has happened, click somewhere else on the Time Slider to move your current time marker out of the way. Notice that on frame 1, there is now a red line; this indicates a keyframe (Figure 10.6).

Now, of course, there is no motion yet. We must have two keyframes to do this.

FIGURE 10.6   Our first keyframe at frame 1.

Step 6: Create another rotation keyframe at frame 300. Again, the order is important.

First, move the current time marker to frame 300. You can do this one of three ways. You can click on frame 300 in the Time Slider; you can enter 300 in the Current Frame input field, or; you can click the **Jump to Animation End** button in the Playback buttons.

Second, select the object to be animated. Unless you have selected something else, Propeller will still be selected, so no need to do anything this time.

Third, set the rotation value you want. If it does not appear, make sure the Channels box is visible. The Channels box will have the rotation input fields highlighted in a peach/pink color. This is telling you that there are keyframes assigned to these values, meaning that they are animatable. If we want to have

FIGURE 10.7   Entering a new rotation value in the orange input fields that indicate animatable characteristics.

the Propeller spin 10 times in our 300 frames, we need to enter −3600 into the Rotate Z input field (Figure 10.7).

It turns out, the propeller could rotate in the positive direction too, but with the shape of the propeller blades, the negative direction is how it should spin.

Fourth, record a rotation keyframe. Hit **Shift-e** and the keyframe is set.

So, now with two keyframes, one at frame 1 with a Rotate Z setting at 0 and another at frame 300 with a Rotate Z setting at −3600, Maya knows to rotate the propeller 10 times over the 300 frames.

Step 7: Playblast the animation. Now, unless you have a real beast of a machine with a huge video card, you will probably not be able to see this animation play in real-time. This is because by now, the project is fairly large. If you hit the Play Forward button, there would be no change in the Workspace, although you would see the current time marker jumping across the Time Slider. There is just too much data to deal with.

Rendering would take too long as well. As slow as stills are to render, imagine waiting for that time multiplied by 300. Much too long to just get an idea of what we have done.

Playblasts are Maya's way of letting you do a quick rendering of the Workspace using the OpenGL algorithms. It creates and quickly assembles a short animation for you to view. You can choose to Playblast the entire animation or just sections of it.

Before we start to use Playblast, we need to narrow our Time Slider a little bit. Because all that is happening for the entire 10 seconds (300 frames) is the same turning, we do not need to Playblast the entire thing. Enter 180 in the Range End Frame input field, or grab the right Range Bar Handle and drag to the right so that the Time Slider is only showing 180 frames (Figure 10.8). Remember that this does not affect how many frames are in the animation; there are still all 30. It only affects how many we can see in the Time Slider.

To tell Maya to Playblast, choose Window>Playblast…(Options). We want to be able to define exactly what it is putting together (Figure 10.9).

Figure 10.9 shows what the settings should be. We only want to see the 180 frames in the Time Slider. Using the Fcheck, which is a kind of media player inside of Maya is fine. You can define a Display Size but because the motion is small, just leave the Scale setting at 0.5; this will create the Playblast at half the size of your Perspective view. Leave the last part alone as we only want a temporary file—no need to save the files for this Playblast.

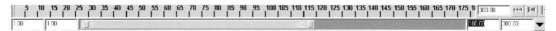

FIGURE 10.8   Reducing the amount of frames shown on the Time Slider.

FIGURE 10.9   The Playblast Options window with settings to check out our animation.

Hit the Playblast button.

Your UI will do some funny things here. You will start to see some motion in the corner of your Perspective view and you will see the current time marker marching across the Time Slider. When it is all done, a new window called FCheck will pop up playing the animation.

By default, FCheck is playing every frame as fast as it can. If you have a slow machine, this may not be in real-time. Hit **t** on your keyboard and FCheck will jump to playing the animation in real-time, even if that means dropping frames (Figure 10.10).

Close the FCheck when you are done previewing this animation.

FIGURE 10.10   FCheck in action.

Step 8: Animate the Birdie flying into the room and around the middle pillars stopping at a picture. Grab your Range Bar handle and stretch the Range Bar back out to show all 300 frames. Move the current time marker back to frame 1. Make sure and select the entire group, Birdie (from the Outliner), and move the bird to match Figure 10.11. Record keyframes similar to the following:

- Frame 1 (Figure 10.11).
- Frame 60 (Figure 10.12a).
- Frame 90 (Figure 10.12b).
- Frame 120 (Figure 10.12c).
- Frame 160 (Figure 10.12d).
- Frame 200 (Figure 10.13). Move the Birdie so that it comes right up to any of the frames on your walls, whichever you pick. The picture we chose is shown in Figure 10.13.

For now, do not worry about the direction Birdie is facing, just move it. Remember, the steps are current time marker; make sure Birdie is selected; move to new location; and hit **Shift-w**.

FIGURE 10.11 Position for frame 1.

FIGURE 10.12 Position for frames (a) 60 (b) 90 (c) 120 and (d)160.

FIGURE 10.13   Move Birdie up close to an image in the room.

So, the idea here is that the Birdie flies into the room, weaves through some pillars, and then flies up to a picture. Display the Top view as a Wireframe (hit **4**) and hit the **Play** button in the Playback Controls. The Birdie should animate close to real-time with its motion following something like that shown in Figure 10.14. If you are getting a very slow playback, hide some layers in the Layer editor (hide the `Ceiling_Floor`, `Windows`, `WallHangings`, and `Furniture`).

Step 9: Have the bird hover in front of the picture for 60 frames (two seconds) through copying and pasting a keyframe. So, now we have the bird flying into the room and up to a picture. To let the bird take a second to look at the picture, we want to have little or no motion. The way to accomplish this is to have two keyframes that are identical. We could do this by moving the current time marker to frame 260 and, without moving Birdie, record another keyframe. However, let us look at another method.

FIGURE 10.14   The path of the Birdie so far.

Move the current time marker to frame 200 (it is probably already there) and RMB-click-hold to show the pop-down menu (Figure 10.15). Included here are a number of different options that allow you to alter keyframes that are present. You can also find tools to control playback and other miscellaneous animation tools.

Of interest to us is the Copy command. Select **Copy** to load the keyframe into memory. Now, move the current time marker to frame 260 (enter 260 into the Current Frame input field) and again RMB-click on the current time marker and select **Paste**.

A new keyframe will appear on frame 260—a duplicate of the one copied from frame 200. In theory, you would think that there would be no movement. However, take a look in the Top view (displayed as Wireframe) and play the animation. Notice that between frame 200 and 260 (supposedly, two identical

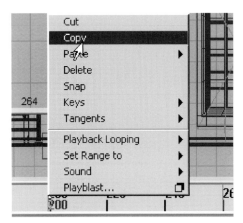

FIGURE 10.15   RMB-clicking on a keyframe.

frames) there is indeed movement; not what we had in mind. This is because of how Maya is assuming you want it to create the in-between frames.

Step 10: Adjust the in-between frames with the Graph Editor. When you create keyframes, Maya does its best to guess how you want to create the frames in between. The Graph Editor (Window>Animation Editors>Graph Editor), displayed in Figure 10.16, shows how Maya fills in the frames.

FIGURE 10.16   The Graph Editor showing the interpolation for Birdie.

By default, Maya uses something called *Spline Tangent types*. This means that between the keyframes (the black dots), Maya attempts to create very curvilinear lines of motion. The benefit of this is smooth and natural motion. The problem with this is that it can sometimes be a little over ambitious and place motion between keyframes that should not be there. In the Graph Editor, you can determine how Maya defines what happens between keyframes.

Dolly into a closer view of the last two keyframes so we can get a better idea of what we are doing as shown in Figure 10.17. (You move around in the Graph Editor the same as any other editor in Maya—**Alt**-LMMB-drag will zoom you in.)

As indicated at the right, the different colored lines represent various directions of movement. In this case, there is a distinct S-shaped curve in the path between keyframes for the Translate X line. If this line were straighter, the movement would be eliminated.

To do this, **Marquee** around the last keyframe on the Translate X (red) line. This will display Bezier handles similar to what you would use within Illustrator. These Bezier handles define the shape of the curve and are called the animation curve's *tangents*. To flatten out these handles, you can either select Tangets>Flat (from within the Graph Editor's pull-down menus) or hit the button hightlighted in Figure 10.18.

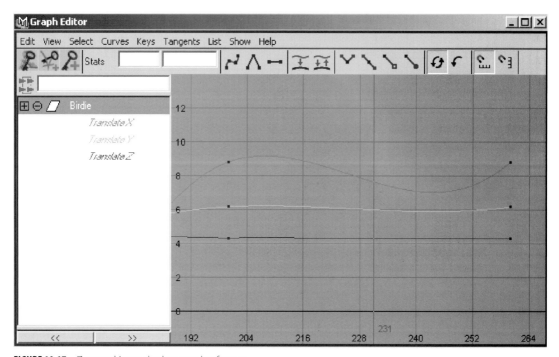

FIGURE 10.17   Zoomed in on the last two keyframes.

FIGURE 10.18   Flattening the tangents of an animation curve.

Repeat this step for the second-to-last keyframe on the Translate X line. We also want to do this for the keyframes on the Translate Y and Translate Z lines. To do this a bit quicker, marquee around all of the last two keyframes on all three Translate lines. Hit the **Flat Tangents** button and the keyframes' tangents will all adjust (Figure 10.19).

Play the animation and notice that the motion between the keyframes at frame 200 and 260 are gone.

FIGURE 10.19   Flattened tangents for a collection of keyframes.

Note that to the right of the Flat Tangent buttons are buttons to let you create tangents that are Linear and Spline. You can change the nature of any keyframe's tangents by clicking these buttons. Linear allows you to create sharp motion that snaps from one keyframe to another (great for mechanical motion).

Step 11: Add 30 more frames to the animation. We will be making one more move to get Birdie out of the room, but to do this, we need more frames to work with. To add more frames to an animation, just enter the new length of the animation in the Animation End Frame input field (Figure 10.20).

Drag the right Range Bar handle out to view all 330 frames.

FIGURE 10.20 Adding more frames to an animation is quick and easy by changing the Animation End Frame value.

Step 12: Move Birdie back out the door she came in from at frame 330. Move the current time marker to frame 330. Select Birdie and move her directly back out the door she came in and record a movement keyframe (**Shift-w**).

Step 13: Create a camera that focuses on Birdie. You probably have seen by now that from the Top view you can get a good idea of the movement of Birdie. However, from the Perspective view (the view that counts), you have to dolly and tumble around continually to see the new position. We need to create a camera that always keeps its "eye" on Birdie.

Use the Create>Cameras>Camera and Aim pull-down menu. This will create a group in your Outliner called `camera1_group`. If you expand this group, notice that it contains a camera and something called `camera1_aim`. This little aim object is what the camera looks at. By default, both the camera and the aim object are in the same group. However, by rearranging the aim object's hierarchical organization, we can keep the camera on focus.

In the Outliner, MMB-drag `camera1_aim` onto the group, Birdie (Figure 10.21). This will move the aim object out of the camera group and make it a child of the group, Birdie. This means that when the group, Birdie, moves (which it does quite a bit now), then the aim object will move as well. The problem is that the aim object is nowhere near Birdie.

Move the current time marker back to frame 1. Select the object, `camera1_aim`, in the Outliner and move it in the Workspace so that it is sitting

FIGURE 10.21   MMB-dragging the camera1_aim object out from the camera1_group and into the Birdie group.

right on Birdie (Figure 10.22). Make sure to do this in a multitude of views so that it is on Birdie in all three directions.

Next, select `camera1` in the Outliner and move it up so that it sits approximately in the middle of the west end of the room (Figure 10.23).

Finally, we want to be sure that when we are looking in the Perspective view that we are seeing through this new camera. To do this, go to the Perspective view's pull-down menus and select Panels>Perspective>camera1. This tells this panel to show us what `camera1` sees.

Now, if you play the animation (even in the Perspective view), the camera will always follow Birdie.

FIGURE 10.22   Moving `camera1_aim` into position on Birdie.

FIGURE 10.23 Moving the camera1 that is focused on `camera1_aim` and thus on Birdie to a better position in the room.

Step 14: Add rotation keyframes to Birdie to get her turning the right directions. So, now we have Birdie moving. We have a camera looking at her the whole time she does so. The problem is that she is always facing one direction as she moves. Luckily, we can refine our animation of Birdie to be more true to the direction she would need to be facing.

Move the current time marker to frame 1 and hit **e** (just **e** to activate the Rotate tool). Select Birdie in the Outliner and rotate her around so that she is facing into the room (Figure 10.24).

Hit **Shift-e** to place a rotation keyframe for Birdie. This tells Birdie, "Ok, you are going to be turning over the course of the animation and this is the angle you are going to start out at."

Hit the **.** (**period**) key to jump to the next keyframe for Birdie; in this case, it will jump to frame 60. We know that Birdie is about to head eastward in the room, so rotate Birdie in her heading and bank her a bit to the side (Figure 10.25). Hit **Shift-e** to record a rotation keyframe.

FIGURE 10.24   Rotate Birdie so she faces into the room.

FIGURE 10.25   Creating banking for Birdie so she turns in the direction she is flying.

Repeat this trick—hitting **.** to jump to the next keyframe for Birdie; rotate her to anticipate her flight path; and record a rotation keyframe (**Shift-e**). Do this for all her keyframes.

Note: When Birdie finishes looking at the picture, you might find that you need to alter her animation to make the movement believable. Place one position and rotation keyframe at frame 280 and another at 300 to give her a more arc-like movement.

Step 15: Playblast the animation to get a look at your animation. Hopefully, you are excited and pleased with what you see. The finished Playblast from the tutorial as followed here is contained on the CD-ROM in Tutorials/ Chapter10.

Step 16: Adjust Render Globals to render the project. There are several things that are important to adjust in the Render Globals window when you are ready to render an animation (Figure 10.26):

- **File Name Prefix** `Chapter10Final`**:** This is just the name that you want Maya to use as it saves the individual frames or completed clip.

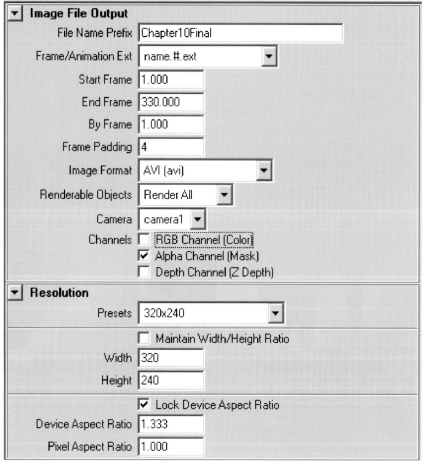

FIGURE 10.26 Consult the Render Globals window to get an early rendered test.

- **Frame/Animation Ext `name.#.ext`:** If you plan on rendering as anything but an AVI, you want to make sure to select an option with # (pound sign) in it. The # means that Maya will name the sequential stills that it renders with a number attached to it. This becomes very important when it comes time to assemble the stills in a video editing system. For our purposes here (because we are rendering to an AVI), this is a less important detail but it is important to note.
- **Start Frame `1.000`:** This can be set at anything and should be if you only want to render a chunk of an animation. For us, we started our animation at frame 1.
- **End Frame `330.000`:** Again, this can be set at any value you wish when you want a part of an animated clip. For us, we want to render the entire project, so we put the last frame we animated.
- **By Frame `1.000`:** We want to render every frame and only one rendered frame per animated frame.
- **Frame Padding `4`:** When Maya gets ready to render animations, it does so as a collection of stills. The frame padding is essentially how many zeros go before the frame number. This makes the numbering of the frames right when you get ready to import the sequential stills (if you are rendering to stills) into a video editing package.
- **Image Format `AVI (avi)`:** This can be changed to have Maya render to sequential tiffs, jpegs, or a whole slew of other formats. For what we are doing here, we want Maya to render a movie file. AVI files are movie files that will play in a media player or Quicktime player as soon as you are done rendering; no need to import a large collection of sequential stills. When you finally get ready to render a project that is destined for broadcast, sequential tiffs that will be assembled in a nonlinear digital video editing system are a good idea.
- **Camera `camera1`:** The default here is Perspective. However, we have cleverly worked out a camera that stays focused on Birdie (`camera1`), so we want to make sure that Maya is rendering while looking through that view.
- **Resolution/Presets `320×240`:** Although this size will definitely change when you are preparing for final output for initial renderings, 320×240 is a good preview render.

The rest of the settings can remain as they were set for the stills. It is important to notice that when you are ready for final output, you will want to make refinements in the settings such as turning up the Anti-aliasing Quality. You might even choose to use Raytracing. Also, there is a section for Motion Blur that allows Maya to blur shots as it renders to simulate "real" footage. Unfortunately, all of these options add significant rendering time, so use them sparingly and only when you know you have what you want.

On the CD-ROM, you will find a rendered version of Tutorial 10.1. Also, feel free to pick apart the actual tutorial file contained on the CD-ROM for details on how we animated and made adjustments to that animation.

Finally, when all the Render Globals have been set it is time to let Maya do its rendering magic. To render the animation, go to Rendering|Render> Batch Rendering (Options). If you have multiple processors, make sure to check the **Use All Available Processors** button. Hit **Batch Render** and Maya will begin rendering the project. If you look at the bottom-right corner of your screen, you will get updates on where Maya is in the rendering process. It will be slow, but sooner or later, your finished piece will be ready to play.

By default, rendered clips are stored in the Images folder in your Project directory. Watch for it there and play it in your media player of choice.

CONCLUSION

We have covered an awful lot through the pages of this book. Through the course of the tutorials, you have looked at basic modeling techniques of NURBS surfaces, Polygon objects, and subdivision surfaces. We looked at how to create visual interest through color, bump, and other attributes assigned to materials that were placed on our surfaces. We explored Maya's lighting scheme—how to create lights, alter them, and fake complex lighting schemes. Finally, we have taken an overview of how to animate in Maya.

Unfortunately, we have just scratched the surface of all of these areas. The great power of Maya is complex. The techniques and tricks of Maya are wide and varied, and must be explored. However, with the information gained in this book, you now have the vocabulary and the theoretical knowledge to understand the discussions and advanced tutorials you will find throughout the Internet and in other volumes.

Although you are probably not a Maya master quite yet, you should feel confident in the skills you have explored in this volume. Like any 3D package, successful mastery of Maya takes constant vigilance in continued practice. Work with Maya often—daily, if possible—to keep the skills gained here, and explore new corners of the vast realm called Maya.

A

WHICH HARDWARE TO USE?

Appendix A's title is a complicated question. Without a doubt, Maya is a demanding piece of software not for the faint of heart or weakling hardware setup. Further, different animators will have different levels of need. If you are a hobbyist and are using Maya as an interesting toy to fool around with shapes and basic animation, you probably have no need for the $5,000 super-duper-show-7-trillion-polys-per-second-render-film-resolution-scenes-in-less-than-a-second system. But, if your animation jobs are lined out the door, and quickly realizing projects in Maya is the key to your success, the previously mentioned system is probably a necessity.

Because of this complexity, it's difficult to define what system or type of system you *need*. In this appendix, we will look at "Qualified Hardware" and break down the basic components of a computer that are necessary for using Maya effectively. Remember that this discussion is by no means exhaustive, and many parts of it will be largely subjective. As with any large purchase, make sure to do your homework, ask trusted experts, read reviews, and research carefully before upgrading your existing system or buying a new one.

MAYA'S QUALIFIED HARDWARE

Alias|Wavefront includes an "official" list of "approved" systems that are certified to run well with Maya. This chart is usually located on the Alias|Wavefront Web site under the title of "Qualified Hardware Chart" or in the Support section under "Qualified Hardware." These lists represent hardware solutions that have been tested successfully by Maya. Now, this definitely does not mean that Maya will not run on other systems—in fact, Maya will run on multiple systems not remotely mentioned on

Maya's Qualified Hardware list, including some that were built from scratch. However, if you have more money than time, purchasing these qualified systems makes sure that you are up and running with Maya out of the box.

Mac Systems

If you are among the Apple faithful, or are looking for an alternative to Windows-based machines, the choices are clear and fairly limited. As of this writing, the qualified Macs for running Maya are as follows:

SYSTEM	GRAPHICS CARD	OS X
G4 Systems, 800 MHz and faster	ATI Radeon 8500 Mac Edition	10.1.3 (5Q45)+ Driver 1.1.5
G4 Systems, 800 MHz and faster	nVidia GeForce 4 MX	10.1.3 (5Q45)
G4 iMac Systems, 700 MHz and faster	nVidia GeForce 2 MX iMac	10.1.3 (5Q45)
G4 Systems, 450 MHz and faster	nVidia GeForce 3	10.1.1 (5M28) 10.1.2 (5P48)
G4 Systems, 450 MHz and faster	nVidia GeForce 2 MX	10.1.1 (5M28)
G4 Systems, 450 MHz and faster	ATI Radeon Mac Edition	10.1.1 (5M28) 10.1.2 (5P48)
G4 Systems, 450 MHz and faster	ATI Rage 128 Pro	10.1.1 (5M28)
Powerbook G4 [Titanium]	ATI Mobility Radeon "Rage M6"	10.1.1 (5M28)
Powerbook G4 [Titanium]	ATI Mobility Rage 128*"Rage M3"	10.1.1 (5M28)

* Significant limitations exist for this card.

An important thing to note is that everything but the highest-end Macs usually come with video cards that you will want to replace. The video card list in the machines listed above are full of caveats (make sure to see the Alias|Wavefront Web site for details). If you have the cash after purchasing a good Mac, you should seriously look into upgrading the video card. Although the latest round of Macs include the nVidia Geforce 4 Titanium (not a shabby card), most Macs still have comparatively weak cards. If you are serious about using Maya on Mac, consider upgrading to as nice a card as possible. See the video card discussion later in this appendix.

Now, this means that if you have or plan to purchase an iMac or Powerbook, you are stuck (as there are really no video card upgrade options). For this reason, I would really not recommend buying either of these two types of systems for serious Maya work. Although they will seem to be snappy when placing a few quick primitive shapes, they will become entirely too slow for poly-heavy projects down the road. If you are serious about using Mac for Maya, get a robust G4 tower system. With the recent announcement of all dual-processor systems for towers, you can purchase decent horsepower for reasonable prices.

LINUX SYSTEMS

Ah, the Linux lovers. Folks who know Linux typically know more about hardware than people should. So, besides listing the approved systems here, we will leave the Linux discussion alone.

COMPANY	MODEL	WEB
sgi	Visual Workstation 230/330/550	www.sgi.com
HP	HP Workstation X1000/X1100/X2000/X2100/X4000	www.hp.com
IBM	IBM MPRO 6850	www.ibm.com
Compaq	W6000/W8000	www.compaq.com

A great thing about the Linux community is that they tend to be well connected. Make sure that if you plan to run Maya on Linux that you put out the feelers amongst your Linux contacts to find the ideal system for you.

PC SYSTEMS

As of this writing the "qualified" systems were listed as follows:

COMPANY	MODEL	WEB
sgi	Visual Workstation 320, 540	www.sgi.com
sgi	Visual Workstation 230, 330, 550	www.sgi.com
sgi	Visual Workstation Zx10	www.sgi.com
Boxx	3DBOXX R1	www.boxxtech.com

(continued)

COMPANY	MODEL	WEB
Compaq	Professional Workstation 6300	www.compaq.com
Compaq	Professional Workstation AP 400, 500, 550	www.compaq.com
Compaq	Professional Workstation SP700	www.compaq.com
Compaq	Professional Workstation 6000	www.compaq.com
Compaq	Professional Workstation EVO 6000, 8000	www.compaq.com
Dell [1]	Precision Workstation 210, 410, 610	www.dell.com
Dell [1]	Precision Workstation 220, 420, 620	www.dell.com
Dell [1]	Precision Workstation 330, 530	www.dell.com
Dell [1]	Precision Workstation 340	www.dell.com
Dell [1]	Precision Workstation M40 (with nVidia Quadro2 Go)	www.dell.com
HP	HP Workstation X1000, X1100, X2000, X2100, X4000	www.hp.com
IBM	Intellistation E Pro 6836, 6846	www.ibm.com
IBM	Intellistation M Pro 6868, 6849, 6850, 6229	www.ibm.com
IBM	Intellistation Z Pro 6866	www.ibm.com
IBM	Thinkpad A31p (with ATI FireGL 7800 mobile)	www.ibm.com
Intergraph	TDZ 2000 Graphics Workstation	www.intergraph.com

This list will undoubtedly be updated again soon as new systems will continue to be developed and tested. As Maya 4.5 matures and more folks use it, new systems will look to be certified.

Remember that many times manufacturers have other systems that work great with Maya that they (the manufacturer, not Alias|Wavefront) have tested extensively. For instance, Boxx Technologies has certified their R1 series of Dual-Athlon machines. Indeed, these machines work great (it is the machine this book was written on). However, if you are strictly an Intel computer user, Boxx Technologies also make the S-Series that are Dual-Xeon equipped. Of course, these Dual-Xeon systems also run Maya like a dream—Boxx has tested the setup extensively. Now, just because a manufacturer makes a certified system does not mean that all of their systems play well with Maya. However, if you can talk to a living knowledgeable person at the manufacturing companies, they will be anxious to tell you of other feasible alternatives. So, do your research, but make sure that you do not limit yourself to the models shown earlier in this section.

IMPORTANT COMPONENTS

If you purchase a system off of Maya's Qualified Hardware list, you will receive a machine (minus a monitor, probably) that has all of the things you need. However, if you are more adventurous or cannot afford the systems listed on Maya's "official" list, there are some general guidelines of hardware that you *must* have, and guidelines of hardware that you *should* have.

Processor(s)

This is definitely a must have, although there is a fairly wide range of possibilities here. As you know, the *processor* is kind of the like the brain of your 3D station. It makes the calculations necessary for creating complex 3D in real time, and especially for rendering your projects. Although there are areas of calculations when you are building a project that make heavy use of the processor (like dynamics); the biggest difference you will see in different speed processors is in rendering times.

What you need and what you want in processors is an interesting question. There are some true *needs* depending on what platform you are working with. For instance, if you are a Mac 3D artist you *need* a G4 processor. I have run Maya fairly smoothly on a 667MHz as well as a dual 1.25GHz machine. The leap in price is substantial but the leap in performance (except for rendering speed) is not that noticeable.

Similarly, if you are running a PC, you will be surprised at how small a machine will run Maya successfully. A P3 is usually plenty of firepower when you are first getting started. I have even used Maya on a Celeron-equipped machine, although this begins to really push things. Naturally, if you can use a P4 or similar generation AMD chips, you get much better performance and especially better rendering speeds. However, when you are learning Maya, there's no need to drop four grand on the latest and greatest machines. In one of our labs here at the University of the Incarnate Word, we run Maya on P3 800MHz machines quite well. These machines do have decent video cards (nVidia Quadro 2) and that makes for fairly smooth operation.

Usually, the bleeding edge processors have an inexplicably heavy jump in price over the next fastest processor choice. In general, the absolute fastest processor is rarely worth the price for most Maya users; especially because that same processor will drop by hundreds of dollars in six weeks when the next speed bump occurs. However, most folks cannot buy a new machine very often, so you want to make sure and purchase a machine that stays with you long enough to get your money's worth. So, a general rule that I use is to find the absolute fastest machine available, and then look for its little brother. Typically, the little brother is still a strong machine with good legs that still comes at a huge discount over its top-of-the-line counterpart.

A Note on Multiple Processors

Maya is one of several 3D software packages that will actually make use of more than one processor. Although this is never truly a "double-the-speed" situation, there is usually a very worthwhile drop in rendering times when you have two processor brains calculating those light rays. Typically, dual processors render 1.6-1.7 times faster than a single processor unit. Although you do not see a jump in the speed of the interface, dual processors help a lot if you do not have a render farm at your disposal.

Video Cards

Video cards are responsible for many things, but the most important is how quickly Maya interacts with you, the user. A larger, faster video card can display more polygons at once and refresh the screen more quickly than smaller ones. If you are coming from a 3D package other than Maya and have dealt with large projects, you have undoubtedly experienced the move-your-camera-wait-five-seconds-for-screen-redraw dilemma. Usually, you fix this problem by turning off lights, or viewing things as isoparms or wireframes. Maya is much better at providing a great OpenGL accelerated experience when moving models or moving around models. However, this is still dependent on how much muscle your video card has.

As always, bigger is typically better. Putting good money into a video card is usually worth the investment. Having a snappy interface makes the work much more intuitive and the computer appears to think as fast as you do.

Luckily, the cost of video cards has continued to drop as the speed of the cards continues to rise. Remember that not all consumer cards are appropriate to work with Maya. As of this writing, Alias|Wavefront includes the following cards as "Qualified."

COMPANY	GRAPHICS CONTROLLER	DRIVER VERSION ON WINDOWS XP PRO	DRIVER VERSION ON WINDOWS 2000 PRO (SP2)	DRIVER VERSION ON WINDOWS NT 4.0 (SP6A)
3Dlabs	Oxygen GVX1		2.16-0676	
3Dlabs	Oxygen GVX1-Pro		2.16-0691	
3Dlabs	Oxygen GVX210		Not qualified.	2.16.0388
3Dlabs	Oxygen GVX420		2.16-0691	
3Dlabs	Wildcat 4110		05.03.01.15	04.02.03.02
3Dlabs	Wildcat 5000	06.04.01.10	06.04.01.10	
3Dlabs	Wildcat II 5110		05.03.01.15	04.02.03.02
3Dlabs	Wildcat III 6110	06.05.01.16	05.05.02.09	
3Dlabs	Wildcat III 6210	06.05.01.16	05.05.02.09	
HP	FX5		1.08	1.08
HP	FX10		1.08	1.08
nVidia	Quadro2 Pro	5.13.01.1570	5.00.2195.1241 or 5.13.01.1420	
nVidia	Quadro2 MXR		5.00.2195.1241 or 5.13.01.1420	
nVidia	Quadro2 EX		5.00.2195.1241 or 5.13.01.1420	
nVidia	Quadro DCC	5.13.01.1570	5.00.2195.1241 or 5.13.01.1420	
nVidia	Quadro2 Go (in Dell Precision M40)	5.13.01.1427		
nVidia	GeForce2		**NOT QUALIFIED**	
nVidia	GeForce3		**NOT QUALIFIED**	
nVidia	Quadro4 700/750/ 900 XGL	29.80	29.80	
ATI	Fire GL1		5.00.2195.1118	
ATI	Fire GL2 (or the Dell 2077 driver)	5.12.2195.2082	5.12.2195.2082	
ATI	Fire GL4		5.12.2195.2074	
ATI	Fire GL4-DUAL		5.12.2195.2074	
ATI	Fire GL7800 mobile (In IBM Thinkpad A31P)		5.13.1.6080	
ATI	Fire GL8800	6.12.10.3035	5.12.2195.3035	
sgi	cobalt		5.1.0 / 5.2.1	5.1.0 / 5.2.1
sgi/nVidia	VPro 32/64		5.00.2195.1241	4.00.1381.1241

A discussion of important details about these graphics cards follows.

This of course does not mean that all consumer level cards are incompatible. It also does not mean that all of these professional cards work without flaw; in fact, when you look at this list on the Alias|Wavefront Web site, you will also find a huge list of issues that exist with each card.

In general, if you can afford a "professional" grade card (especially 3D Labs, Elsa, FireGL, nVidia, and Oxygen cards), buy it. If not, purchase the biggest, fastest card you can afford but keep your receipt. Make sure to experiment with all sorts of objects and all your pull-down menus within Maya, and return the card if necessary. It really is not that scary a process to use an unapproved video card but issues do arise.

The process of picking a video card does indeed seem mysterious. There appear to be hardly any cards that are perfect for all aspects of Maya, so do not worry about small issues. The up-front pains are worth it when working with video cards, as once you have the card that is right for your work flow and budget, Maya will feel more smoothly interactive than any 3D applications you have ever worked with.

If you had to choose where to put your money as you built a Maya system, this would be the place. A good video card is vital to effective Maya use.

RAM

Only one piece of advice here: get lots of it. RAM is cheap these days and anything less than 512MB can get downright painful. As your skills increase and the complexity of your projects rises, your RAM requirements will blossom. Insufficient RAM can really slow you down so if you have the budget, max out your board. Besides the video card, this is the second most important place to put your money as you develop your Maya box.

Monitor

The monitor is the one piece of hardware that you spend the most time looking at. However, many users scrimp on their monitors in an attempt to beef up their central processing units (CPUs). Spend some good money on your monitor. Going into all the dot-pitch, refresh rates, and other issues of the monitor, and whether to go cathode ray tube (CRT) or liquid crystal display (LCD) is beyond the scope of this volume. However, remember that the size of icons remains the same, so if your monitor only does 640×480 or even 800x600, your actual working space is severely limited.

In general, make sure your monitor does 1024×768 with a high refresh rate (75-85KHz) at *the very least.* You will be much happier and your eyes and head will thank you when running a nice size (19-inch to 21-inch) monitor running at 1600x1200 at 85KHz. A good monitor can last you through several generations of CPUs. Remember, you will be looking at that piece of machinery for countless hours as you learn and master Maya–get something you are really happy looking at.

Mouse

Three-button, three-button, three-button (and that does not mean two buttons and a scroll wheel). Honestly, the standard two-button mouse or the "luxury" two-button with a middle scroll wheel are just not what you need when using Maya. As was discussed in Chapter 1, Maya uses a very quick, effective method of moving the camera around your digital world. However, it does this by combinations of all three buttons on your mouse. A true three-button mouse is not a huge expense but can really speed along your work process.

CONCLUSION

People get passionate about the computers they build or buy. Everyone has an opinion about what machine/video card/RAM brand/platform/OS is the best. In reality, your Maya box, whether it be an out-of-the-box-ready-to-go Apple, Dell, HP, or Boxx, or built from scratch to match the specs of these other boxes, it can and should be a help in your 3D creation process. Make sure that you are not cheating yourself in the long run by selling yourself short on the machine as you learn.

B

CUSTOMIZING THE MAYA USER INTERFACE

Throughout the earlier chapters, we have looked briefly at various ways to change the user interface (UI) of Maya to accommodate a particular work flow. This appendix serves as the workout gym for your Maya interface. Although it does not cover every single way to modify the Maya UI, it does provide steps on the methods that are most commonly used and most helpful in trimming down the interface fat present in some areas and building up the interface muscle needed in others.

GENERAL OVERVIEW

There is a lot going on when you open Maya. As discussed throughout this volume, there are so many things going on that Maya hides many of the available tools just to keep things cleaned up a bit. Through hotboxes, Marking menus, and other such tricks, Maya allows you to get to those options that are not immediately accessible rather easily. However, sometimes this is just too slow. Sometimes, you want a collection of tools to be *right there*—easy to grab, easy to use, easy to find.

Additionally, the individual panels that are present and created by default when you first open Maya may not provide you with the spaces and tools that you wish to use. A great thing about Maya is that nearly every panel is customizable; nearly every tool can be organized where you wish it. You can really create the interface to match what you would like it to be.

Windows

When Maya is first opened, all of its tools, pull-down menus, and panels are contained within one large customizable window. However, because there is a limited amount of screen real estate, you will find only a limited number of the vast types of tools available in Maya. As we discussed throughout this volume, Maya allows you to create and edit a large variety of functions and characteristics of your scene through collections of editors. There are *a lot* of editors. Because of this, most are hidden until you choose to call them up.

All editors may be called up as floating windows that you can move wherever you wish within the interface. To access any editor, see the Window pull-down menu where all of the editors are organized by General, Rendering, Animation, and Relationship options. Figure B.1 shows a

FIGURE B.1   The Window pull-down menu (accessible in any module) allows you to access editors and other important tools like the Outliner and Hypergraph.

quick breakdown of what each sub-menu of the editors presents. Many of these particular editors are used throughout this volume.

Notice also that within the Window pull-down menu, you can access the Settings/Preferences sub-menu. This is a huge part of customization and later in this appendix we will be looking exclusively at these tools.

Managing Panels

Maya's interface is divided up into easily recognizable panels. *Panels* are the large sections that contain either editors (Outliner, Hypergraph, Trax Editor, Relationship Editor, and so on) or camera viewpoints. In general, panels are a bit different from the windows we just looked at as panels are *docked* into place within the interface. For instance, when you select Window>Outliner, the Outliner that appears is a window—it floats through the interface. These windows have the advantage of being easy to move around when you need them out of the way. However, this also means that this window is always on top of some other part of the interface. You can also view things like the Outliner as a panel—that is, the window gets nestled into the interface occupying its own real estate and is never in the way.

When Maya is first opened, there is one large panel in the middle of the screen generally referred to as the Workspace. Notice that this Workspace has its own collection of pull-down menus (Figure B.2).

We already looked at and made extensive use of switching from one view to four views by quickly hitting the **Spacebar**. This divides this main Workspace panel into four smaller panels—each with a different

FIGURE B.2 The main Workspace panel has its own collection of pull-down menus. These menus allow for the modification of the content of the panel.

view of the scene. An important thing that happens here is that each of these new panels has its own collection of pull-down menus. Among these is the Panels pull-down menu (Figure B.3). This allows you to control what exactly is contained within each individual panel, or even control how all the panels are rearranged.

The most general change you can make is to select Panels>Layouts and then choose one of the many split options that are available. The names of the options are fairly self-explanatory, so we will not detail them here. Suffice it to say they allow for a multitude of organizations for your panels (Figure B.4).

Still within each panel, and within the Panels pull-down menu, there is Panels>Saved Layouts. Here, you are given several options to select a variety of prepared collections of panels. These collections of layouts will

FIGURE B.3   The Panel pull-down menu is the source of rearranging the Workspace.

FIGURE B.4   A quick look at a few variations possible through the pull-down menu within each panel, Panel>Layouts.

FIGURE B.5   A few examples of some of the Panels>Saved Layouts options. Notice that many of these saved layout combinations include panels containing things like the Hypershade, Outliner, or the Trax Editor.

also include various editors. You may find that at different times of your work flow, some of these saved layouts will be just the ticket (Figure B.5).

New to Maya 4.0 and later are a collection of buttons along the left side of the interface (in the Toolbox) below the QWERTY tools (Figure B.6). These contain collections of saved layouts that can be selected with a quick click.

FIGURE B.6   Saved layouts available in the Toolbox.

To change or add new saved layouts to these buttons within the Tool-box, simply RMB-click any of the extant icons for layouts and select the new desired layout (Figure B.7).

Notice that the last option within Panels>Saved Layouts is Edit Layouts. The resulting dialog box (Figure B.8) allows you to create custom layouts that can be pulled up again at a later time. Once you begin to establish a work flow and find where you prefer to have each of your panels for various times, this option becomes very handy.

Finally, still within the collection of pull-down menus in each panel, notice the Panels>Panel option (Figure B.9). Here, you can define manu-

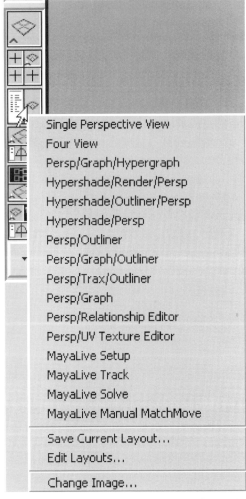

FIGURE B.7   To customize the Toolbox's collection of saved layouts, RMB-click on the tool to change and select the new desired layout.

FIGURE B.8   You can create your own saved layouts with Panels>Saved Layouts>Edit Layouts to be called up again at will. Remember that Maya saves these created layouts within the defined project file.

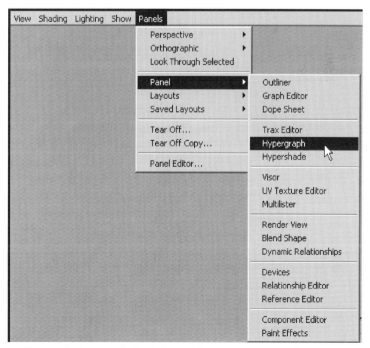

FIGURE B.9   To define an individual panel for a temporary panel arrangement, you can define one at a time what each panel should contain.

ally what each individual panel will contain. For temporary setups, this works well.

SHOWING AND HIDING PARTS OF THE INTERFACE

In the first image of this appendix we looked at a general overview of the Maya UI. Maya works hard to minimize the tools used for visual tool buttons and maximize the Workspace. However, this might not be enough for you. Sometimes, you might want to get rid of (or show) parts or all of the UI.

The standard way to pick and choose what parts of the interface are visible is with the Display>UI Elements pull-down menu, and then by selecting or deselecting the parts of the interface you wish to show or hide (Figure B.10).

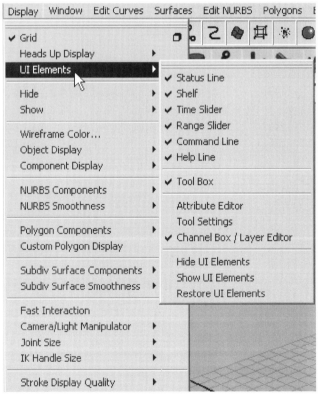

FIGURE B.10   The Display>UI Elements pull-down menu allows you to define what parts of the UI are to be seen and what is to be hidden.

Of interest is that the first two options (Status Line and Shelf) are elements of the UI that appear at the top when activated. The next four (Time Slider, Range Slider, Command Line, and Help Line) are all parts of the UI that appear across the bottom. The next one (Tool Box) is for UI elements on the left and the last three (Attribute Editor, Tool Settings, and Channel Box/Layer Editor) are for panels that will be nested along the far right edge.

Notice the last three options of Hide UI Elements, Show UI Elements, and Restore UI Elements (which restores all of the default elements). Hide UI Elements hides all the elements leaving you with a Workspace that takes up the entire screen (Figure B.11). Show UI Elements brings all the elements back into the UI.

FIGURE B.11 Hide UI.

ADJUSTING UI ELEMENTS THROUGH PREFERENCES

We have looked at a wide variety of interactively altering the user interface to suit our needs. The obvious method of optimizing the interface is through the method you are probably used to in most other 3D applications—editing preferences.

To access Maya's UI Preferences, select Windows>Settings/Preferences>Preferences. Now, this collection of preferences entails more than just the user interface. For this appendix we will only be discussing the first three sections: Interface, UI Elements, and Misc.

The first set of interface preferences shown in Figure B.12 allows you to define what will be the default module (Modeling, Animation, and so on) when you first open the application. In addition, this Preferences window allows you to gain further screen real estate by choosing to show or hide things like the Menubar (in both the Main window and in Panels) and the Title Bar. If you want to have the main Workspace take up absolutely the entire screen, you can use Display>UI Elements>Hide UI Elements (as we discussed earlier) and then here in the Preferences, you can uncheck the Show Menubar and Show Title Bar options. The result will be an interface devoid of everything but the Workspace.

FIGURE B.12 Windows>Settings/Preferences>Preferences allows you to define further issues of how the interface will be displayed and interact with you, the user.

If you indeed hide every bit of the UI, remember that holding the **Spacebar** still allows you to access the various pull-down menus you will need. Be aware though, that there are sometimes problems with the hotbox. I have been unable to pin down the problem. However, in one of our labs at the University of the Incarnate Word, Maya consistently crashes on our Dell systems when students attempt to make heavy use of the hotbox. Fortunately, using the new Maya 4.5 on my Boxx R1i, I have yet to experience a crash related to the hotbox.

Other options in this dialog box are self-explanatory, so we will move on to the second window of this Preferences window—UI Elements (Figure B.13).

This window allows you another way to define which UI elements to display. This is just like the Display>UI Elements> collection of pull-down menus.

The last part of the UI preferences is largely not of note except for the Panel Configurations area. This allows you to define whether your collection of panel organizations created for a specific project will be saved with the file or not. Similarly, you can set the default interface layout to the one you work in most comfortably at early parts of your work flow.

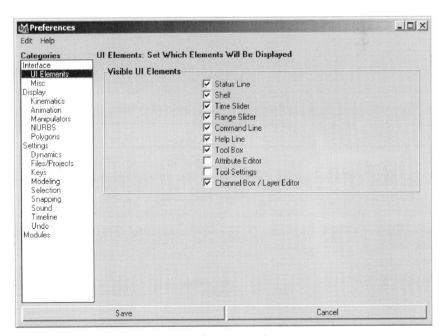

FIGURE B.13 The second pane of the Preferences window.

FIGURE B.14   The final UI preferences pane.

EDITING INTERACTION

Up to now, we have been looking at adjusting the visual UI of Maya. The rest of this appendix will be looking quickly at how to optimize the way that Maya interacts with you, the user. Although this is not a visual interface alteration (for the most part), it still can dramatically affect your work flow and consequently, the effectiveness of Maya as a tool for you.

EDITING HOTKEY CONFIGURATIONS

Also within the Window>Settings/Preferences> is the Hotkeys option. Selecting this opens the Hotkey Editor (Figure B.15). Simply put, this editor allows you to choose the command you wish to assign a hotkey to by finding the pull-down menu where the command is located in the Categories column. Then, find the command in the Commands column. If the command already has a hotkey assigned to it, this will be displayed in the Current Hotkeys column. If not, you can enter a hotkey in the Assign New Hotkey area of the pane. Notice that you can change the modifier here as well. If the key or key-modifier combination is already in use by some other command, you will be warned within the Assign New Hotkey

FIGURE B.15   The Hotkey Editor. Of primary use to us is the top part of this window. It allows you to define any command to a hotkey of your choice.

area. If all is well, or if you are willing to overwrite an extant hotkey setting with a new one, click the **Assign** button and your new hotkey is ready for use.

CHANGING INTERFACE COLORS

OK, so we may be getting a bit esoteric here but being able to change colors also has some very legitimate functional issues as well. Depending on the textures you are using within your scene, you may want to have different colors represented on your screen as you work. Or, maybe you are colorblind and the blues and greens just do not work for you; or perhaps you just do not like working in a gray world. No matter what the reason, the Window>Settings/Preferences>Colors option allows you to change the color of just about every single part of the interface. Want a black background as you work? No problem. In the mood for pastel colors on the X, Y, Z transform tools? Again, easy to switch here. Do you find the CV purple annoying or the isoparm blue deceiving? All of this is easy to change within this one window. For this book, we will leave all the colors as their defaults, but be aware that this is the place to colorize your Maya interface world (Figure B16).

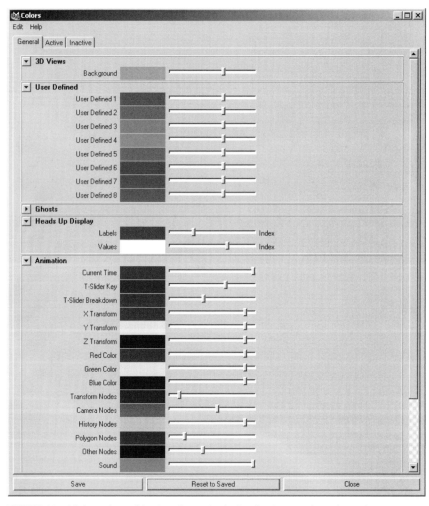

FIGURE B.16 All the colors of the interface—including backgrounds, tools, and components—can be changed through Window>Settings/Preferences>Colors.

CUSTOMIZING MARKING MENUS

Marking menus, as discussed earlier are ways to bring collections of tools, or even pull-down menus, to the visible forefront of your interface upon demand. Marking menus are pulled up by clicking on them and holding down a particular key on your keyboard. For instance, some Marking menus are located within the hotbox (pulled up by pressing and holding the **Spacebar**). These Marking menus are set up around the perimeter of the hotbox itself (Figure B.17).

For instance, Figure B.17 shows the hotbox activated. By clicking the LMB on the north quadrant of this space, a Marking menu that allows you to choose the panel layout appears. Although we will not go through all the extant Marking menus here, take a minute to look and explore them; they are located around the hotbox.

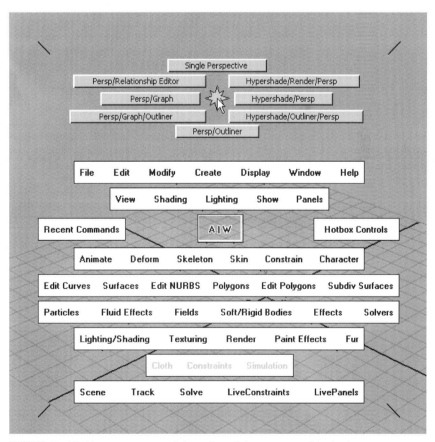

FIGURE B.17   Marking menus around the points of the compass of the hotbox.

The important thing that we will talk about here is how to edit the Marking menus that exist. Using Window>Settings/Preferences>Marking Menus, you will be presented with a window that lists the extant Marking menus, where they are, and how they are manipulated when pulled up (Figure B.18).

To edit an existing Marking menu, simply double-click the name of the menu, or select it, and hit the **Edit Marking Menu** button. A new window will open (Figure B.19) that will show the Marking menu. You can test the Marking menu by clicking any of the menu items shown and Maya will act as though the Marking menu is in use. Or, if you RMB-click on one of the menu items, you will get a pop-up menu allowing you to edit, delete, or add a pop-up submenu to the menu item (Figure B.20).

Notice that this window shown in Figure B.19 also allows you to see what the Marking menu will look like with the box in the bottom-left corner. You may also change the name of a Marking menu.

Click **Save** to save your changes or **Close** to discard them.

FIGURE B.18 The Marking Menus editing window gives you the opportunity to alter existing Marking menus or even create your own.

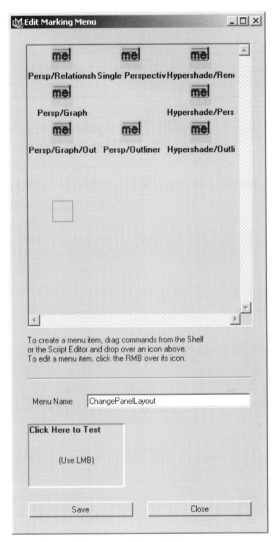

FIGURE B.19   Editing an existing Marking menu.

FIGURE B.20   Changing a menu item within a Marking menu.

CREATING MARKING MENUS FROM SCRATCH

In general, it's probably better to leave the existing Marking menus as is. However, the window shown in Figure B.20 can do more than just edit existing menus.

Notice that besides **Deleting and Editing Marking Menus**, there is also a button for **Create Marking Menu**. When you click this button a window similar to the editing one shown in Figures B.19 and B.20 opens as a blank canvas (Figure B.21). This allows you to create a Marking menu of your favorite tools from scratch.

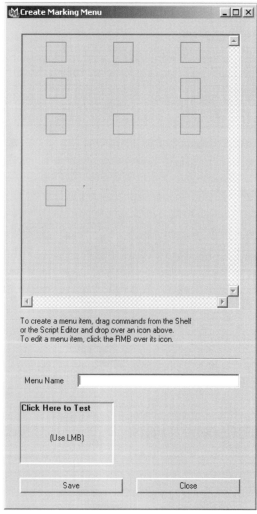

FIGURE B.21   The empty Marking menu window allows you to begin creating your own collection of vital tools.

Each of the empty menu item boxes can be filled by MMB-dragging a tool from a Shelf. This, of course, means that if you wish to add any tool to the Marking menu, you must first add it to the Shelf (select the tool while holding down the **Shift-Ctrl-Alt** buttons). You can always delete the tool or item from the Shelf afterward.

Figure B.22 shows a new menu called FrequentPrimitives that has a collection of frequently used shapes. Notice that this new Marking menu's name has no spaces (a typical Maya convention). Also notice that the figure shows a test of how the Marking menu would appear.

After clicking **Save** and **Close**, you can decide in the main window how to pull up this Marking menu. In the Settings section, you can

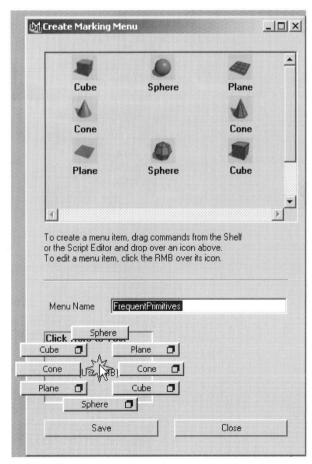

FIGURE B.22 A custom created Marking menu. Each of the primitives shown here were first added to the Shelf and then MMB-dragged into position within the Marking menu.

choose to have the Marking menu be part of the hotbox or, more effectively, choose to assign it to a new hotkey (Figure B.23).

If you choose to assign a Marking menu to a hotkey, you need to be
sure and pull up the Hotkey Editor (Window>Setting/Preferences>
Hotkeys). Here, you can find User Marking Menus in the Categories column. Select the **Marking Menu in the Commands** column and then
assign your desired hotkey within the Assign New Hotkey area (Figure
B.24). Upon saving and closing, your Marking menu is ready to use. In
Figure B.25, when pressing **Ctrl-F** (as assigned in the Hotkeys Editor)
and LMB-clicking the interface, the Marking menu indeed appears.

FIGURE B.23 Choosing how to access a Marking menu.

FIGURE B.24   Assigning a hotkey to a newly created Marking menu within the Hotkey Editor.

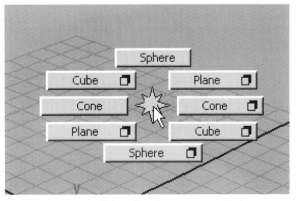

FIGURE B.25   Successful results of creating new Marking menu and assignment of custom hotkey.

CONTROLLING SHELVES

By default, Maya's interface displays the Shelf. The Shelf is a tool where frequently used tools can be stored for quick access. We have looked at how to hide and show this shelf, and we have alluded to how to add elements to the shelf while discussing the creation of Marking menus.

Window>Settings>Preferences>Shelves brings up a window that allows for the creation and organization of custom Shelves (Figure B.26). However, because Shelves are a visual tool, this editor is a rather clumsy way of editing a Shelf. Instead, in this section, we will look at how to do the same things within the interface.

FIGURE B.26 Editing Shelves.

Editing Shelf Content

Figure B.27 shows the default Shelf visible when Maya is first opened. It contains a smattering of commonly used tools from all sorts of modules. To add a tool to the Shelf, simply hold down **Shift-Ctrl-Alt** (okay, so it's not so simple after all), and select the tool you wish to add. You can select a tool from any pull-down menu (remember to keep the **Shift-Ctrl-Alt** keys held down). The tool will appear on the Shelf.

Using the MMB, you can click and drag any tool to a new location on the Shelf. This allows you to organize a collection of tools into clusters. No-

FIGURE B.27   The default Shelf.

tice that to the far right of the Shelf is a small Trashcan icon. You can re-move a tool from the shelf by MMB-dragging the tool to this Trashcan icon.

Creating New Shelves

At the far left of the Shelf are two small tools (Figure B.28). The bottom allows you to create or edit Shelves (Figure B.29).

Of interest to us is the New Shelf option. Selecting this will prompt you for a name of the new Shelf. You may wish to nest a collection of your favorite modeling or lighting tools. No matter what your Shelf will hold, enter the name with no spaces or "strange" characters.

You will then be shown an empty Shelf ready to be filled with the **Shift-Ctrl-Alt** method.

Once you have begun creating custom Shelves, you can move through them with the top button at the far left of the Shelves. Clicking this pops up the extant shelves allowing you to choose which one to bring forward (Figure B.30).

FIGURE B.28   Buttons nesting tools to control the Shelves.

FIGURE B.29   Pop-up menu allowing for creation of new Shelves or editing of extant ones.

FIGURE B.30 Choosing which Shelf is to be visible.

Remember that all of this could be done with the Shelf Editor but is accomplished more intuitively by using the visual methods listed here.

CONCLUSION

These are not all the ways to alter Maya's interface. However, the methods listed here are by far the most commonly used. In most applications, altering the interface is typically not part of the game plan. However, because of the sheer number of tools within Maya, and the layering and nesting that goes on to get to them, you can increase your productivity tremendously by taking a few moments to organize your panels, windows, and shelves to match your work flow. Notice that in the Shelves Editor (Window>Settings/Preferences>Shelves) and the Panels Editor (Window>Settings/Preferences>Panels), you can save and load previously organized configurations allowing you to bring your interface organization from project to project—or even machine to machine.

You might not want or need to organize your interface any differently when you are first learning Maya. You will notice that in this book, we are using the default UI organizations. However, as you become more familiar with Maya and your own work flow, customize Maya to your style. Doing so helps make Maya do your bidding and not the other way around.

C

CREATING EFFECTIVE TEXTURE MAPS

I n Chapters 7 and 8, we looked at how to create materials that could be placed on surfaces to give them color, bump, and other believable attributes. Besides just adding color to these various attributes, we also looked at how to bring in textures that defined further what the material should look like. Although Maya has some procedural textures, and even has some canned Shaders, the best looking models make use of custom-built materials that come from custom textures.

ON THE CD

In Chapter 8, we spent a bit of time applying a custom texture of a tile floor to our room. That texture was included on the CD-ROM (Tutorials/ Chapter08/Textures) and it was set conveniently to lay right on the floor and behave in all the ways it should. However, to get such a texture requires a little bit of work outside of Maya. This appendix is essentially a Photoshop tutorial that discusses how to create textures appropriately.

Creating a believable texture usually starts out with a believable photograph. Figure C.1 is a shot taken with a digital camera of the tile in our entry way (yes, that's my foot in the corner). This shot has some good things about it and some problems.

Among the good things about this shot, and things that you should keep in mind when taking photos for use as textures, are the following:

- **The pattern is fairly "straight on."** The vertical lines of the grout between the tiles are all parallel to each other. It is important when creating a texture map that you have no perspective visual in the shot at all. You want to let the 3D application do that for you.
- **The parallel lines are fairly straight in the frame**. This is not a big deal, but you get the most out of a frame if you are careful to have the camera square with any straight elements in the scene.

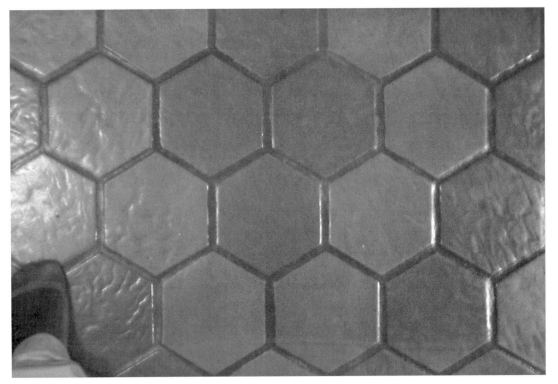

FIGURE C.1   Shot from a digital camera.

- **The scope is wide**. This shot could be focused on one tile but that would create a fairly unsuccessful texture map. The reason this would be unsuccessful is that all the tiled tiles would look exactly the same with no natural variation or interest. If your camera is sufficiently high resolution, you should get as broad a shot of a texture as you can so you have lots of variation to the pattern.

  Some problems include the following:

- **The flash highlights**. If you look on the left side of the photo, there is a yellow highlight from the light in the room. Similarly, the right side has a bit of a highlight along the edge of the tiles from the light in the next room. Although this helps to define the shapes of the tile to our naked eye visually, it causes great havoc when you need to create bump maps from this image.

- **Relatively low contrast**. The image is largely monochromatic. When time comes to create bump maps from it, monochromatic images make it tough to get sufficiently white whites and sufficiently black blacks to get appropriate definition.

FIGURE C.2   Because this image is not prepared, it is seamed and unfit to be replicated across a surface.

- **The image is seamed**. That is, if you took this photo and then added another where it ended, and another after that (Figure C.2), you would be able to see the *seams*—definitive lines that show when each copy of the image starts and ends.

    Luckily, none of these drawbacks are terminal. We can fix all of them with a little bit of Photoshop wizardry. Follow the next tutorial to learn how.

TUTORIAL

ON THE CD

C.1 CREATING SEAMLESS TEXTURES

Step 1: Open the file, `Raw Photo.tif`, from the CD-ROM in Photoshop. It is located at Tutorials>AppendixC.

Step 2: Crop the photo to get rid of feet and bad highlights. My foot in the scene is definitely a problem. Also, the highlights at the extreme left of the image cause some problems. So, to start out, we want to crop those out.

FIGURE C.3 Getting ready to crop the image to get rid of poor sections and create roughly seamless imagery.

Before just cropping too roughly, take a bit of time to look at how you can find ways to crop so that the edges meet (Figure C.3).

Notice that on the left side, the cropping bounding box comes to the edge of the grout, while on the right side, it cuts the grout out and comes to the edge of the tile. Similarly, on the top of the image, we have the bottom of the diamonds of tiles, while the bottom corners of the bottom tiles are cropped out. Finally, notice that you might need to rotate the cropping bounding box slightly to make up for any crookedness that might have snuck into the photo from not having the camera straight on. The cropped image is shown in Figure C.4.

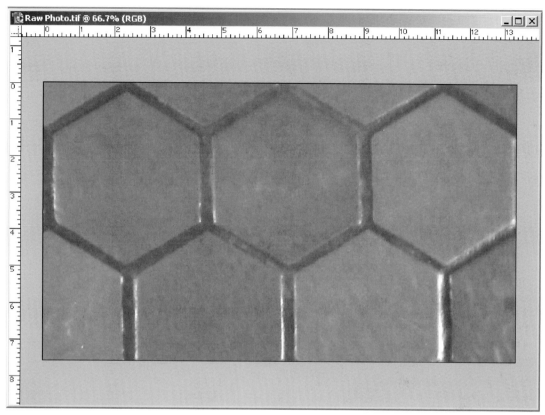

FIGURE C.4   Cropped image.

Step 3: Offset the image to see the seams. Now, even though we have carefully cropped the image, there are still undoubtedly seams where the right edge of the image does not match up perfectly with the left edge. However, it is difficult to see these problems and work them out when they are on the opposite sides of the image. To move them where we can see them and deal with them, select Filter>Other>Offset.

When you do so, a new dialog box will appear similar to Figure C.5. The values of how far to offset are arbitrary but it is important to have the Wrap Around option checked (Figure C.5).

This takes the image and slides it all sideways off the canvas. However, with the Wrap Around activated, it takes the parts of the image that have been offset off the canvas, wraps them around, and brings them onto the other side. The net effect of this offset in both directions is that the seams of the image are now in the middle of the screen where you can work with them. Meanwhile, the edges of the image now are truly seamless.

FIGURE C.5   The Offset Filter dialog box.

You should be able to see the seams fairly clearly, but if not, adjust the levels (or brightness/contrast) until you can see them a bit more clearly.

Step 4: Clone Stamp the seams away. To get rid of the seams, we need to soften the area where they exist. The easiest way to do this is with the Clone Stamp tool (Figure C.6).

FIGURE C.6   The Clone Stamp tool.

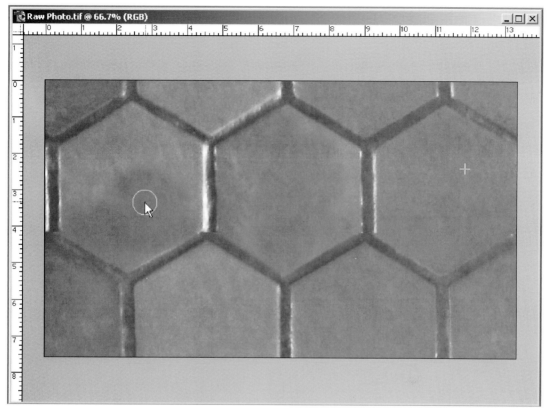

FIGURE C.7   Using the Clone tool to work seams out.

The way this tool works is to define an area you wish to clone from by holding the **Alt** key down (**Option** on a Mac) and LMB-clicking. Then, move the mouse over an area that you wish to clone to, and click-drag. This will clone your source pixels to this new location. This works great because it clones the texture and surfaces of the image (Figure C.7).

Step 5: Offset again. Sometimes, in the process of working seams out, you can accidentally create new seams if you clone too close to the edges. To make sure that things are all on the up and up, select Filter>Other>Offset again and look to see if you can distinguish any seams. If you can, fix them and offset again.

Once all the seams are worked out and repeated offsets reveal a seamless image, you are set. Save the file as `TilesColor.tif`; make sure to save it as a tiff although jpegs and other formats will work in Maya. This image is what we used in the Color attribute of the material we put on the floor of the room tutorials.

Step 6: Create a bump map from this seamless color map. Although Maya will use colored images as a bump map, the best bump maps are grayscale. Select Image>Mode>Grayscale and hit **OK** when Photoshop asks you if you wish to discard color information.

Step 7: Work out artificial bumps created through highlights. A nice thing about the grayscale image is the grout is dark already. For some images, such as bricks, the grout is white. Because Maya interprets grayscale images as the whiter the color, the higher the bump while the darker the color, the lower the receding, you often need to invert images where the whites and blacks are backward.

Because this one is alright, there is no need to do this. However, there are some highlights along certain parts of the tiles (circled in Figure C.8). These

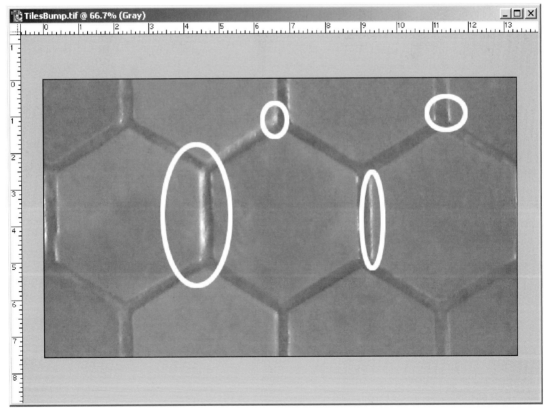

FIGURE C.8 Hightlights created from the light of the photo that will make for inappropriate bumps.

highlights would be interpreted as actual raised sections when Maya looked at them as a bump map. Because of this, we want to calm down these highlights so they do not create undesired artificial hightlights.

There are several ways to do this, but one of the easiest is to use the Clone tool to clone edges of tiles without highlights (Figure C.9).

FIGURE C.9   Getting rid of unwanted highlights.

Step 8: Deepen the grout by adjusting levels and using the Burn tool.
Select Image>Adjustments>Levels to be able to increase the contrast of the document (Figure C.10). You might find again that after level adjustment, you need to work out some too-high highlights.

Finally, use the Burn tool to darken the grout a bit more. Make sure that the Burn brush size is slightly larger than the grout is wide. Also, make sure that

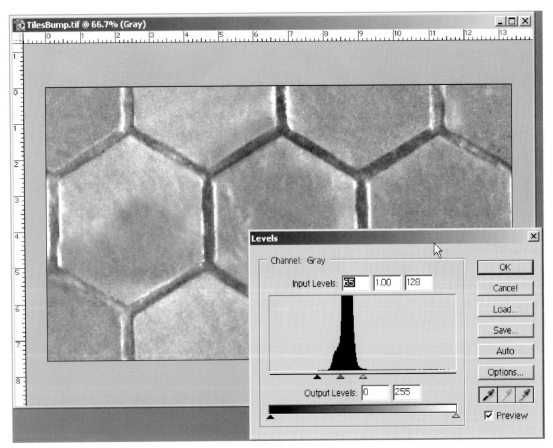

FIGURE C.10   Adjusting levels to create higher contrast.

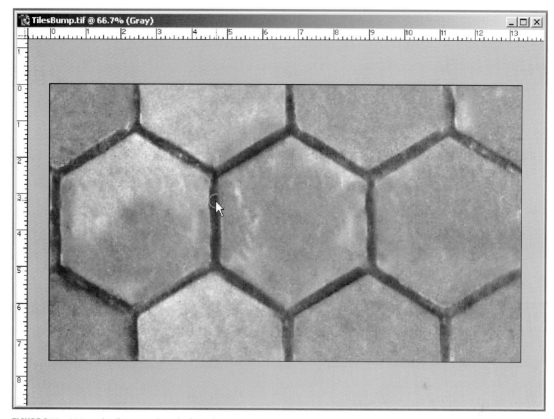

FIGURE C.11   Using the Burn tool to darken the grout.

you have a soft edge on the brush and that you have an opacity of around 40 percent. This way, you get gentle edges and you don't blacken anything too quickly (Figure C.11).

Step 9: Save this image as `TileBump.tif`. Of course, this is the image used as the bump map for the Bump attribute for the floor.

CONCLUSION

Creating good texture maps is an art and takes lots of practice. Remember to prepare the images properly and work out the seams so you will have much more believable images to import as textures. Remember to build each variation texture map off the base color map so that all of your various textures imported into attributes line up.

D

ABOUT THE CD-ROM

Included with this book is a CD-ROM that includes several important things to help you as you work through the concepts and tutorials. When you first open the CD-ROM, you will see two folders: Images and Tutorials. The Images folder includes all the figures contained in the book in full color. For several areas of the book—particularly the ones on texturing and lighting—these full-color images are especially important, so you might want to have them available as you work.

The second part of the CD-ROM is the Tutorials folder. Contained here are all the finished files that show the results of the tutorials we cover. You might find it helpful to pick apart these files to discover details that you feel were left out of the descriptions. Also contained in the Tutorials folder are additional texture maps and other files used in the course of the tutorials.

To use the CD-ROM, just drop it in your CD-ROM drive and open it. All the tutorial files are Maya binaries so they will only open in Maya. The color images are all jpegs and should open with just about anything.

If your machine runs Maya, it will run the CD-ROM. Use it often to augment the descriptions and figures included in this volume.

SYSTEM REQUIREMENTS

To use the CD-ROM, of course, all you need is a machine with a CD-ROM drive and software to view jpgs. However, if you wish to use the Maya binary files included on the CD-ROM, you must have and be aware of the following:

- Maya 4.5 Complete or Unlimited.
- Maya 4.5 is qualified officially to run on Intel Pentium II, Pentium III, Pentium 4, AMD Athlon Processors, and Apple G4 processors.

- Maya will run with Windows XP Professional, Windows 2000 Professional, and Mac OS X.
- Run Maya with as big a video card as you can get. Officially, Maya does not have definitive video card requirements, but if you have less than a 32MB card, you will be too slow to work efficiently.

Remember, as stated in the Preface, Maya has an official list of what hardware setups it will run on. Although these officially "qualified" setups are great to have since you know Maya will run on them, you can run Maya efficiently on other less expensive systems.

INDEX

A

Align tool, 44–45
Ambient color, material attribute, 177
Ambient Lights, 233–234
Animation
  Animation Preferences Button,
    284–285
  Auto Keyframe Button, 284–285
  cameras and, 298–300
  defined and described, 4, 280–281
  frame padding settings, 303
  frames-per-second (fps) settings,
    280
  Graph Editor and, 295–298
  keyframe animation, 281
  Playback Controls, 284
  playback speed settings, 282–283
  Playblasts, 289–291
  Range Bar, 284–285
  setup for, 282–283
  Time Slider and Current Time
    Marker tools, 284
  tools in Maya, 283–285
  in workflow, 4
Animation Preferences Button,
  284–285
Anisotrophic materials, 176
Anti-aliasing Quality, 272–273
Architectural elements, modeling
  arched walls, 79–90
  ceilings, 59
  columns, 115–117
  crown molding, 106–107

doorways, 90–96, 141–145
floors, curved floorboards with
  NURBS, 102–106
frames, 109–112
Primitive Room Forms tutorial,
  42–61
spiral staircase, 122–126
walls modeled with Cube primitives,
  43–44
windows, 112–115, 141–145
Area Lights, 239–240, 252–253,
  260–263
ATI video cards, 311
Attenuation (decay attribute) of light,
  230–231
  Directional Light and, 235
Attribute Editor, 30, 177–180,
  210–211
Auto Keyframe Button, 284–285
.avi output files, 303

B

Blinn materials, 176
Boolean functions, 141
  difference functions, 141–145
Boxx Technologies, 307–308, xv
Bump maps and bump mapping, 177,
  190–195, 222–224
  seamless textures creation, 346–347

C

Cameras, creating, 298–300
CD-ROM contents, 351–352

Ceilings, modeling, 59
Center of Interest (CIO) manipulator, 241–245
Chairs, modeling, 131–132
Channel Box, 29–30
Clone Stamp tool, 344–345
Collapsers, 9
Color
 Color attributes of materials, 187, 210–211, 214
 interface colors, 327–328
 .jpg files and, 210–211
 light attribute for, 230–231
 materials and, 177
Color attribute of materials, 187, 210–211, 214
Columns, modeling, 115–117
Command Line, 31
Compaq systems, qualified hardware, 307, 308
Component mode, 11
 Select by Component: Type, 16–17
Conceptualization phase of work flow, 2
Construction History, 20–21
 On / Off controls for, 22–23
Control Vertex (CV) curves and CV Curve tool, 65, 68–74
Control Vertices (CVs) of NURBS, 74–75
Couches, modeling, 127–131
Crown molding, modeling with NURBS, 106–107
Cube primitives, modeling walls with, 43–44
Current Time Marker tools, 284
Curves
 animation curve tangents, adjusting, 296–298
 closing curves, 71
 creating and manipulation, 65–74
 CV (Control Vertex) curves, 65
 editing existing curves, 73–74
 EP (Edit Point) curves, 65–68
 tutorial on, 66–74
Cushions, modeling, 132–136
CV (Control Vertex) curves and CV Curve tool, 65, 68–74
Cycloramas, 263–266

D
Decay attribute of light, 235, 237–238
 Point Lights and, 249–250
 Volume Lights, 240–241
Dell systems, qualified hardware, 308
Depth Map Shadow Attributes, 231–232
Difference, Boolean function, 141–145
Diffuse, material attribute, 177
Directional Lights, 235–236, 258–259
Disable All Inputs, 21–22
Display options, 39–41
Dolly movement, 36
Doors and doorways
 Boolean difference function to create, 141–145
 modeling trim for, 90–96
Duplicate Options, 44
 keyboard shortcut for, 47
 tutorial, 122–126

E
Editors and editing
 access to Editors, 316–317
 Attribute Editor, 30, 177–180, 210–211
 Graph Editor and animation, 295–298
 Hypershade editor, 181–183
 isoparms and, 137–141
 Layers Editor, 60
 Relationship Editor, 267
Edit Point (EP) curves and EP Curve tool, 65–68
Enable All Inputs, 21–22
Environment Fog, 274
EP (Edit Point) curves and EP Curve tool, 65–68
Extruded surfaces, modeling with, 106–107
Extrude Face options, 153–156
Extrude NURBS surfaces, 90–96

F
Field Options, 272
Files
 animation output, 303
 finding files for import, 207–208

importing and organizing texture files, 204–205
output formats, 270–271
Floors
modeling curved floorboards with NURBS, 102–106
texturing with tiled floor materials, 221–224
Fog, light fog effect, 231
Frames, modeling, 109–112
Frames-per-second (fps) settings, 280
Fur, shading / shadowing, 232
Furniture, modeling
art lamps, 254
couch, loveseat, and chairs, 127–132
cushions, 132–136
sconces, 250–251
table lamps, 98–102

G

Glass and glasslike materials, 176, 198–200, 213–214
light and, 258–259
Glow, attribute of materials, 180
Graph Editor and animation, 295–298

H

Handles, manipulators and, 37–39
Hardware
Linux systems, 307
Mac systems, 306–307
monitors, 312–313
mouse specs, 313
PC systems, 307–308
processors, 309–310
video cards, 310–312
Help Line, 31
Hiding extraneous objects, 53–54
Hierarchy mode, 11
Select by Hierarchy: tools, 14–15
Highlight Selection mode, 17–18
Hotkeys
assigning, 326–327, 335
for Duplicate option, 47
for Move tool, 49, 285–286
HP systems, qualified hardware, 307, 308
HP video cards, 311

Hulls, 76
Hummingbird
animation tutorial, 286–304
subdivision modeling tutorial, 156–171
Hypershade Editor, 181–183

I

IBM systems, qualified hardware, 307, 308
Incandescence, materials and, 177
Index Manipulator for lights, 243–244
Inputs to Selected Object tools, 21–22
Interactive Photorealistic Rendering (IPR), 23, 275–276
Interactive Placement tool, 219–220
Interface, 5–26
Attribute Editor, 30, 177–180, 210–211
Channel Box, 29–30
color settings, 327–328
Command Line, 31
customizing, 27–28, 315–338
Editors, access to, 316–317
Help Line, 31
interaction customizations, 326–327
Layer Box, 29–30
menu bars in, 7–9
modules in, 5–6
panels, managing, 317–322
preference settings, 324–326
Shelf tool, 336–338
showing and hiding parts of, 322–323
Status Line, 9–26
Time and Range sliders, 31
windows, customizing appearance of, 316–317
Workspace, 28
Intergraph systems, qualified hardware, 308
IPR (Interactive Photorealistic Rendering), 23, 275–276
IPR Render the Current Frame tool, 23
Isoparms, 39, 76
editing models and, 137–140

K

Keyboard shortcuts
  assigning, 326–327, 335
  for Duplicate option, 47
  for Move tool, 49, 285–286

L

Lambert materials, 176, 185
Lamps
  art lamps, 254
  lampshades, lighting of, 248–249
  modeling with NURBS, 98–102
  Point Lights in, 247
  Spot Lights in, 241–245
Lathing (Revolve surfaces), 98–102
Layer Box, 29–30
Layers, 59–60
  rendering and, 276
Layers Editor, 60
Layouts, saved, 319–322
Lens flare effect, 231
Lights and lighting
  Ambient Light, 233–234
  Area Lights, 239–240, 252–253
  Center of Interest (CIO)
    manipulator, 241–245
  color attribute of, 230–231
  daytime room lighting tutorial,
    258–269
  Decay attribute, 230–231, 235,
    237–238
  default lighting in Maya, 228–229
  Directional Lights, 235–236,
    258–259
  fur shading / shadowing, 232
  general control and positioning of,
    241–245
  glow attribute of materials, 180
  incandescent materials, 177
  Index manipulator, 243–244
  intensity of, 230–231
  lens flares, 231
  light attributes, 230–233
  lighting lab, 229
  lights effects, 231
  nighttime room lighting tutorial,
    245–258
  Object Display options, 233
  penumbra adjustment, 244

Point Lights, 236–237, 247, 251–252
  rendering and, 246
  shadow tools, 231–232
  shape attribute of, 230–231
  Smooth Shade with Hardware
    Texturing option and, 40
  Source manipulator, 241–245
  Spot Lights, 238–239, 255–256
  sunlight, 258–259
  Volume Lights, 240–241
  in workflow, 3
  X Light attributes, 230
Linux systems, qualified hardware,
  307
Lock Current Selection tool, 17–18
Lofted surfaces, modeling with,
  109–110

M

Mac systems, qualified hardware,
  306–307
Make the Selected Object Live tool,
  18–20
Manipulators
  handles and related movement,
    37–39
  for lights, 241–245
  tutorial, 36–37
Marking menus, 50
  creating, 332–335
  customizing, 329–331
Materials
  attributes of, 177–180
  Blinn materials, 176
  Color attribute of materials, 187,
    210–211, 214
  glass and glasslike materials, 176,
    198–200, 213–214, 258–259
  Hypershade editor to create,
    181–183
  Lambert materials, 176, 185
  names and naming of, 185–187
  painted wood, 195
  Phong and PhongE materials, 176,
    210
  shaders and, 175
  specular highlights and, 176
  textures and, 175
  types of materials in Maya, 175–176

MEL scripts, 274
Memory, 275
 RAM recommendations, 312
Menus
 converting to floating menus or
  palettes, 7–8
 Marking menus, 50, 329–331,
  332–335
 menu bars in interface, 7–9
 Options boxes in, 8–9
 pull-down menus, 7
Metals, shiny materials, 176
Modeling
 defined, 2
 maneuvering through space while,
  35–36
 NURBS room modeling tutorial,
  74–96
 Primitive Room Forms tutorial,
  42–61
 project set up, 34–35
 subdivision surfaces modeling
  tutorial, 156–171
 in workflow, 2–3
 see also Architectural elements,
  modeling
Modules, 10
 in interface, 5–6
Monitors, 312–313
Motion Blur, 274
Mouse, specs for, 313
Move manipulator, 36–39
Movement
 maneuvering in Maya, 35–36
 Move tool, 285–286
Move tool, keyboard shortcut for, 49,
 285–286

N
Names and naming
 material names, 185–187
 objects during modeling, 45–47
 Quick Rename tool, 25
New tool, 10
Nodes, Construction History and,
 20–21
Numeric Input: Absolute tool, 25–26
Numeric Input: Relative tool, 26
Numeric Input tool, 23–24

NURBS (non-uniform rational
 b-splines)
 Control Vertices (CVs) of, 74–75
 curves, creating and manipulation,
  65–74
 Extrude NURBS surfaces, 90–96
 floors modeled using planes, 42
 hulls and, 76
 isoparms, 39, 76
 Revolve surface, tutorial, 98–102
 room modeling tutorial, 78–96
 SubD (subdivision) surfaces, 65
 surface points and surface patches,
  76–77
 tessellation, 64
NVidia video cards, 311

O
Object display, states of, 39–41
Object mode, 11
 Select by Object: Type, 15–16
Objects
 defined, 175
 display states of, 39–41
Open tool, 10
Orthographic views, 50
Outliner, 46
Outputs form the Selected Objects
 tools, 22

P
Panels, managing interface panels,
 317–322
PC systems, qualified hardware,
 307–308
Penumbra, 244
Performance, 275
Phong and PhongE materials, 176
 creating, 210
Photograph, texture maps created
 from, 339–340
Playback Controls, 284
Playblasts, 289–291
Point Lights, 236–237, 247–249,
 251–252
Post-rendering effects, 180
Primitives, Cube primitives, 43–44
Procedural textures, brownian1
 swatch for changing, 191

Q

Quick Rename tool, 25

Quick Selection tool, 25

Qwerty tools, 26–27

R

Radiosity, faking, 239–240, 252–253, 260–262

RAM, system recommendations, 312

Range Bar, 284–285

Range slider, 31

Raytracing, 199–201

  Raytrace Shadow Attributes, 231–232

  Raytracing Quality, 273

Reflection and refraction, in glass and glasslike materials, 199–200

Relationship Editor, 267

Render Current Frame tool, 23

Render Globals window, 23

  animation renders, 302–304

  options in, 270–276

Rendering, 270–276

  animation, 302–304

  Interactive Photorealistic Rendering (IPR), 23, 275–276

  layers and, 276

  lighting and, 246

  post-rendering effects, 180

  Ray Trace Shadows and, 232

  raytracing and, 273

  Render Current Frame tool, 23

  Render Globals window, 23, 270–276, 302–304

  targeted renderings, 189–190

  in workflow, 4

Render Layer / Pass Control, 276

Resolution, 271, 303

Revolve surfaces, 98–102

Rooms, modeling

  NURBS modeling tutorial, 78–96

  Primitive Room Forms tutorial, 42–61

Rotate manipulator, 36–39

Rotation

  adding rotation keyframes to animation, 300–302

  of placed textures, 212–213

Rotate tool, 285–286

S

Save tool, 10

Saving, texture files, 204–205

Scale manipulator, 36–39

Scale tool, 285–286

Scripts and scripting, Command Line, 31

Select All Inputs tool, 21–22

Selection Masks, 10–11

Setting up projects, 34–35

Sgi systems, qualified hardware, 307

Sgi video cards, 311

Shaders, textures and, 175

Shading. *See* Textures and texturing

Shadows

  Depth Map Shadow Attributes, 231–232

  fur shading / shadowing, 232

  Ray Trace Shadows, 232

  Raytracing, 231–232

  shadow tools, 231–232

Shadows, for Point Lights, 247–249

Shelves, "The Shelf," 26

  creating additional shelves, 209–210

  custom Shelves, 336–338

Smooth Shade display options, 39–40

Snap to Curves tool, 18–20

Snap to Grids tool, 18–20

Snap to Points tool, 18–20

Snap to View Planes tool, 18–20

Source manipulator, 241–245

Specular highlights, 176

Spirals, modeling, 125–126

Spot Lights, 238–239, 241–245

Stairs, modeling, 122–126

Status Line, 9–26

Subdivision surfaces

  creating, 150–151

  hummingbird modeling tutorial, 156–171

  polygon mode, 152–156

  standard mode, 151–152

SubD (subdivision) surfaces, 65

Surface points and surface patches, 76–77

System requirements, 351–352
  see also Hardware

T

Tables, modeling, 117–118
Tessellation, 64
Textures and texturing
  Color attribute and textures,
    210–211, 214
  creating and editing, 181–184
  defined and described, 3, 174
  importing texture files, 204–205
  Interactive Placement tool, 219–220
  map creation, 339–349
  procedural textures, 175, 191
  room textures tutorials, 184–201,
    204–225
  rotating placement of, 212–213
  seamless texture creation tutorial,
    341–349
  texture maps, 175, 339–349
  tiled textures, 221–224
  veneers, 3
  in workflow, 3
  see also Materials
Textures tab, 207
3Dlabs video cards, 311
Time Slider tool, 31, 284

Toolbox
  quick setup options, 27–28
  Qwerty tools, 26–27
  saved layouts in, 319–322
Track movement, 35
Translucence, attribute of materials,
  180
Transparency, 258–259
  materials and, 177
Tumble movement, 35

U

UV coordinates, 175

V

Veneers, 3
Volume Lights, 240–241

W

Walls, modeling arched walls with
  NURBS, 79–90
Web addresses, Boxx Technologies,
  xv
Windows, Boolean difference
  function and, 141–145
Wireframe objects, 39
Work flow, 2–5
Workspace, 28